STARTLING
BEAUTY

REAL LIFE STORIES
Two Timeless Books in One

Startling Beauty

My Journey from Rape to Restoration

HEATHER GEMMEN

KINGSWAY PUBLICATIONS
EASTBOURNE

First published 2004
This 2-in-1 edition 2008

This book is based on a true story.
To protect identities and for ease of reading, some names have been
changed, some characters are composites, and the chronology of some
events has been adapted.

Unless otherwise indicated, biblical quotations are from the
New International Version, copyright © 1973, 1978, 1984 by the
International Bible Society.

ISBN 978 1 84291 400 7

Cover design: PinnacleCreative.co.uk
Front cover photo C Manamana | Dreamstime.com

Published in the UK by David C. Cook
Kingsway Communications Ltd
26-28 Lottbridge Drove, Eastbourne BN23 6NT, UK
www.kingsway.co.uk

Printed in Great Britain
1   2   3   10   09   08

Many thanks to…

Mary McNeil, my excellent editor and best friend:
for reminding me that since God has called me to this task,
he will equip me to do it.

Dan Benson:
for your gentle but persistent nudges toward excellence.

Jeannie St. John Taylor, my writing coach:
for sharing your time and expertise to help shape this book.

Barb Reinhard and Vicki Caruana, my critique group:
for helping me craft words and ideas.

Bob Bever:
for catching the vision of the ministry of this book
and for passing it on to others.

Kim Brandon and Jeff Barnes:
for your expertise and your encouragement.

The entire team at Cook, especially
Terry Whalin, Janet Lee, Craig Bubeck, Jeff Dunn,
Michelle Lowder, Phyllis Williams, Karen Athen, Joni Costa,
Michele Tennesen, Kerry Park, Susan Parsons, Lori Jackson,
Dick Frieg, Ted Ehrlichman, Ken Lorenz, Les Jones,
Mary Chapman, Jeff Ray,
Chris Robinette, David Cura, Kelly Becker,
Patsy Edwards, Jeff Francisco, Jeremy Potter,
Pam Steinberg, Sue Giordano, Pete Zickefoose, Keith Franklin,
Mike Mason, Kathy Guist, Judy Krafchak.

Ray and Linda Bert, Dan Lenahan, and Danny and Mickey Jantz,
my prayer group:
for praying this book into existence.

CONTENTS

Contents

POETRY

POETRY

How else will you rape my life?

P oetry is escape into truth." She smiles sadly as she reads, and the wrinkles on her face deepen. She does not look at the other members of our small writers' group gathered in her immaculate home. We know we are the privileged few to enter her truth.

The group sits silently, savoring language, slowly building the stack of word pictures into an invisible pile before us.

"Poetry articulates abstraction." He is young and white and confident. Once he had terrified us with a short story about what he would do if he were God.

"A poem laughs at despair." Tasha smiles discreetly at me, and I have to take a deep breath. She knows which poem I will be reading tonight.

"The poet coaxes a soft brook out of the frothing river of words." She teaches kindergarten and serves as an elder at her church. Her laughter is as beautiful as her sentences.

"The poet is a sagacious fool." Blonde dreadlocks bounce as this newlywed grins around the circle. Her favorite word is *paradox.*

I watch the faces around me and then offer my interpretation: "A poem is the place where familiar beauty becomes startling."

Some of us barely sit in our hardback chairs, as if ready to spring into the places we have created. Some of us retreat into the cushions of the oversized couch, as if longing to fade away from reality. Some of us peer into the eyes of the others, as if expecting to find ourselves there. All of us reach into the stack of words piled in front of us and sift through it, passionately searching our souls.

These are my sisters and brothers. They will understand.

When the silence empties, I clear my throat. It is

my turn to read first. Tonight I will read out my soul. For three years our carefully crafted words had brought our unnamed group to intimacy deeper than lovers, and yet I had never revealed to them my secret. Tasha knew the story—had helped carry me through it—but the others here had unwittingly provided a haven for me from the many who knew. I speak over the thick sound of my fear.

> Sire:
> *Strange that I should remember you …*
> *You whose face I never saw,*
> *Whose words I barely understood.*
> *Your life crossed mine for mere moments.*
>
> *I'm sure by now you have forgotten …*
> *You whose breath reeked of beer,*
> *Whose words slurred almost beyond comprehension.*
> *You had no idea what you were doing.*
>
> *I know what you have done …*
> *You stole my courage;*
> *Your words, filthy and threatening, penetrated my soul.*
> *I grasp in vain at a missing part of myself.*
>
> *How could you not have known?*
> *You scorned a closed door;*
> *You scarred me with your words.*
> *I can still feel the knife pressed against my throat.*
>
> *I won't forget your laughter …*
> *You who slapped me when I begged to pray,*

Whose words mocked what could have set you free.
I did still pray.

And there is more that you don't know ...
You created more than fear;
Your words are not the only thing you left behind.
I have gained more than I have lost.

Strange that I should forgive you ...
You who do not even know you need it,
Whose words displayed your pathetic need for grace.
You didn't know what you were doing.

The silence throbs once again, and I know my words are between the fingers of my friends, like play dough under the scrutiny of a group of preschoolers. I look at the floor as I wait.

How many times had I been taught grace? "God so loved the world that he gave his one and only Son." Familiar. Startling. "I am with you always." Familiar. Startling. "Love your enemies."

I see toes with sky-blue nails wiggle in thick-soled sandals. I nod almost imperceptibly. The postmodern concept that two opposing truths can exist simultaneously is as ancient as God.

But then the soft sound of a full-length skirt rustling in the chair across the room jars me into sudden insecurity. My lofty thoughts are instantly replaced by a frantic concern that I have foolishly opened the door for yet more people to judge me by that which is beyond me.

The cowboy clears his throat. Even he must silently mock

my grandiose proclamation of impossible forgiveness.

My fingers fondle the waxy oak at the base of the armrest, and I notice the subtle scent of roses rising from the candle beside me. I am surrounded by flawlessness. I have revealed too much.

Do you see? Your few minutes of ecstasy haunt my entirety.
Because of you, even words turn against me.
How else will you rape my life?

My mounting fear creates a foothold for bitterness. Does my forgiveness still hold?

"Read it again, Heather."

I do. This time, I need to pause between words as I fight to get them out of my throat.

When I look up I see emotion, raw and potent, in the faces of these people who love me. I accept the salve of friendship's passionate sorrow and anger, and my soul is caressed smooth again. Bitterness slinks away.

I will not be your captive.

As I listen to my friends' words of encouragement and endearment, anger and sorrow, I am overwhelmed by abundance, I who was once empty and lost. My heart is changed within me.

CHAPTER ONE

STATIC
IN THE
STORM

I reached for
Steve's hand, but he must not have
noticed;
he didn't reach back.

The havoc you wreaked in my life was not the first storm I endured. Another struck two years prior to my even being aware of your existence. It started in the sterility of a doctor's office. I remember listening to my own heartbeat in the silence of that examining room.

W hat's wrong, Maryann?" My whispered words screamed.

I searched my doctor's face, desperate for the reassurance of the familiar crinkles around her soft blue eyes. She murmured some word of comfort, in vain.

A streak of lightning sliced the sky.

"You can't find the heartbeat, can you?" I asked quietly. She was my friend more often than she was my doctor, and I would not accept anything less than the full truth.

Maryann looked up at me, and then a smile caught the edge of her lips. "This baby is definitely your child, Heather. I'm sure he's dodging the Doppler just to frustrate me."

Her teasing didn't entirely relax me, but I accepted her attempt and tried to smile. "When have I ever frustrated you? I have been the calming source in your life, the sunshine after the rain, the wind beneath your wings—"

"Right." She snorted. "Okay. Maybe *frustrate* is the wrong word for it. Perhaps *torment* would work better."

"Word choice, eh? I knew you would bring it around to Scrabble sooner or later." This was my soul sister. "The only reason I let you win was so Byron wouldn't have to go home ashamed that his esteemed wife was beat by—"

"Let me win? You need a psychiatrist, girl, not an obstetrician." Maryann's sandy brown hair maintained a tousled look, whether in the office or at the beach, and her intimidating brilliance was disguised by playful kindness. "Now hush. I want to hear your son."

"It's a girl, Maryann."

"It's a boy. Shh." She raised a finger to her lips and held the silence. Her eyebrows were furrowed. The thunder growled. "So, why didn't Steve come with you today?"

"Come on, Maryann. You know him."

"Yeah, but he hasn't even heard the heartbeat yet."

"I know. But he doesn't take time off work for things like this."

"Did you ask him to come?"

"Well, no. But I know he wouldn't want to."

"Heather," she touched her fingers to her forehead, "you have to do your part. Listen, Steve may be emotionally inaccessible at times—I'll give you that—but that doesn't let you off the hook. You could have at least asked him to come."

"But then he'd come out of obligation and I'd feel guilty."

"Nah. He wouldn't complain."

"Okay. He probably wouldn't say a word, but he'd be ticked off inside. I'm sure he would be."

"You can't jump to conclusions, Heather. It doesn't help."

"Well, what am I supposed to do? I don't know what he's thinking. Either he has no feelings whatsoever or he just doesn't want to tell them to me. Yesterday he felt the baby move for the first time, and I don't even know if he thought that was exciting or not."

"You felt the baby move?"

"Oh, yeah. I forgot to tell you. Lately I've been feeling her flutter all the time, way more than I did with the boys at five months."

"Hmm. I'm surprised. That's early." She rested cool, gloved fingers gently on my belly for a moment. "But, Heather, I'll bet Steve was just as excited as you were. You can't let his poker face fool you."

"Right. If only this were a card game. I'd let him win every hand if only we could have some interaction while we played." I waved my hand. "Anyway, I was pretty excited." I put my hand on my belly, too. "Oh, Maryann, I think it must have been her little elbow poking up against me. And she didn't pull away until I moved again."

"No doubt a little boy wanting his daddy." Her words smiled, but Maryann's face looked serious as she spread more gel on my belly and started moving the monitor over it. She turned the volume up and we listened to the swishy noises inside me. After a few minutes she clicked it off and looked at me, but her eyes looked right through me as her thoughts roved. "This Doppler must not be working."

I felt a sprinkle of fear fall over me again. "You still can't find the heartbeat? What are you going to do?"

"Well, I'm going to get a newer one from the other room. This one's older than you are." She winked.

I laughed. But when she left, I lay back, gently massaged the protrusion that represented my baby, and waited for the fluttering to begin. She had measured up exactly right and had moved just yesterday. Nothing could be wrong.

I watched the nimbus clouds pile on top of each other. Occasionally an escaped raindrop splattered against the window, but the sky was not yet ready to release its fury. I've always believed that we each choose our own path, but as I stared out the window in that quiet examining room,

I realized for the first time that we don't get to choose the obstacles we face on the journey.

Oh, God, don't let this be my obstacle. Let me learn about life another way.

Maryann was silent for nearly five minutes as she moved the cool plastic plate back and forth over my belly, pushing gently and then more firmly, listening to the creaks and groans, rumbles and churnings.

"Wait. I heard it," I said after an especially loud whoosh.

"No. That did sound somewhat like a baby's heartbeat, but it's actually the blood flow through your arteries. Listen." We heard some more whooshing sounds. "It's much slower than the baby's heartbeat." She waited a moment longer and then turned off the monitor. I watched her long, smooth fingers fold the tool neatly into the drawer and then float upward to slide through the soft curls over her eyes. She glanced at the clock and then put the lid on the gel and straightened the instruments beside it. Finally, she looked at me, pulling the white jacket tight around her athletic shoulders as she crossed her arms in front of her. "Well, Heather, we're going to have to get you to the hospital for an ultrasound."

The storm broke and propelled its wrath against me. I knew the truth without being told.

I have heard the question from little kids and from old ladies: Why does God let bad things happen to good people? I've known a mother who left her fourteen-month-old son home alone in his crib for sixteen hours; she laughed when the child was taken away from her. Steve and I had chosen names for our baby before she was the size of a pea; before she was as big as a banana, I had blankets and diapers and pajamas folded neatly in the room that would be her home.

Our first two children had been conceived accidentally, at times inconvenient for us; we loved them no less for it. This child had been prayed for and anticipated, our reward for a job well done.

The illusion of control shattered before my eyes.

"Don't give up, Heather. We might be able to pick up the heartbeat at the hospital." I nodded heavily and prepared to leave while Maryann personally made arrangements. Just before I left the office, she grabbed my arm and pulled me into a spontaneous hug. She almost squeezed the tears out of me.

Moments after stepping outside, I felt my hair pressed slick against my scalp, but I did not pop open my umbrella or run through the rain. And I sat quietly before I turned on the car. It's hard to believe that God knows our prayers when we do not even know what to say. My wipers slapped the rain that dumped on my windshield, and I thought about the baby pushing up against me the day before. No wonder she hadn't moved away when I touched her. She couldn't.

I called Steve when I got home. "What are we going to do?" I lamented quietly.

Over the thick static threatening our connection, I heard Steve's answer. "We'll go ... hospital like ... said and find out if every ... alright."

I wanted *connection*.

"Oh, Steve, what's going to happen?" The dim yellow glow encircling the porch light was nearly swallowed up by the sheet of rain streaking into it. "What are we going to do?"

Steve didn't hear my question.

"I'll ... home in ten minutes and we'll ... the boys to ... parents' house. Then we'll meet ... with Maryann...." The connection was broken.

I set down the phone and stared at my reflection in the window. The paleness of my round face was hidden in the dark glass, but I could see the effects of the rain on my long, straight hair. Dark eyes looked sadly back at me and full lips twisted downward. I leaned my forehead against the cold window. Does rain hurt when it smacks against a window? Does it want to mingle with the brown hair that is pressed into the glass? The rain and I, like my husband and I, nearly touched each other.

When Steve came home, he threw an odd expression toward the red spot on my forehead—and I felt foolish for my meandering thoughts.

An hour later I lay on a doctor's table again, intently watching the screen, asking the technician many questions about what I saw as he wiggled the camera over my belly. He pointed the heart out to me when I asked: a little black blip on the screen, perfectly still. He must have known I understood my baby's status, but I didn't cry. Steve stood silently by my side while I joked about having to pee.

The curse of gregarious people is that our extroversion sometimes shows up at inappropriate times. I remember respecting Steve's taciturn nature, maybe for the first time since our wedding, when our neighbor showed up at our door a few years ago, her bag stuffed with clothes and her left eye badly swollen. "Can I stay with you a few days?" she asked. I, embarrassingly, responded with delighted enthusiasm to the opportunity for enjoyable company rather than, like Steve, extending hospitality and then sitting back quietly, ready to listen to words that would express her apparent suffering.

In this situation, as I stared at the screen that proved my

baby had died, I used humor as a shield. Laughter might keep away sorrow.

The technician told us to wait while he took the pictures to the doctor. We waited, and my own black blip of a heart could stand no more. Resistance crumbled. I had struggled against the sweeping sorrow—and felt as if I were pushing my way through the wind that shook the world outside—but now I wept. Our precious baby had died.

When Maryann entered the little room only minutes later, looking very disturbed, she knew she was saved the work of breaking the news to us. Instead she sat down and waited until I had finished sobbing.

"Maryann," I croaked, "do you know if it was a girl or a boy?"

Maryann shook her head. "I don't think we got a clear view of that from the ultrasound"—I nodded with acceptance—"but we'll find out in a little while."

A blast of truth hit me. The storm wasn't over yet.

I craned my neck back to see him, but Steve looked straight ahead as he pushed me in a wheelchair down the hallway. Oddly, I felt surprised by his perfect features that I had come to know so well: soft brown hair falling neatly into place; thick eyelashes extending over deep brown eyes; muscular arms complementing his slim body; tall legs moving confidently forward.

The storm did not seem to touch him.

Would resistance eventually crumble for him, or did he have nothing to resist?

We passed a few moms groaning in the pains of labor, the nursery housing several newborns, and the nurses' station where one woman grinned at me as we descended to the far end of the obstetrics hall.

I stopped looking around. Instead, I ventured back to the moments (was it only a few hours ago?) that I had pressed my head against the glass, comparing my marriage to raindrops on a window—and no longer felt foolish. Rather, I envisioned myself punching the glass, shattering it, so the rain, so Steve's love, could drench me.

I envisioned but did nothing more.

Maryann came in and sat down with us again. She didn't seem in a hurry to start the procedure, and I was thankful for that. Things were happening much too quickly already.

"I'm going to give you medication to induce labor," Maryann told me. "We will wait for full dilation to occur and for your water to break, and then you will deliver this baby as if everything were normal." She looked at me sympathetically before she continued. "I need to warn you that this will be painful and long. You are physically unprepared for this. Your body thinks it still has a few months to go."

I nodded. For once my body and mind were in agreement.

"I'm sorry, Heather and Steve. This is really tough."

I reached for Steve's hand, but he must not have noticed; he didn't reach back.

Maryann was right. Bare minutes after taking the medication, I felt my first labor pain. I gasped in surprise as I was plunged into an all-night, agonizing ordeal.

When it came time to push, I didn't bother to call for help. Steve sent for a nurse when he saw what was happening. "Try to wait until Maryann gets here, Heather," he begged. But I pushed. What difference does it make? The baby's dead anyway.

Maryann came in time to help deliver the placenta and to care for me. The silent infant was set aside.

Exhausted, I closed my eyes and wished for sleep. Maybe now it would all be over. I didn't care about the gender of the baby, about whether or not Steve loved me, about what Maryann was doing. I had no desire to pray—neither to cry out in anger nor to breathe in God's peace. I just wanted to sleep.

A nurse touched me on the shoulder. I turned, and in her arms was the baby, so tiny, dressed in a blue gown and a white woolen hat far too big for him. "It's a boy. Would you like to hold him?"

A boy? He seemed alien to me, and I could hardly acknowledge that this baby before me was my own child. I shook my head.

But Steve reached out for him. "A boy," he crooned as he pulled back the hat to better see the little head. I watched a half-smile creep over Steve's face, and I couldn't help peeping at our child. He was precious. So delicate and so small. The nurse encouraged us to undress him, to examine him thoroughly, to embrace our little one with the pride only new parents can have. We did, and the nurse left us alone.

I did not feel sad during those brief moments with our son. I had emerged into the calm of the storm. I marveled at how perfectly he was formed, how each of his tiny toes was wrinkled just right, how soft his cheeks felt, how round his belly was. His death did not diminish his beauty.

"You did a great job again, Heather," Steve told me. I soaked up his favor like parched ground soaking in a late summer rain.

"It was worth it." My words surprised me. I looked at the

27

little fingers resting on mine. "An hour ago I wouldn't have said that, but now—well, he is absolutely amazing."

"Yes. Casey is amazing."

We smiled at each other. The rain poured down, and I stood with head back and mouth open to take in as much as I could. "Steve, would you ever have believed that our hearts could be so full and so empty at the same time?" A beautiful paradox. Steve turned his head to look out the window. I put my hand on his arm. "The emotion is almost too much, isn't it?" Steve didn't say anything for a moment. Finally, still looking out the window as if preparing to face the storm we were reentering, he shook his head. "I'm confused."

I murmured agreement.

"No, it's different," he said. I couldn't read the look in his eyes when he turned to me. "I don't feel anything at all. I mean, I'm amazed that this child is so perfectly developed, but I don't feel strong love or sadness. I wish I could agree with you that the emotion is too much, but it's not."

I let go of Steve and lifted Casey to my shoulder, patting his back as if listening for a burp. "You must be numb still, from the shock."

"No, it's not that." We shifted uneasily in the silence.

I made another attempt. "Well, you hadn't even felt the baby move until yesterday. It makes sense that you're not feeling the loss like I am."

He looked out the window again, staring right through the drizzle. "No, it's not that, either." Steve slumped into the stiff hospital chair. "I never feel things strongly. Sometimes I wonder if I'm even able to love at all." He almost whispered the words. I softly pressed my cheek against Casey's cold body.

28

Raindrops don't hurt when they smack against a window; they don't even notice the brown hair pressed into the glass. No, I had felt the extent of Steve's rain in his brief smile moments ago.

When the nurse stole into the room a while later, I kissed Casey's cheek and reluctantly handed him over to her. Then I turned my head to sleep. I could not consider my husband's emptiness just yet.

I slept as Steve signed the papers that released our child to the funeral home for cremation and as he made the appropriate phone calls to family and friends. I barely woke when nurses checked my vitals. I slept through visitations from our pastor and friends. I groaned when I had to eat; I cried when I had to urinate; and I bawled when my milk came in.

I laid in bed begging God to transform me into a stoic so I would not have to feel the pain of loss, to help me gain comfort from people's words that little Casey was cuddled safely in his arms, or to convict me that this—like "all things … for those who love him"—would turn out for good.

But grief overcame me. The repercussions of my loss were strewn before me like broken branches on a windswept street.

Steve wheeled me out of the hospital the next day. My arms were full of flowers, cards, and candy, but I held only emptiness.

CHAPTER TWO

HEAVY EMPTINESS

If God wants us
to stay here, I thought,
we'll just have to
disobey him.

The extent of the darkness you would deliver a few months from now was beyond my ability to fathom. I thought today I had reached an impenetrable depth already.

I t's negative." I slumped onto the bed. I'm surprised."
Steve slathered shaving cream on his thick stubble.
"You've sure been acting pregnant." His grin was like a stick in the hand of a twelve-year-old boy probing an injured dog. He meant no harm, but I snarled.

"What's that supposed to mean?"

"Oh, don't be so sensitive. I'm kidding."

Our house throbbed with the heavy bass of rap music coming from a car illegally parked at the playground across the street. I watched Steve slice through the foam on his face and wished I could slice through him myself. Instead I rolled over to the window and slammed it shut despite the July afternoon heat—but not before I caught a glimpse of our inner-city neighborhood where litter fluttered in the breeze, houses banged up next to each other, groups of kids loitered beside school fences, and cars squealed and sped their way down the residential streets.

Steve flicked the excess shaving cream off his razor and

began washing his face. "After the game, I'm going grocery shopping. Is there anything else you want to add to the list?"

"Steve!" I raised an arm in exasperation. "What is your problem? Didn't you hear what I said? The pregnancy test was negative!" I thought about whipping a pillow at him to wake him up.

"I heard." He dropped beside me on the bed and draped an arm over my belly. "So we keep trying." He kissed my shoulder. "I like trying to get you pregnant." His hand stole under my top.

"Cut it out." I rolled over, turned my back to him, and gave in to my despair. "How can you think about sex at a time like this?"

I could feel him shrug.

"You don't get it, do you?" The windowpane vibrated as it tried to hold out the offensive noise from the street below. "It's been almost a year since Casey died, and I'm still not pregnant. What's wrong with me, Steve?" I whispered.

"Nothing's wrong with you."

"Then why can't I get pregnant?" The words would hardly come out because of the sadness that wallowed in my throat.

I didn't notice Steve's silence until he spoke a few moments later: "Maybe we aren't supposed to have another kid."

"Don't even say that." I turned toward him to search his face. "We'll keep trying."

"I think this is becoming too much for you." Steve looked at his hands. "You don't laugh anymore. I miss that. I want the old you."

It seemed so long ago that I laughed. The Heather who

34

threw spontaneous parties to celebrate someone's promotion or to try out a new recipe or to acknowledge the first snowfall, the Heather who convinced friends to give up the safety of the bench for the thrill of the roller coaster and the comfort of the beach for the fun of the waves, the Heather who turned mundane jobs into community shindigs—that Heather seemed far removed.

"Maybe we should quit trying," Steve said quietly.

I felt my face contort as I absorbed his words. "Quit? How can you say that?" Suddenly I hated the intense heat and stood up to yank the trembling window back open again. "We can't quit, Steve."

The steady *thud* of a bouncing basketball pounded in my ears, but Steve's words smacked me in the face: "We have to."

"Steve!" I choked. "Are you kidding?"

"We have two kids already. It feels good to be leaving the baby stage behind. Besides—" he pointed toward the window "—we've got to save up enough money to move out of here."

"Yeah, but that doesn't mean—"

"Be realistic."

I stared at my perfectly cool and aloof husband in disbelief. "But we always said we'd have three." His eyes patronized me—waiting for me to acknowledge his truth against my pathetic hope—but I couldn't stop. "You really don't want another kid?"

"I don't. I'm happy with two." Happy.

Fleetingly I wondered if it was I, and not Steve, who needed a pillow whipped at me. But self-pity smothered the joy I longed to have.

35

"The emptiness is *heavy*, Steve." I held out my arms. "Can't you feel it?"

His eyes said no.

I gulped for air. "So all this time you've been hoping the tests would be negative?" I knew the question was not fair, but I didn't care.

"Well, it's not—" He pushed himself up on one elbow and tried to touch me. I pulled away.

"I can't believe it." I spat the words at him as the sadness that had been hovering exploded into fragments of anger, pain, betrayal. I couldn't sit near him anymore; I couldn't stand that he peered into me like I was a case study to be figured out. "You really don't care about me, do you?" Hot, angry tears embarrassed me, and I turned my face from him. "Have you ever cared?" From deep in the pillow my smothered voice wailed out to him: "Have you ever cared about anything?" It was the first time I acknowledged the confession he had made at Casey's deathbed—and I used it against him. I hated my own cruelty more than I hated him.

The reflection in the mirror when I looked up showed my red eyes and ugly scowl. I stared at that image of myself and cried bitterly, unguarded. The sorrow spilled out of me like the rap music that spilled out of the Jeep below: harsh and uncensored. Killing. Cursing. Raping. Screaming. The ugliness of words paralleled the ugliness of my despair.

I glanced at Steve beside me on the bed. I knew he wanted to go.

Yes, the emptiness was heavy. It was about time I started helping Steve carry his load. *God, help me.*

A moment later, I heard the bedroom door squeak open. "Mommy?"

I brushed away my tears and held out a hand to four-year-old Chad. "Hi, honey."

"What the matter, Mommy?"

"Oh, Chad, I've been feeling sad. But I'll be better pretty soon, okay?"

"Okay. Mommy, what 'white boy' mean?"

I caught Steve's eye and he shrugged.

"It means that whoever called you that wants to look like you." I justified the loaded statement to myself by claiming rights to protect my child from emotional harm. But Chad didn't question my reasoning.

"Oh. Can I play outside?"

"In the backyard, okay? Don't go into the front yard. And don't wake Simon." He kissed me and ran off. I looked at Steve. "We've got to get out of here, Steve. Yesterday I saw a kid throw sand in Chad's eyes when he was sitting by the sidewalk. They don't want us here."

"Why was he in the front yard?"

"I was working in the flower garden." I shuddered. "Eeh. It was awful. I felt like everyone was looking at me." I sat up and looked out the window. "What do these people do, anyway? They sit on their front porches and watch each other. It gives me the creeps."

"Just forget about the garden," Steve told me.

"Okay. Fine. As soon as we sell the stupid house!"

"Yeah." Steve nodded his head, thinking. "But I don't really want to lower our asking price."

"Who cares about money? What if some gunman comes running through our yard again? We can't live like this."

"Yeah, I know. It's just weird that we've had this house on the market for almost a year and nobody has even looked at it."

I snorted. "It's not weird. I can't believe we were such suckers!"

"I don't know. Maybe God's trying to tell us something."

I cocked an eyebrow. "Like what?"

Steve remained silent for a moment before he spoke: "What if he wants us to stay here?"

He couldn't have meant it. He hated this place more than I did.

We had been living in the house only a couple months when we were initiated into our neighborhood: We were drinking eggnog and licking the fudge off our fingers at my parents' house hundreds of miles away that Christmas Eve when my dad walked into the room holding out the phone to Steve. "It's the police." The front door of our house had been swinging open, and some officers driving past were suspicious. They entered our home and saw clear evidence of a break-in: shattered glass, an empty entertainment center, a floor strewn with half-emptied drawers. Even our sweaters had been carted off in our laundry baskets.

Steve, sitting in a living room so far away, recognized his own powerlessness to defend his home or to pay retribution to those who violated it. Resentment was born.

One evening a few months later, Steve heard some commotion in the yard. He went to the window and saw some teens slinking over our fence and slipping through our neighbor's back door. "Hey!" he hollered. "What are you guys up to?" The kids scattered. Steve, armed with a baseball bat, followed the intruders, yelling at me to call the police. I did, terrified at what Steve was getting himself into. By the time a unit pulled up, Steve had pinned one of the kids and told him, in his gently intimidating way, that he and his gang were not welcome in our neighborhood.

Now, to think that Steve thought we ought to stay was laughable.

"Yeah, right." I looked out the window at the yellow grass below. "Why would God want us to stay here?"

Steve shrugged and waved the idea away. "I don't know. It's crazy."

I laughed a little too loudly in agreement. *If God wants us to stay here*, I thought, *we'll just have to disobey him.* I had learned enough—too much—during our four long years in the city.

They say the first step to overcoming racism is to admit you have it. Well, then, I was well on my way to recovery. The black culture that surrounded me seemed nothing short of pathetic, and I had no problem discussing my opinion with anyone who would listen: Two-year-olds wandered unattended at the playground across the street. Teens were getting pregnant or hauled off to jail. The local convenience store was robbed five times in one summer. Murders in our neighborhood didn't even make the evening news. Ebonics was not a course to be studied, but the only language known. Money was spent on stereo systems rather than milk and eggs.

I hadn't expected to feel so bitter against my black neighbors when we moved into the area. I had never had much contact with people outside my Dutch, Christian Reformed circle and assumed all people were just like me, no matter what race they were. So when people more knowing than we were warned us against purchasing the quaint house that was impossibly cheap, we ignored them. Steve loved the economics, and I didn't comprehend the implications of living as a minority.

My naïveté held for a year or so. I loved the river of kids that flooded my home to gush over my pretty house and soft hair and sweet baby. I scoffed at my white friends who advised that I check the pockets of my "darlings" as they walked out the door. I was delighted to see neighbors chatting on porches with as much familiarity as I had had in my small hometown. The richness of community contrasted with the poverty of material wealth. The words and mannerisms of my neighbors intrigued me: I found the black culture to be lovely, beautiful—just as a poet from the countryside would find beauty in the dance of cars moving through a busy intersection. Common beauty was startling through my eyes.

I'm not sure when my attitude changed—maybe I was convinced by the skepticism of others, maybe protective mothering instincts heightened my awareness of danger, maybe I was watching the world instead of heaven—but I lost my innocence by the time Chad turned one: Our family walks eventually started at a distant park rather than our front step; a high wooden fence soon replaced the chain link fence surrounding our backyard; blinds covered the unpainted oak window frames and blocked out the sun.

By the time Chad was two, I had become bitter: I didn't allow neighbor kids to play at our house anymore because too often I couldn't find some of my belongings, and I wanted to rule out theft. Once I took a young boy called Deshawn firmly by his hand and rang his mother's doorbell. The smell of marijuana and the noise of rap fell out of the darkness of her home when she answered the door.

"Hi," I said with tight lips. "I'm your neighbor. I need to tell you that Deshawn may not come on our property

40

anymore. He has broken our porch light twice this week, and he plucks every tulip before it can even open. I am terribly busy with my college classes and raising my own kids, so I don't have time to baby-sit yours." It was my first time on her doorstep, but I didn't stay for chitchat.

As I walked back home, I wondered if I had been too harsh; but it made me angry that she could laze around while I worked so hard. *She doesn't have to be the way she is just because she's black. Look at Tasha!* I muttered to myself. Tasha was my friend who lived on the other side of the schoolyard, provided a well of wisdom from which I often drew, and seemed always to know exactly what I needed to hear. *She pulled herself out of this mess.*

I didn't enjoy my resentment—I hated it—but I didn't know how to change my heart. I wished I could go back to innocence—and I thought I could if only we would move out of this ghetto.

Anyway," I shot at my husband, "now I have another reason for wanting to get out of here." The after-crying breath caught in my chest, and Steve looked at me.

"You know, we can keep trying to have another baby if you think you can handle the stress. It's not like I would hate to have another kid."

It took a few moments for me to answer. "I wasn't crying about that."

"What?" He wearied of these conversations.

"I'm not crying because you don't want a baby," I snuffled. "Okay, it's about that, too, but it's more about us."

Steve closed his eyes. As my emotions snowballed, his tolerance for me dwindled. As he grew colder, I grew more desperate to be understood. "All I'm asking is that you say

41

you love me once in awhile, that you kiss me without wanting sex, that you tell me how you're feeling. Sometimes your eyes hate me, Steve. Am I that awful to live with?"

For the first time, I wanted to know the answer even though I was scared of what I'd hear.

"Oh, honey." Those intolerant eyes softened as they looked at me from beneath long lashes. "I'm sorry." I suppose he meant it, but for once I wasn't ready to hear it. This time I wanted first to understand how to resolve the issue. I had to look away or I would give in, accept the apology, and continue in our well-worn pattern.

"I know. Me too. We're always sorry. But tomorrow everything will be back to how it always is." I watched him sit up slowly and swing his feet over the side of the bed so his broad shoulders faced me. "You'll say that you'll try to be a better husband, but tomorrow I'll still feel like a moron every time you give me that look—you know which one— without saying anything." I touched the thick muscles on his arms and smelled his cologne. My words lost their thrust. "I'll say something, and you'll ignore me or you'll attempt to win the grand prize for insulting me to tears in five words or less." Steve turned around and smiled a little. I wasn't sure if I wanted to kiss him or hit him. "You're such a jerk and I love you so much. I'm sorry I'm such an emotional wreck. But, Steve," —I started to etch my name on his back with my finger— "I really need love from you." Steve reached for a tissue and handed it to me. "I want things to work between us. Heather,"—he paused and I held my breath in anticipation—"I … I will do better, okay?"

"Okay." I tried to smile as I nodded and got out of bed— even though I knew he wouldn't be able to do any better. He wouldn't be able to love me.

"Now, is the grocery list done or do you still want to add stuff?" I sighed. A plaque hanging over the dresser caught my attention:

> *O Master, grant that I may never seek*
> *so much to be consoled as to console,*
> *to be understood as to understand,*
> *to be loved as to love with all my soul.* *

"It's done," I told him.

"Okay. Say hi to Tasha for me."

I smiled at his retreating back. He was right, and I loved him for knowing me so well: I was aching for some of Tasha's balm.

I picked up the phone as he drove out the driveway.

* Francis of Assisi, "Make Me a Channel of Your Peace"

CHAPTER THREE

PAINFUL
HEALING

I grudgingly opened
my eyes and peeked out from
the covers.
The man standing in my bedroom was
not Steve.

The only white woman among a crowd of black people. I wonder how long ago you noticed me. I wonder how often you were watching me. I did not think about that as I sat on the park bench with Tasha.

I don't think I can handle this whole marriage thing, Tash!" I wailed as we watched Chad push Simon on the swing. Simon's eyes were bright with delight, and Chad was asking him if he wanted to go higher. Each time Simon swung back, their blond heads would align, and their smiles looked identical.

"Steve's gettin' under your skin, is he?"

"Well, no. I don't know why I'm frustrated with him. He's so wonderful, really."

"Mmm-hmm." Tasha nodded. "He sure do help out a heap around the house. I know many womenfolk who'd give up an arm for a man like that."

"Yeah. And he's so good with the kids."

"What's wrong then? You been fighting?"

"No. It's not that." I sighed heavily. "It's just that it feels like we're not even together." I raised my hands dramatically in the air. "Is it too much to ask him to treat me like a woman instead of a roommate?"

"Romance ain't everything, honey."

"I know. But love is. Besides," I continued, "you know how I always say that our strengths are our weaknesses. Well, that's something Steve doesn't get. He's authentic, but only because he doesn't care what others think of him. He also doesn't care how he makes others feel. I want him to care what people—well, at least what I—think of him."

I might have gone on, but Tasha interrupted me. "Alright. Try single parenting and see if you like that."

"No, I don't want that, of course."

"So, what do ya want?"

I liked Tasha's no-nonsense attitude—though I knew some folks at our church didn't.

Tasha and I had met at Sherman Street Church a couple years earlier. I had been sitting near the back row where I could easily slip out with one of the boys if they needed some extra attention. A second grader had lit the Christ candle during the first verse of the opening hymn. The bulletin that had been placed in our hands after a warm greeting indicated that praise singing came next and that we should stand for this portion of the service. But I didn't need to read the bulletin to cue me in. I shifted Simon to the other arm while I spoke the Lord's Prayer in unison with my brothers and sisters in Christ. I lowered my head respectfully while I received the blessing offered by the pastor. I sat simultaneously with those around me when the homespun quartet walked to the front to offer "special music." This church and its customs were as familiar to me as my own living room.

But then something changed. I glanced over my shoulder when the back door opened silently, and I saw a smashing woman move into the seat in front of my family. Her age was hard to determine because her stylish exterior seemed so much younger than her aura of easy confidence, but I figured she was probably in her early forties. Her ebony skin looked polished against the red velvet dress that clung to her alluring figure. Her full lips were thickly painted to match the long, red fingernails that rested on her folded arms. She briefly surveyed the primarily white congregation that met in the primarily black neighborhood and then began to nod her head in time to the music. As if surprised at their skill, she turned her full attention to the musicians and began to clap so that the whites of her hands slapped loudly in the still room. "Oh yes!" she moaned. "Alleluia!"

If heads turned or if whispers started, I didn't notice. All I saw was hope. The dream of our church, for as long as I had been part of it and despite our long history of failure in achieving the dream, had been to breach the chasm that separated the parish community from the constituents of our church. We wanted this to be the place where all nations could worship together, reconciled with each other and God: the place to set aside our differences as easily as we would take off our winter coats in front of a warm fire. A cozy place. A peaceful place.

We hadn't imagined that racial healing would hurt.

We prayed regularly that people from the neighborhood would join us, and we welcomed them fervently when they trickled in. We couldn't understand why they rarely interacted during the service and even more rarely came back. Personally, I sometimes wondered if the core group of people at Sherman Street—we who developed our mission statement and organized the block parties and attended the evangelism committee meetings—didn't truly represent the church body. It made me uneasy. How could our dream be realized if the majority of the church wanted things to stay the same? It frustrated me. We weren't asking folks to move into the city (heaven knew, if they wanted to do that, they could buy my house); we were asking them, for just one hour of the week, to be welcoming to people different from themselves, to build friendly relationships with the guests.

Ironically, I blamed other people for running off our neighbors, but I never suspected that I was the scariest white of them all. I was the kind of person black people avoided: I knew enough to realize that a problem needed to be solved, but I didn't care enough to find out how to solve it.

In truth, I had been told how to work toward racial healing: build relationships. I had heard it over and over again, at each racial reconciliation meeting I had attended with my other white friends. "The only way to overcome the disease of racism," I had been told, "is to get to know people who are not from your own skin color and culture." But I didn't get it. I thought church, because of the base in faith it provided, was the only place I had to do that. I could see no commonality with my neighbors.

And so, before her seat was warm, this woman whose white teeth flashed and whose large, gold earrings dangled wildly, had unwittingly obliged me to make her acquaintance. I squirmed in my seat, wondering what I would say after the pastor walked to the back door of the sanctuary where he would shake hands with us as we filed slowly out. But I didn't need to worry. As soon as the sermon started, Tasha heard Simon's gurgle and turned around to gush over his soft cheeks and his ready smile. "Can I hold him, honey?" she whispered loudly in her thick black accent. I gladly handed him over and then quietly stole out of my pew and squeezed in beside her. By the time the service was over, Natasha Desiree Peterson had won my heart.

Actually, by the time the service was over, she and I were in the cool basement of the church swapping birthing stories. Steve found us laughing heartily together with Simon snuggled soundly in my new friend's arms and Chad staring adoringly up at her. Honestly, I don't know if our friendship started because I wanted to minister to a guest or because God sent her to reach into my soul and to pull out nuggets I hadn't even known were there. Whatever the reason, a few years later we sat on a park bench deep in conversation.

So what *do* ya want?" she wisely asked me. I don't want to be single, that's for sure." I shuddered. "I really don't think I could do it on my own. Especially living here." I saw a black man walking toward us and wished I had a car door to lock. Instead, I got up to help Simon out of the swing.

Tasha folded her arms over the silver hoop piercing her belly button and slowly rocked side to side, humming. Her slim shoulders moved easily under the strings of her halter-top. Chad and Simon ran off to join a group of boys in the sandbox. It seemed apparent that they, at ages four and two, hadn't yet noticed how different they were from their neighbors.

I wandered back to Tasha. "Did you know that we bought our house in the winter? We didn't even realize we were in the 'hood until spring when suddenly the whole tribe swarmed outside and beat their bass drums on their car stereos until winter came again." I laughed.

Tasha didn't. It really was a stupid joke.

"I don't mean *you* when I talk like that, Tash. You're different."

"Am I?"

"Yeah. I don't even think of you as black."

"Just like Steve don't think of you as a woman." Tasha batted her lashes at me and then turned her head to hum some more.

I don't even think of you as black. That wasn't just a bad joke. That was a revelation of my true self. I hushed and watched the kids for a little while, letting my friend's words sink in. The splinters in my throat from that morning's confrontation with Steve gathered to form a giant lump. My paradigm was shifting.

A boy threw sand at Chad. I almost jumped up, but then I saw Chad grab his own face and pretend to fall over. They both broke out into giggles.

The man I had dodged stood patiently behind a two-year-old girl wearing Winnie-the-Pooh overalls as she painstakingly climbed the ladder to the top of the slide. I watched him hold up his hand protectively as he moved to the foot of the slide and then murmur encouraging words to the delighted child who wouldn't budge.

A sixteen-year-old boy bounced a basketball to a younger boy with the same toothy grin. "You all dat, boy," the older one hollered out. "Yeah, buddy." The younger one dribbled the ball, glanced at his brother, and missed the hoop. The older boy caught the ball and tossed it back. "Try again." The younger boy stuck his tongue between his lips in concentration as he aimed. This time the ball swished through the hoop. They both hooted with pleasure while they ran their hands in a quick succession of motions that ended in a handshake.

As I watched the scenes playing out before me, I found myself thinking that if this were a movie, the camera would be panning from each of the characters in the park to my face, which would be slowly growing more and more pale. The audience would be holding their breath as they squeezed the hand of whomever they were with. "Yes," they would be wanting to shout out at me, "you're getting it!" But instead of feeling the excitement that imaginary viewers might be enjoying over my epiphany, I felt only a sickening twist in my stomach as the implosion that had started that morning continued.

Something needs to change, God. Is it me? Again?

Tasha broke the silence. "So, what started all this trouble with your man?"

I felt dizzy. "It doesn't really matter." I tried to look at her without moving my head. "Oh, Tasha. I'm sorry. I'm just a stupid white person."

She laughed, and it surprised me. It surprised me even more when she scooted closer to me and gave me a sideways hug. "You is stupid, girl, but I still love ya."

I looked at the ebony fingers of her right hand intertwined with the white ones of my left hand. "Look how black you are."

Tasha's voice seemed to vibrate from deep within her chest when she laughed. Usually I have to laugh with her when I hear it. This time I wanted to cry.

Shame overwhelmed me.

"Oh, Tash, I can hardly bear myself. I am so … Oh, Tasha, I'm so racist, aren't I?" Tasha kept her left arm around me while I pulled my hands to my face and curled my shoulders down. "When I was in college I lived with a girl from Nigeria, and I loved feeling so … so cosmopolitan. I thought that meant I wasn't racist." I laughed sourly. "I really didn't get to know her that well."

Tasha was humming again. I noticed the song was an old hymn that we hardly ever sang at Sherman Street: "Let My People Go."

"I thought that since *you're* my friend, I wasn't racist." I laid my head on her shoulder and let myself cry. "I thought that since I was involved in a church that preached racial reconciliation, I wasn't racist." My tears flushed down my face. I grinned through them at Tasha. "Now I'm surprised you keep coming back."

Tasha nodded. "Everybody sure love me at Sherman Street, but I wonder if it ain't just 'cause I'm black. Still, I keep hoping they'll eventually love me for being me."

"I used to love you just because you're black." I blushed at my confession and stared at the dirt under my feet.

Tasha pulled a tissue out of her purse and dabbed my cheeks. "I know, sister. But that's alright. You a changed woman now."

Suddenly, my shame dissipated. I took a deep breath and felt myself straighten and soften at the same time.

"Strange." I suppose I was speaking to Tasha, but the words would have floated out of me regardless of the audience as I immersed myself in this new revelation. "Strange. Why have I always thought reconciliation was something sweet and gentle?"

Tasha shook her head knowingly. "It ain't easy."

"Hmmm. I've always thought black people were stubborn when they wouldn't come to racial healing classes and when they seemed to avoid conversations about race. Wow." I shook my head as I absorbed this wonder. "I've been so dense!"

Tasha turned to look at me directly, her eyes slightly squinted.

I stood up and stretched, as if trying out new limbs.

Tasha also stood up. "I'm glad we stuck with each other, Heather. You a good friend."

Chad was driving a Matchbox car around the shoulders and head of his playmate, making wonderful motor noises. His new friend laughed jubilantly as he pressed Chad's nose with a muddy finger. At four, they didn't *care* about their differences.

I kissed Steve passionately when he came home from the store. "I'm gonna cook you up some chicken, baby," I told him as I started pulling groceries from the bag. He raised his eyebrows.

"Oh, yeah." The laughter in me couldn't be contained. "If God wants us to stick around, then we'd better learn how to fit in."

"Daddy," Chad burst out, "we went to Deshawn's house! His mama teached Mommy how to make chicken."

Steve's eyebrows curved even more.

I nodded. "You know what I like about the people around here?"

Steve stared at me.

"Wait. That may be a generalization. Do you know what I like about Dolores so much?"

"Dolores?"

"Deshawn's mom. She forgives so easily. She even gave me some corn bread."

"Corn bread?"

"Yeah." I stopped reaching into the brown bags and

looked up at Steve. "Something happened to me today."

"I see."

I grinned widely. "Oh, hey. Do you mind if Deshawn spends more time with us? He's such a sweet boy. And his mom ... wow." I looked around at my beautiful family and my cozy home. Dolores's rotting furniture and smoke-filled rooms matched the painful childhood she flippantly revealed to me; her current drug- and boyfriend-related problems happened before my eyes. "Well, I don't know how she survives with the life she has."

He leaned over the counter to kiss me. "I think that would be wonderful."

That week I asked the kids who hung out at our house to help me plant perennials in the black, spring soil—and a new tradition was birthed. They proudly joined me in watering and weeding the flowers rather than plucking them. Cuss words were rare because no one could bear to watch through the fence all afternoon.

Our family began walking to church on Sunday mornings. By the end of the summer, we were able to greet several neighbors along the way by name. One of them started coming to church with us.

Watching the sunset and greeting our neighbors from the front step became a regular habit.

Bunk beds replaced the twin bed in Chad's room so we could make Deshawn's frequent sleepovers more comfortable.

Pumpkin bread baked from the bright orange vegetable that grew beside my garage was exchanged with neighbors for tips on where to buy the best greens in town and how to fix them.

An afternoon of chatting with Dolores one stormy

Saturday led to cornrows in my pin-straight hair. "And you gotta wear tighter pants on that big booty of yours, girl," she told me as I walked out her door. "Oh ho. You just keep them hackles down. I'd give up my own sweet granny for a foundation like that."

Comments on the arrogance of white people bounced off me regularly. I struck back by disparaging the loud level of noise coming from the mouths of black folk. As we criticized each other, our arms held each other's shoulders more tightly and our smiles broadened. One warm October evening after taking Chad to the playground across the street and chatting with the other moms who congregated there, I walked into the house with a swing to my step. "Oh, Steve. We laughed until our sides ached." I lifted Simon up and gave him a kiss. "It's amazing—I never thought this would happen—but I *like* living here." Steve nodded. "Yeah. I've been thinking about that. Some-one at church asked about the house. He'll be at the council meeting tonight. Shall I tell him we're not selling anymore?" He shrugged his shoulders. "I don't think we can afford to move anyway." I almost giggled. "I guess we're staying." When Steve left, I put the boys to bed and dropped into bed myself, exhausted and happy. Everything was lovely. I wouldn't have believed, had I been warned, that my life would be interrupted so grossly in so short a time.

But what seemed like only moments later, the light in my bedroom turned on. I groaned and pulled the blankets over my head. "Turn off the light, Steve." The room went dark again, and I grudgingly opened my eyes and peeked out from the covers.

The man standing in my bedroom was not Steve.

CHAPTER FOUR

THE
PAINTING

"You better not

wake your babies.

I don't think you want them to get

hurt."

T**hrough** the dim light reflecting from the hallway, I saw your silhouette—and vaguely understood that a tall, black man with thick arms stood a few feet away. "Who are you?" I asked sleepily. I might have rolled over and disappeared back into my dreams, but the ugliness of your voice ("Don't you worry 'bout dat,") shocked me into wakefulness. Suddenly, I was not only awake, but keenly aware.

I sat up quickly, and you yanked a knife out of your pocket.

"Oh, no," I whispered, holding my hands up toward you as if sheer willpower would keep you away. "No, don't do this."

You could have stopped. God carefully paints each detail of our lives onto a giant canvas with the desire of creating a beautiful picture, but he lets us determine each stroke of his brush. "Don't do this," I told you. "Let me pray for you." I flung the words at you as you slowly pushed me back down onto the bed. "I can pray for you," I shouted desperately.

You laughed—and the sound was wicked, mocking what could have set you free, reveling in the illusion of power.

Suddenly angry, I sat up and tried to get out of bed. My protest grew louder. "Stop!" I screamed at you. "Go away!"

We wrestled only briefly. You needn't have wrestled at all, for your next words subdued me entirely. "You better not wake your babies. I don't think you want them to get hurt."

The darkness hid your visage from me, and I was glad, for I was spared from looking into the face of evil. I moaned as you shoved me back onto the bed. I sobbed for my children, not knowing if you had hurt them already. I prayed for protection. I begged God to free me.

You chuckled as you sat at the edge of my bed, acting as though you had a right to be there. You touched my hair gently, as if your other hand did not threaten me with a knife. "You gonna like this, baby." Your breath reeked of beer, and your words fell on me like vomit. Slowly, so gently, you pulled the blankets off me and let your free hand roam over my body, over the long, flannel nightgown I wore. At first I resisted your touches by slapping your hands and moving away any way I could, but that only increased your pleasure. "You'll be flying, baby. You never had it so good, baby."

Could you really have believed the words you spoke?

When your fingers found their way under my gown, I felt each touch as deeply as a burning coal against my skin. "You gonna be begging for more, baby." The hardness of the knife against my neck was barely noticeable against the sick sound of your words. I reflexively jerked away from you and experienced momentary freedom. I nearly escaped from the bed.

And so, in your panic, you lost all pretense of charm. You called me "bitch" and slapped my face. You grabbed me violently and scraped the knife over the flesh on my neck. You swore that I would die if I moved again. You snatched off my panties and yanked my gown up around my neck.

I endured the filth of your mouth on my breasts.

I endured your fingers and tongue penetrating my body.

I endured your sweat dripping on my belly.

Your play with my body finally found satisfaction, and so you moved into the final act. I sensed the change coming and whimpered audibly. I doubt you heard me over the sound of your grunts and heavings.

Perhaps the agony would have been too much for me if I hadn't discovered a Place in myself where the Comforter dwelt. I might have screamed and struggled hysterically, driving you to worse measures. I might have mustered up the strength to kill you with your own knife. I might have willed myself to die. Instead, I entered the Place that had been newly revealed to me and leaned into Holy arms. I prayed without words and communed with God. The tears rolled down my face, and my very soul wept, but I was safe. I endured.

I silently called out to the God who lets me face only that which I can handle. But I wasn't calling out for protection any longer. I wasn't calling out for freedom from your pollution. Instead, I was calling out for salvation—for you. "Forgive him, Lord." The words were not even my own.

Once, for a brief moment, you stopped, and I felt your head turn to look toward my face. Were you responding to the Holy Spirit's prompting to quit and repent of this act, or were you simply looking for the knife you had dropped?

You returned to your perilous quest for power.

You found exhilaration by forcing entry into another soul and didn't know you were actually on a roller coaster ride heading straight into the pit of darkness where you would crash into eternal doom. At the end of your ride, you would experience far worse than rape. I knew even then that you and I, though intertwining our souls in a deeply personal way that would remain forever embedded in our hearts, were as far apart as two humans ever could be. And so my heart mourned for you. "Forgive him. He doesn't know what he is doing." My brother, you should have listened to the prompting.

I didn't come out of the Place until you jerked my arm and told me to get you some money. I got out of bed quickly and pulled my gown over my body, thankful for the privacy.

You cursed, for you had lost the knife.

Oh, how I wish I had been in a frame of mind to protect myself then. I might have seized the moment and run away so you would have had to abandon your quest for the knife. I might have used strength fueled by adrenaline to knock you over or to rush to the phone. I might at least have memorized your appearance to describe you to the police later.

Instead, I sank onto the foot of the bed and put my face in my hands. Reality eluded me. I did not consider that I might be moments from death. I did not consider that my children might be dead already. I did not consider that a rapist walked freely in my home. I knew only that my heart was searching, searching for something that was lost and would never be found.

Awareness faded away.

I   did not know that it was your arm that pulled me close. I did not know that it was your voice that soothed me. I did not know that I wept on the shoulder of the one who caused the pain. I knew only that I longed for comfort to replace my brokenness.

I wonder what color God used as he painted on your canvas in those moments of embrace. Did the dark shades of scarlet soften to rose in reflection of your gentleness? Or did he swirl the crimson streaks into an ever-thickening blackness as you sought control of me in yet another way?

We went downstairs after a moment. I no longer felt a protective arm, but a threatening knife. Anxiety enveloped me as we descended the stairs—your giant presence hovering behind me, my mind racing for a way to appease you. We had no cash in the house except some coins in a pottery jar that held various oddments, but I dumped everything out to you as a peace offering. Too late I remembered that Steve's wedding ring nestled among the quarters. He kept it there during the week to avoid shocks in his work as an electrician. You stuffed a handful of the treasure in your pocket, snatched the car keys, and then turned me back toward the stairs.

Not again, my thoughts wailed. Not again!

The stench of your body surrounded me, but the choice was not mine to make. Dread seemed to grow into a tangible force that pushed against me as we ascended, but you shoved me until I collapsed onto the bed. I felt myself sliding back into myself, back to the Place.

"When's your husband coming home?" you asked, your face close to mine in the darkness—and I remembered my desire to survive. Steve! He would save me!

"Soon!" I blurted with renewed hope. "Soon!"

We heard a noise. You covered my mouth and held the knife in front of you, transforming my hope into terror, until the silence proved that Steve had not returned. You would have killed him.

"Go!" I told you with new urgency when you uncovered my mouth. "He'll be home soon. Go." You yanked open dresser drawers until you found some pantyhose. "Go!" I shouted as you jerked me over to my stomach and tied my hands behind my

back. "Go! Quickly!"

I held my wrists slightly apart as you bound me. Did you notice my self-protection and allow God to paint with gentle strokes? Or were you simply negligent because of your hurry?

The point of your knife again found the nape of my neck. I heard venom spew out of your mouth, but the slur of drunkenness and rush of passion hid the meaning from me. I remained silent. Your face came closer and you snarled the words again, but I still didn't understand. "I don't know what you're saying," I sobbed as you increased the pressure of the knife to indicate you wanted a response.

This time I heard you: "I'll kill you if you tell anyone 'bout dis."

Understanding was worse than not understanding, for I knew your words to be true. "What do you want me to say?" I whispered—and then you were gone.

The sounds of silence echoed around me as I held my head slightly over the pillow, listening. My temples throbbed. Tension pulled tightly at my scalp. Darkness clawed at me. When I dared to move, I pulled my hands out of their binding and then stopped to listen again. I swung my legs over the edge of the bed and then stopped to listen. I walked cautiously to the door and listened. Finally, I let out my breath. I rushed to the boys' bedroom, terrified at what I might find.

May God forgive you entirely for what you did to me— I bless you! For you spared my babies.

My babies! I couldn't stay long at one bedside but rushed back and forth between them, crying, touching the sweet, restful eyes and cheeks and shoulders of my peaceful boys. They were safe.

Full joy sparred with empty despair.

I stumbled down the stairs, hardly able to see for the tears in my eyes. The back door was wide open. I slammed it shut and locked the deadbolt. I found the phone through my blurred vision and called the church.

Maryann's husband answered the phone. "Byron!" I made no attempt to hide my terror. "I need Steve!" I didn't care that the sobs rose out of me for my friend to hear. He asked no questions, and Steve's voice soon replaced Byron's.

"Steve." I had no words. "Steve .. "

"What's wrong?"

"Come home." My voice shook.

"What happened?"

"I've been …" My throat ached. "A man came …"

"Heather …" His voice weakened. "What happened?"

"Steve," I whispered. "I've been raped."

I cowered in the corner of the kitchen, pressed against the wall, holding the phone to my chest, and didn't move even when I felt Steve take the phone from my hands, even when he rubbed my stiff arms and held my face.

I was empty again.

CHAPTER FIVE

VIOLATED AGAIN

My eyes dared him

to accuse me of

the very thing I accused myself of:

negligence.

It was my fault.

You could not have tied me tight enough to match the prison I created for myself in those moments I cowered in a corner of the kitchen.

I felt Steve's hands on my face and heard his voice trying to call me out of myself, but I stayed where it was safe—deep in my corner, deep in myself. His words were garbled and his touch cold. His image blurred before my eyes, though I shed no tears.

I noticed he was gone when he left my side, for fear suddenly loomed over me. My need to know where he was yanked me from my reverie. I began to feel the cramps in my bent legs and the tightness of my own grip on my arms.

"Steve," I cried softly, desperately. "Where are you?" I loosened the hold I had on myself but dared not move.

Steve rushed into the kitchen. "I'm right here." His voice cracked. "The boys are asleep."

I nodded. His arms held me again.

"Oh, Heather." Steve's face twisted with emotion. His eyes, wide and wet, held me.

Suddenly the doorbell rang—and it seemed to me like a shriek from the bellows of a hellish demon. We had been sitting in full view of the glass front door—exposed. I covered my ears, screaming, running, hiding. Steve's grasp failed, and his call fell into the empty space between us. "Heather—"

I stood with my shoulders pushed against the back door, shaking.

Steve found me and took my hands in his. "I'm going to answer the door. Stay here."

"No!" I whispered the word in terror. "It could be him!"

The porch light was on, and Steve had glanced up before coming to me.

"It's Maryann. She was at church tonight."

I looked suspiciously around the dark entryway. "Turn on the light." I still whispered.

He turned the light on. "See, it's just you and me here." He hushed his voice also. "I'll be right back." He touched my twitching face.

I heard their voices ("Is everything alright?" she asked), and I struggled over what to do. Should I go to Steve? I was terrified without him. Should I reveal myself to Maryann? I cringed at the thought.

But Steve was back before I could decide.

"Heather, I'm calling the police." He held both my hands.

"Police?" I didn't understand.

"Yes. Do you want to get dressed?"

"Dressed?"

"Yes. You should put some clothes on before the police come."

"I should put some clothes on." My words thudded

like an abandoned racquetball bouncing to a corner of the court.

"Heather, are you okay?"

"I'm okay." An echo only.

He took my hand and directed me out of the entryway. When we got to the phone, he let go of my hand and gently pushed me on. "Go get dressed."

I looked up the stairs and shuddered. Steve stood by the phone, watching me. "Go." *Go.* I had said that word.

I glanced up and then took a deep breath. The hall light was on, and pictures of Chad and Simon smiled at me. Steve still watched me, but he picked up the phone and waved me away.

Alright. I scrambled up the stairs, using my hands and feet like a young child would. I didn't stop outside my bedroom door, but plunged in and yanked open my closet to grab some jeans and a sweatshirt. I threw my gown and panties on the bed and then stepped into the bathroom to put on the clean clothes.

The shower beckoned me—promising hot, clean water that would wash away the filth that covered me. I touched the faucet but then heard a floorboard creak. I screamed and threw on my clothes. I smashed into Steve in my frantic sprint to the stairs and screamed again. He caught my fist before I swung at him.

"Shhh," he told me gently. "Don't wake the boys."

Better not wake your babies.

A sob caught in my throat.

"Come on," he said as he eased me down the stairs. "They'll be here in a minute."

"Who?"

73

"The police, Heather. I called the police."

Maybe it was his tone of voice—slightly annoyed, slightly helpless. Whatever it was, I gasped. My vision cleared so that I saw the straight edge of the bookshelf and the fuzz on the couch pillow, but my insight clouded.

"The police?" I stared at him. "Coming here?"

"They might still be able to catch—"

"Oh, no! This place is a mess." I immediately rushed through the living room—tossing newspapers, folding throw blankets, stacking books. "Thank goodness the dishes are done."

"Heather …"

"Grab that teddy bear, would you?"

He picked it up and set it on the couch.

"Listen," he said, "you'll have to talk to—"

"Will you close the door to the laundry room?"

"No."

I looked at him.

"No," he said again. "The house looks fine."

"But—"

"Heather, the police are coming to talk to you about what just happened."

I sat down, a coaster in my hand, and repeated his words: "What just happened …" It wasn't a question, but Steve took it as one.

"Heather! You tell me! What happened?" He nearly shook me.

"Maryann was here." I looked at the blue swirls in the design of the coaster and then shot a look at my husband. "What did you tell her, Steve?" My voice accused him; my heart beat wildly. *I'll kill you if you tell …*

74

"Nothing!" He sat beside me and took the coaster out of my hand. "I didn't tell her anything."

The doorbell rang. I stared at my empty hands while Steve went to the door.

The police officer at the door was a man. Of course he was a man. He sounded friendly, almost happy, as he greeted my husband. "Good evening, sir. Are you Steve Gemmen?" He pronounced the "G" soft, as in "German."

Steve must have nodded. I was pulling one of the blankets I had just folded over myself, up to my chin.

"I understand there has been a disturbance here. Could we come in?"

I could feel Steve look at me, but I wouldn't look up.

"Sir?"

"Uh. Yeah. Come in."

The man strolled over to me, and I sensed his confidence without looking at him. I heard a couple other male voices grunt a greeting to my husband.

"Ma'am?"

I wouldn't look up.

He sat down in the blue denim chair across from me. Steve and the others stood by the door.

"I'm Officer Long. May I ask you a few questions?"

I looked at Steve. He walked over and sat down beside me—I would have bolted if he hadn't—and leaned forward in his seat.

Officer Long cleared his throat.

"Pull up a chair," Steve told the other men. The words sounded awkward from him. He wasn't used to playing the host. They pulled chairs from the dining room and made a

75

semicircle around me.

I was the child at the top of a high diving board with an impatient crowd jostling behind me.

Mine was the face under the lightbulb in the dark, smoke-filled room.

I was the bird flinging myself against the glass, going nowhere.

"Ma'am?"

Steve squeezed my knee through the blanket.

"Mrs. Gemmen, did you experience a crime tonight?"

Steve shifted uneasily.

"Heather." The officer's voice softened just a bit. "You need to answer the question so we can get things in motion as soon as possible. The K-9 unit is waiting outside." He cleared his throat. "Did you experience a crime tonight?"

"Yes," I whispered.

"Were you raped tonight?"

I nodded.

"Do you know who raped you?"

I shook my head.

I heard one of the men stand up to go outside.

"Would you please tell me the events of your evening?"

I glanced up at the three officers surrounding me. Officer Long held a pad of paper in his pudgy fingers, and his blue eyes bored holes in me. The other two sat in disinterested poses—ankle over knee and fingers folded behind head. One of them leaned back so the chair strained on the two back legs.

"I—I can't." I looked at Steve again, searching for some sign that he would save me. Even as I did it, I knew he couldn't help. He wanted me to talk, too—to ease the tension, to explain the impossible, to solve the problem.

"Did the crime happen here?" the officer asked me.

I nodded, but glanced again at the other officers before dropping my eyes back to my hands. One of the men had picked up a picture of our family and was looking at it. The other ran his finger over the grain of the wooden chair where a crack had begun to form.

"Steve," I whispered. They all listened, but I looked only at Steve. "There are too many people here." My whispering felt pathetic, as if I were a small child hiding behind my mother's skirt in a room full of rowdy teenagers. But the alternative was worse.

"Okay, guys," Officer Long said. The guys stood up and moved to the door where they shuffled their feet, looking out the window.

"Did it happen here in the living room?"

I shook my head.

"Where did the rape occur, Heather? Please, help me out here." His tone demanded cooperation.

"Upstairs. In my bedroom."

"Mr. Gemmen, is it okay if we look around a bit?"

Steve told them it was alright, and the two strangers loitering in my living room made their way unescorted into my private rooms, past my sleeping children. They took my panties, my nightgown, my sheets, and my new bedspread. Their fingerprint dusting left grease spots on doorknobs and dresser drawers.

"Now, from the beginning, tell me what happened," Officer Long said.

"A man came and made me have sex with him."

"Did you let him in the house?"

I shot my gaze at him, but saw no battle waiting. Still, I growled. "No." I didn't look away this time. I folded the blanket and swung it over the arm of the couch—and the scared child that had covered me since the attack was put aside.

"So, how did he get in?"

"Maybe through the back door."

"Was it unlocked?" His eyebrows lifted skeptically.

"Yes." I directed all my bitterness toward this officer who seemed to scorn me; my eyes dared him to accuse me of the very thing I accused myself of: negligence. *It was my fault.*

He leaned back in his chair and crossed his fat legs so that his right foot stuck out far in front of him. "What are you folks doing in this neighborhood, anyway?" He shook his head and shooed the question away. "Whatever. Are you in the habit of leaving your door unlocked at night?"

"This neighborhood is our home." I leaned forward as Steve leaned back into the couch.

Officer Long persisted. "Answer the question, please."

I could feel myself starting to shake. "Steve was coming home soon, and I wasn't worried. I don't always lock the door."

"You live on one of the most dangerous streets of the city, and you weren't worried?"

"No. I wasn't." My voice turned defensive. "We have very good neighbors." My voice edged toward offensive.

"Could the man in your bedroom have been one of these neighbors?"

I didn't hesitate to answer the question. "No."

Officer Long leaned further back in his chair, looking too comfortable, and then addressed me again. "Heather, are you sure you do not know the man who came into your bedroom tonight?"

Steve stood up to pace the room.

"I didn't even see his face."

"Please answer the question."

"No! I do not know who it was and I did not want him in my house and I hated every second of his filthy hands on my body!"

"Did you tell him that?"

"Of course! I screamed and hit and told him to leave me alone."

"But he still got what he wanted?"

"He had a knife to my throat, and he threatened to kill my kids if I didn't give him what he wanted!"

Officer Long uncrossed his legs and leaned forward in his chair. I smelled garlic on his breath. "Heather, you are getting upset. Why don't you go get a glass of cold water, and we'll continue this when you have settled down."

"No! Let's get this over with so you can get out of my home."

I looked at Steve to see if I was overreacting, but I couldn't read my husband's expression.

"Alright, then. Why don't you just start from the beginning and tell me what happened."

"Officer—" Steve's intrusion into the conversation surprised me "—my wife called me at church right after the rape. She was clearly traumatized. When I pulled into the driveway, the car door was open and the ignition was on. It looks like the person who was trying to take the car couldn't get it into reverse."

The officer looked at me. "Did you give this man the car

keys?"

"He took them. They were sitting on the kitchen table."

"Okay. Tell me what happened. Start at the beginning."

I nearly mocked him for his patronizing repetition. Instead, I crossed my legs and crossed my arms and looked out the window. "I went to bed early—"

"What time?"

"I went to bed around nine o'clock and went straight to sleep. I woke up when someone turned on the light."

"I thought you said you didn't see his face."

"I didn't. I pulled the covers over my head because I thought it was Steve."

"What time was that?"

"I don't know. Maybe it was nine thirty."

Officer Long looked at his watch. "It's past eleven now. How long did he stay?"

I shrugged. "What time did I call you, Steve?"

"Just after ten."

"And the alleged rapist left the premises before you called your husband?"

I narrowed my eyes. "Yes."

"So, he's had about an hour to get away. Why didn't you call the police?"

"I didn't think of it."

"You didn't think to call the police?"

I shook my head. *Why hadn't I called the police?*

Officer Long's eyes rolled upward as he sighed deeply. "Well, what happened next?"

"I went to bed around nine o'clock and went straight to sleep. I woke up when a man turned on the light." I paused. Officer Long tapped his fingertips on his notepad. His wedding ring was locked in rolls of fat. "He, well, he made it clear what his intentions were."

"The facts, please."

"What else can I say?" I dropped my face into my hands. "He raped me, okay? Do I have to say it?"

"Yes, I'm afraid you do. And you need to tell me everything he did. If we catch this man, we'll throw the book at him for every single little thing he did—if you press charges."

I'll kill you if you tell ...

I said nothing.

"So, when you say *rape,* does that mean he had sexual intercourse with you?"

I nodded. I looked at the blanket but didn't pick it up.

"Did he penetrate your body in any other way?"

I nodded again.

Steve sat down beside me.

"You have to tell me, Mrs. Gemmen." Fingers tapping again.

"Tongue. Fingers. I don't know. I tried not to pay attention."

"How many times?"

I looked at him. He sat on the edge of his chair.

The officers who had been upstairs hustled out the front door with bags in their hands.

"We can charge him for every single entry," said Officer Long.

"I don't know. I don't know, okay!" I looked up at Steve. "Steve! Do I have to—"

I saw fear in my husband's eyes. "No, Heather. You don't have to do this." He held my hand so tightly I thought he

81

would crack my fingers. "Officer, my wife has given her report. Would you please leave us alone now?"

The officer stood up, adjusted his pants on his hips, and put the notepad in his front pocket. "I wish I could say yes, but I'm afraid we're going to have to get your wife to the hospital to get a rape kit together. We'd be happy to escort you folks over there."

"I don't want to go to the hospital, Steve."

"It's your choice, of course, Mrs. Gemmen. But if you want some evidence against this guy, you're gonna have to jump through some hoops."

"What do you want to do, Heather?" Steve asked without looking at the officer.

"I don't know." I wanted to drive far away, find a ritzy hotel where I could soak in a hot, bubbly bath, and forget this night ever happened.

"I think you should go if you can." Steve looked as confused as I felt.

"Okay." I picked up the blanket and covered myself. "What about the kids?"

"Mr. Gemmen, we'd be happy to take your wife to the hospital if you need to stay with the children."

"No!"

"No. We'll find someone to watch them."

Officer Long excused himself. "We'll be right outside if you need us."

Steve went to the phone.

I laid my head against the back of the couch and waited to be told what to do next.

Steve answered the door a little later. I did not listen to

82

the words he exchanged with our friends who had come to pick up Chad and Simon. I did not stand up to accept the hug offered me. I did not kiss my sleeping children good-bye.

I put on my shoes and coat when Steve brought them to me. I walked to the front door.

And then I screamed.

Blue and red lights from a caravan of police units swirled on the walkway; men in uniforms hovered in my yard; crowds of people, including Deshawn's mom and others I knew, hung out on the sidewalk, their shadows looming under the streetlamps.

"I can't." I had retreated to the kitchen. "I can't go past them."

Steve left me standing in the back entryway while he brought the car around to the back door. He drove right up on the grass so I could step from the house to the car. As we pulled out of the driveway, I hid under my coat, clutching Steve's arm in terror.

And, still, the nightmare wasn't over.

the words he exchanged with our friends who had come to pick up. I had and Simon. I did not stand up to accept the hug offered me. I did not kiss my sleeping children good-by.

I put on my shoes and coat when Steve brought them to me.

I walked to the front door.

And then I screamed.

Blue and red lights from a caravan of police units swirled on the walkway, men in uniforms hovered in my yard, crowds of people, including Deshawn's mom and others I knew hung out on the sidewalk, their shadows looming under the streetlamps.

"I can't," I had retreated to the kitchen. "I can't go past them."

Steve left me standing in the back entryway while he brought the car around to the back door. He drove right up on the grass so I could step from the house to the car. As we pulled out of the driveway, I hid under my coat, clutching Steve's arm in terror.

And still, the nightmare wasn't over.

Chapter Six

ILLUSIONS LOST

Death does not seem so

gruesome or final

when you are holding it in your hand

in the form of a tiny, pink pill.

They say that police dogs track the scent of fear.
You can't comprehend how satisfying it is to know
that you were afraid, that your state of mind was as
fragile as mine.

"I can't go in, Steve." We were sitting outside the hospital. I
watched Officer Long walk toward our car. "And I can't
face that cop again."

For a moment Steve looked like he might agree, as if he
were flirting with the idea of taking off out of the hospital
parking lot and never looking back. But he drew a breath
and squeezed my hand. "You'll be okay. I'll stay with you."
He opened his door and then walked around to open mine.
I took a deep breath as well.

The police officer walked a few paces away as we moved
toward the emergency room doors. Before we got to the desk,
he told us to sit down. He would check us in. "I recognize
the need for discretion, Mrs. Gemmen. But may I inform the
hospital staff of your reason for coming here?"

I nodded and walked to a seat in the far corner of the

waiting room. I stared at the television show, unmoved by the alligator attacks and beer commercials playing on the screen, unmoved by Steve's arm over my shoulder. Eventually I turned to the people around me.

An Asian woman rocked an infant in her left arm. The baby had on nothing but a disposable diaper.

A wiry Hispanic rose and sat, rose and sat, clenching a fist and throwing stony glances at the front desk. A bandana around his forearm was wet with blood.

A lovely blonde teen wearing white shorts and a white sweater clung to a handsome black man. He wore a hockey jersey and held a towel to his forehead. They whispered together constantly. Once, when her laughter grew too loud, the girl pressed her mouth against his shoulder until she was able to limit the expressions of her love to face-aching smiles.

An elderly white man clutched the cane on his lap, ignoring the flittering attentiveness of his aged wife. Every once in awhile he would push the dentures out of his mouth and move his tongue over his gums. The wife handed him a cup of coffee. "It's hot, honey." The man harrumphed, but the old woman kept right on talking. "Not many people here tonight."

"I'm here." The husband spat the words.

"I thought it would be packed. There just aren't many people here."

"I'm here."

"Amazing. You'd think with a city this size there would be more people in the emergency room."

"I'm here." The old man hadn't moved from his hunched position.

I'm here, too, I silently hollered at her.

I looked at Steve, whose arm still held me. I noticed the lines around his eyes and the stubble on his chin. He no longer looked like the boy I had fallen in love with almost a decade earlier. He looked much stronger now. I leaned against his shoulder, and he rested his head on mine for a moment.

"Heather Gemmen." The nurse's voice surprised me. Steve stood up and waited silently for me to gather my strength. The nurse looked at the floor when we got closer. "Come right in here, dear," she said. "Is this your husband?" Steve eased me toward the open door.

I nodded.

"Do you want him to accompany you?" Her words were hedged in caution.

"Yes." I reached for Steve's hand. "Definitely." I wondered if Steve's mind, as I fled into his guardianship, wandered back to last Saturday when I sat down at the desk declaring that I would be the family bookkeeper now. Or if he remembered my recent bold defense of our female friend who had become a pastor. Or if he thought about how I generally tend to take advantage of his laid-back attitude. I was aware of the change—and I was embarrassed by my desperate dependence on him. But as he supplied all the billing paraphernalia and signed the papers, as he answered preliminary questions and carefully articulated the reason for hospital care, I thankfully retreated into silence. I needed all the energy I had to hold up figurative hands against this unfamiliar emotion, this fear that danced a circle around me, breaking in and moving out again. Its conquest of me had seemed complete only hours before, but I felt the loss of courage too keenly to give up the fight.

Loss of courage. But that wasn't all. Independence! Tenacity! Trust! They had been ripped from me in an act that left no outward scar. They had been my strengths. What was left?

My strengths. When had I ever depended on Steve before? When had I ever grown comfortable in his harborage? I clung to his arm and found a bond. I trusted his protection and found love. Fleeing into the sanctuary of my husband's care did not mean I was giving in to the enemy that crouched at my door.

The doctor will be a little while yet, Heather," the nurse told me as we walked deeper into the hospital. "Let's get a couple of things done first." I sat on the table and Steve stood by the door as she took my temperature and blood pressure. She asked whether I was experiencing pain and if it was okay if a counselor chatted with me for a few minutes. And then she laid a hand on my arm. "Heather," she said, "will you tell me what happened?"

I didn't want to. "A man came into our home ..." I paused and looked at Steve for help.

"She was raped," Steve said flatly.

"What exactly did he do, Heather?" The nurse's voice was soft and sweet, but her words burned.

"I don't know. He slapped me."

"Do you have any bruises or cuts?"

"I don't think so."

"What else happened?"

"I don't know. He ..." My voice trailed off again.

"She told all this to the police already." Steve's voice cracked.

The nurse turned to him and gently squeezed his arm. "I know, sweetie. I'm sorry we have to do this again." She turned back to me, and I saw a hint of a tear in her eye. Sometimes when I am aware of deep feelings lurking just under my self-control, all it takes is a sympathetic look to transform my courage into pathetic tears. And the more I try to hold back my feelings, the stronger they push to escape. Usually, when I feel this coming on, I'll excuse myself to the ladies' room until I regain my composure. This time, as my emotion tingled under my eyelids, all I could do was let my hair fall over my face to hide my vulnerability.

I watched the nurse's shoes shift in front of me as I whispered the story, in abbreviated form, again.

The nurse tucked my hair behind my ear before she reached for the door. "I've set out a gown for you, Heather. Take your undergarments off and slip into this. The doctor should be coming soon. Meanwhile, I'm going to find a comfortable place for your husband to wait."

We didn't argue, and Steve disappeared behind the closing door. The quiet click snapped the thread that held my security. I was alone.

I wish I could say it was gentle temperament that caused me to resist insisting that my husband stay by my side. If that is what this was, then my "gentleness" is restricted to strangers. I yell at Steve for little things: like starting a load of laundry and forgetting to flip it to the dryer, or ignoring my question in favor of listening to a radio commercial, or neglecting to enforce a rule with one of our kids. I yell at the kids for even smaller things: like leaving toys outside overnight, or crying too long over a stubbed toe, or eating half an apple and throwing the rest away.

It wasn't even fear that kept me from demanding my rights. Fear was why I wanted him to stay. The reason I didn't insist on Steve staying was because I had a warped sense of politeness. Manners had a firm grip on me.

And so, alone and broken in the emergency room, I did what I thought I should do: I folded up my clothes and put on the frail gown. I sat quietly on the examining table with my hands in my lap. Etiquette placed me on the bull's-eye of Fear's assault, and I battled for nearly an hour. Feeling like a child trapped on a bed about which monsters prowled, I believed I would be devoured by despair unless I stayed out of its reach. I remained still and calm, but every once in a while a shiver ran through my body.

"Come in," I yelped in response to the knock at the door.

The face of a black man poked around the door. Thick lips smiled. "Hi! Are you Heather?"

I nodded, and my palms started sweating.

The man stepped fully into the room and turned to close the door. I watched his back, broad and imposing.

"Wait!" a woman's voice called from the hall. "The doctor hasn't seen her yet."

"Oh." The man turned to me and smiled again. "Sorry. I'll catch up with you later." He closed the door behind himself. I battled for another half-hour.

Come in," I whispered to the next knock at the door.
A middle-aged white man wearing a tie underneath his lab coat entered. He didn't smile, but his face revealed gentleness. He looked tired.

92

"Hi, Heather," he said as he closed the door. "I'm Dr. Manz. Sorry you had to wait so long."

"That's okay," my manners answered.

He sat down without looking at the folder in his hand. "Are you doing alright?" He was looking for a real answer.

I shrugged. "Do you know where my husband is?" I immediately regretted asking it. I hated revealing insecurity.

The doctor raised his eyebrows. "He must be in the waiting room or the lounge. Do you want him?"

"Yeah, if that's alright."

"Okay. As soon as we finish up here, I'll ask the nurse to get him for you." He took the hammer and checked my reflexes. They were fine. "Are you experiencing any pain, Heather?"

I shook my head.

He placed the stethoscope on my back and asked me to take deep breaths. I did.

"Can you tell me what happened?" I couldn't see his face, but I felt the pressure of his fingers firmly on my left shoulder. I was surprised to discover comfort in his touch.

"Well …" I shivered.

He waited, still touching my back.

"Well, a man came into my home."

Dr. Manz moved the stethoscope over. "Mmm-hmm."

"And he hit me." I crossed my arms to rub my shoulders.

"Take another deep breath, Heather." I took two.

"Excellent," he said.

"He threatened to kill my kids if I moved, so I didn't." Words raced through my mind; I tried in vain to sort out which to let escape.

"Did he have sexual intercourse with you?" Dr. Manz asked patiently.

I nodded.

"Did you agree to have sex with him?"

"No." I shook my head once.

"Then he raped you, Heather." Dr. Manz's words were not brandished like a sword. Rather they were administered like salve over a fiery wound. "It was not your fault."

I heaved one giant sob and then sucked in air.

Dr. Manz strung the stethoscope around his neck and moved in front of me. He looked me straight in the face and said again, "It was not your fault."

"But I didn't lock the door," I whispered. It wasn't my only thought: *I gave in too easily. I let him hold me afterward as I cried. I didn't call the police.*

"Did you invite him in?" He seemed to know the answer already.

"No." So then why did guilt slide its slimy fingers over my neck and into my scalp?

"Well, then." The doctor raised his eyebrows as if to say *I told you so.* I sucked some more air. "So," he said, "what happened? Tell me."

I did. I told the story for the third time that night.

Dr. Manz seemed unaware of time or responsibilities outside this little room. He asked appropriate questions and showed obvious concern. When I came to the end of the story, he whistled between his teeth. "You're a brave woman, Heather." He passed a hand over his eyebrows. "And now, I'm sorry to say, you have to endure just a little bit more. Can you do that?"

"Do what?"

94

"I need to do a little detective work to see if we can trace this guy. I'm going to call the nurse in to help me. We'll pull a couple of your hairs to compare DNA, and we'll comb your pubic hair to see if he left anything behind. Are you ready?"

I wasn't. "Okay."

The nurse came promptly. The doctor kept talking as he worked.

"Do you remember when your last period was?"

"About two weeks ago."

"You're sure."

"Yes."

"When was the last time you had sexual intercourse before the incident you've reported?"

"I don't know. Within the last week."

"Have you been using contraceptives?"

"No. We've been kind of hoping to get pregnant."

"How about tonight? Did the rapist use a condom?"

"I don't think so."

Dr. Manz took his gloves off, and I tugged the gown around my body. He scribbled out a prescription and handed it to the nurse. She left.

"Okay, we've got a few more issues to look at."

I should have reminded him to call for Steve.

"You may not feel it right now, but you are very lucky that you came out of this in such good condition. I've seen outcomes much worse. I saw it yesterday ..." He dropped his gloves in the garbage bin. "But, Heather, it may not be over yet. You might have more to deal with than just rape."

"What do you mean?" My skin crawled—either from hearing the awful word again or in anticipation of his next comment.

"First, you're right in the middle of your menstrual cycle. Pregnancy is a definite possibility."

"No," I said. "I'm having trouble getting pregnant."

"Okay, but we'll still run a pregnancy test."

"Okay."

"Second, you are at risk of acquiring a sexually transmitted disease."

I had no idea how to respond. I wondered why Steve had not insisted on staying with me.

"We'll get some antibiotics that can prevent many problems, but we'll still have to run some tests after today to stay sure that everything is okay. I will have some lab work done on the specimen I retrieved to rule out any immediate problems."

The nurse came in with a tray. Three plastic cups held three little pills.

"Thanks, Betty," Dr. Manz said to the nurse. "I'd also like to order a urine test to rule out preexisting pregnancy. Can you get that started when I'm finished in here? Also, why don't you send this out to the lab and see if they can't get us any answers tonight yet."

Betty took the swabs and left. No one asked for Steve.

"Okay." The doctor turned back to me. "I'd like you to take this stuff. Floxin and azithromycin will fight any potential infections." He set two cups on the bedside table and pushed them toward me. "Ovral will prevent pregnancy." He set the third cup on the counter. "Don't take this until we get your pregnancy test results back."

He filled a fourth cup with water and handed it to me. I slugged down the Floxin and the azithromycin in one gulp.

"Okay, let's get that pregnancy test done."

Ten minutes later, fully dressed again, I handed the nurse my urine specimen. "I'd really like to have my husband with me. Could you find him for me?"

"Sure, sweetie. It might take me a bit, but I'll run down to the lounge as soon as I can grab a minute, okay?"

"That would be great." I slunk back into my little room and sat on the table.

Though covered by more than a hospital gown, there on my battlefield, I felt more vulnerable than ever. Fodder had been fed to my opponent; it grew stronger with the knowledge of potential consequences. Time deprived me of sleep, of strength.

Come in," I said to the knock at the door. It wasn't Steve.

"Hi again," said the black man.

"Hi." I shifted my weight on the table.

"I'm T.J. I'm a social worker from the rape crisis center here in town. May I chat with you a bit?"

"Okay." I watched him close the door.

"How you doing?" He held out his hand.

I felt my palm rub against the whiteness of his as he placed his other hand over mine in what I imagine he considered a warm and special shake. "Fine," I answered. "How are you?"

"I'm doing alright." He sat on the stool. "I realize you're going through a tough time."

I barely nodded my head.

"Okay. Well, I want to let you know that you're not alone. There are lots of people out there who want to help you and support you—'cause they've been through this, too."

I nodded. I didn't want to notice his blackness.

"I can't pretend to understand what you're going through, but I can honestly say that my heart breaks for you. This shouldn't have happened."

I nodded. I didn't want to notice his masculinity.

"Anyway, is there anything that you want to talk about right now?"

"No."

He nodded his head and threw a compassionate gaze at me. "Alright. I understand." He nodded some more. "I'm gonna give you my card. You call anytime if you just need to talk, alright?"

"Okay." I took the card.

Steve opened the door.

"Oh, hi," T.J. said. "You must be Steve."

Steve shook his hand but looked at me, concerned.

T.J. looked at me too as he reached for the handle of the open door. "I'll be hanging around these halls for a few more hours yet. Holler if you need me. That goes for either of you." He nodded to Steve and then closed the door behind him.

"Who was that?" Steve asked.

"The social worker." I dropped T.J.'s card in the garbage.

"The social worker!" Steve's voice bounced around the little room. "They gave you a black man for a social worker?"

"Yeah. It's okay, Steve."

"No, it isn't! That's the most ridiculous thing I ever heard. He was in here alone with you?" He knew the answer. Steve wrenched open the door and stormed into the hallway. "Excuse me." His voice was quiet, but his anger was evident. "Can I talk to someone about that—" he paused for a moment "—*idiot* social worker who was just talking to my wife?" Steve's anger scared me. I tried to pull him back into the room, but he ignored me.

The nurse stopped.

"My wife has just been traumatized by a black man, and you send another one in to counsel her?"

"It's okay, Steve," I pleaded.

The nurse looked upset. "I'm sorry, sir. I didn't even think about—"

"I know you didn't!" Steve interrupted. Steve never interrupted people. He turned to me. "I should have been with you."

"That's okay ..."

He followed me back into the room. "I should have been with you." He was still angry.

I closed the door on the nurse.

"You're here now." I took his hand. "I'm so glad." I didn't care about being a child.

We waited in silence, leaning into each other.

Dr. Manz knocked before he entered. He introduced himself to Steve and then apologized for the hospital's insensitivity. "We didn't know the race of your wife's attacker, Mr. Gemmen. I hope you can forgive us."

Steve nodded.

"Thank you, sir. We will be more sensitive to this in the future."

I wanted to tell him that we were not racist, but I recognized the absurdity of the statement and so remained silent.

Dr. Manz sat on the stool. "I've got some results for you, Heather. The chlamydia test came back negative. The gonorrhea test came back negative. The syphilis test was nonreactive. That's good news." I nodded in relief. *Good news* were the only words I needed to understand.

"Also," he said, "the pregnancy test was negative." His eyes searched mine. "Do you know what that means?"

"Yeah. I can breathe again."

"No." He shook his head sadly. "It means that before tonight, you were not pregnant. In other words, before your uninvited visitor came by, your egg was ready and waiting for fertilization."

"Oh." I shuddered. "That's not good."

"No, it's not." Dr. Manz reached for the cup on the counter. "Time to take this."

I held out my hand and he dropped the pill onto it.

"What exactly is Ovral?" I asked.

"Basically, it's a hormone that changes the environment of the uterus so the egg cannot implant."

"The fertilized egg?"

I could feel Steve's eyes on me.

"Ye-es." The doctor held onto the word with expectation. He must have known what I would ask next.

"And isn't that abortion?" Truthfully, I knew the answer. I suppose I was looking for a loophole.

"Well ..." He hesitated. "I think it's more accurate to say you're simply preventing pregnancy. Right now we don't even know if the egg has been fertilized. It's about as early in the game as you can get, Heather. Even if the egg is fertilized, it's only one cell at this point. Better to get rid of it now than later."

"One cell? Where does the DNA come from then?"

"It acquires a full set of DNA from the sperm before the sperm disintegrates."

"Only one cell?" *That's not a baby, is it?* "It must be a big cell."

"The biggest in the body. But it doesn't stay one cell. It divides as it travels toward the uterus. And then it looks for a place to implant so it can continue to divide."

"And then it turns into a baby." My voice betrayed my despair. Could the grime that immersed me yet cling to me, grow in me, reshape me? I ached to feel clean again, to strip off all remains of my trauma. As desperately as I had once longed to be pregnant, I now craved barrenness.

"It doesn't have to." I heard the promise in Dr. Manz's words. The hot tub in a ritzy hotel might not be such a far-out dream. Doctor Manz handed me a cup of water. "Go ahead. Take it."

Death does not seem so gruesome or final when you are holding it in your hand in the form of a tiny pink pill.

"I think I'll wait a minute," I said.

"Take your time. I'll come back in a few." He stood up and held the door handle. "It's the right thing to do." And then he was gone.

I looked at Steve.

"Take it," he said in answer to my silent question.

I wanted to.

"Do you think I should?"

He looked at me as if I were insane. "Yes."

"But it's abortion, Steve."

"That not what the doctor said."

"Yes, he did."

We were quiet for a moment.

"What if you get pregnant?" Steve asked.

I shuddered. "I won't get pregnant." Maybe believing would make it true.

"Still." The edge in his voice surprised me. "Take it anyway."

I was not sure what caused my uncertainty. I was not questioning my beliefs. I did not doubt that taking this pill was abortion, and I did not wonder if abortion in this case was acceptable. I did not waver from my conviction that human life is holy. And yet, I sat in that white, sterile room staring at the pill in my hand with a longing that seared my soul. *I need this pill, God!*

The doctor knocked before opening the door. I don't know how long he was gone. "How are you doing, Heather?"

"I don't think I'll take this." I kept my hand open as I moved it toward him.

He didn't take the pill. He just looked at me.

"Please," I said, my hand swaying before him. "Take it away." If he waited much longer, I thought I would give in.

"Listen,"—he closed my fingers over the pill and gently pushed my hand back—"why don't you keep that for a little while. It will be effective for the next seventy-two hours, and you might change your mind."

It seems possible that I was born with the belief that killing unborn babies is wrong. As a child, I had eaten warm stew from a thermos at many cold and wet Right-to-Life walks and protests. In high school, when hypothetical situations had black-and-white answers, I had discussed long into the night my passionate beliefs on this volatile issue. In college, I earned a perfect A on a paper that lobbied against abortion. And the experience of holding a "fetus" as perfect and beautiful as my other children had clinched my untried conviction.

Integrity is so much more than claiming noble ethics. It is more than holding passionate conviction. Integrity is living out expressed beliefs. It is making choices that accurately reflect core values.

The garbage can was within reach.

I put the pill in my pocket.

CHAPTER SEVEN

KNOWING BETTER

The next person I called was my mother.

Do you have a conscience? Do you ever wake up in a cold sweat at night and wonder what you have done? I do. You have raped, but I attempted murder.

Steve and I talked about my choice on the way home from the hospital. Dawn had not quite crept up on us, and the darkness encouraged softly spoken words. "So, why didn't you take it?"

"Do you think I should have?" I didn't remind him that I had the pill in my pocket.

"Well …" We were at a traffic light, and the red glare streamed over Steve's face.

"But it's abortion."

"Even if it is, it must be okay in this situation."

I let the words penetrate. "And it's only one little cell," I murmured.

The red light on his face turned green, and the car eased forward. "It would not be good if you got pregnant," he said quietly.

We remained silent the rest of the ride home.

The house was dark and empty. I was glad the kids were gone. They didn't belong in this place. "Do you think the kids will be okay?" I asked.

"You mean, tonight?"

I shrugged.

"Yeah, they'll be okay."

Steve held my hand as we went up the stairs to our bedroom where we both fell asleep with our clothes on.

I woke before Steve did. The sunlight was pouring in the window, shining brilliantly as if nothing evil had happened only a few hours earlier. I took a long, hot shower and dressed into pressed slacks and a soft sweater.

The first thing I noticed downstairs was the empty coin jar. Some of the coins still sat on the table and some had fallen to the floor. I collected what was left and put the jar away. Steve's ring was gone.

I wiped the counters and emptied the dishwasher and tidied the magazines. I opened the windows to let cool air refresh the house. I browsed through my CD collection and played Enya softly. I dusted the furniture in the dining room and living room. I washed the windows.

My house shone, but cleanliness eluded me.

I started upstairs to wake Steve—I needed to talk about what happened. I wanted to lie beside him on the bed and feel his fingers intertwined with mine; I wanted to tell him my feelings and hear his thoughts, to cry and eventually laugh together. But I stopped halfway up the stairs—he had slept only a few hours. I knew Steve needed silence as much as I needed discussion. He needed isolation as much as I needed fellowship. He wouldn't be ready to talk yet anyway, not about something so personal and painful. He would need time, years maybe, to think things through. I did not feel strong enough to endure his silence, his separation from me, so I turned and retreated to the living room.

The pill sat on the kitchen table beside my tea. It insisted on being addressed, but I knew I couldn't address it alone. I picked up the phone and dialed the home number of our pastor. "Hi, Mark. Do you have a minute?"

"I have as many as you need. Lori was just about to send me outside to rake leaves. You called in the nick of time."

I laughed and sat on the edge of the couch. "Actually, I'm looking for someone to rake my leaves. I heard you were volunteering for the job." The easy conversation now counterbalanced the anticipation of the difficult one to come.

"Right. And I heard you were going to preach on Sunday. The sermon title is 'Predestination, Justification, and Sanctification Made Clear.'"

"I could do that." Our laughter cheered me. "Maybe we'll get out of church on time for once."

"*Touché!*" Mark laughed loudly, and I could envision his white teeth flashing through the dark, well-groomed beard. I imagined his pale-blue eyes dancing in his handsome face. "So," he asked after his laughter subsided, "what's up?"

"You know, raking leaves won't be so bad today. It's gorgeous out there."

"True ..." Mark chuckled again. "You're up to something, Heather."

I remained silent for a moment, wondering how to break into the next portion of our conversation.

"Hey, Heather." Mark's voice sounded cautious. "Why'd Steve rush out of council meeting last night?"

What could I say? *I'll kill you if you tell* ... But I already had.

"Is that what you're calling about?" Mark asked.

"Yeah. I don't know how to say this." I wished we could go back to chitchat.

"Heather, what's wrong?"

For a moment I wondered why I had called. What was I looking for? Mostly I needed someone to cry to; also, I needed advice. "Well, I need to decide whether to take this pill the doctor gave me." I picked it up and looked at it.

"What pill?"

"It's the morning-after pill. To make sure I don't get pregnant."

"I thought you and Steve were trying for another."

"Yeah, but I was raped last night." I resisted saying the words, so they came out garbled. I'm surprised Mark understood them.

"Oh, Heather." His groan was as healing as his previous laughter. "Oh, Heather."

He and Lori came over while Steve was still sleeping. At the door, I started to joke about getting Mark out of his morning chore, but he just pulled me into a hug and held me until I abandoned myself to his intense, genuine compassion. Lori rubbed my back and murmured comforting words.

Unconditional love has always been embarrassing to me. The first time I noticed my reluctance to accept it was when we were newly married, making just enough money to appreciate the luxury of hotdogs in our macaroni and cheese once in a while. My father-in-law slipped twenty dollars into my hand and whispered, "Go out to eat tonight." I couldn't say no, and I couldn't pay him back. I had to smile as graciously as I could, go out to eat, and accept the fact that he did not want me to return the money. This time, broken and scared and confused, someone whom I honored and respected—someone who knew my faults—pushed me beyond my comfort zone of friendly banter into intense, genuine compassion. I needed it desperately, so I accepted this gift I could never pay back. But once I got past the humbling part, I realized that this kind of love was something I couldn't live without, and I wondered why I had resisted it for so long.

Mark and Lori's love knocked me into grace. I would have fallen sooner had I known how soft the landing would be. Eventually we found our way to the living room, where I'm sure I forgot to offer coffee.

"So tell me about this pill," Mark prompted.

"Steve wants me to take it."

"But you don't want to?" He seemed surprised. I didn't blame him.

"It doesn't make sense," I agreed. I didn't expect them to relate to the bizarre emotions raging through me. I didn't know how to explain—I didn't know how to understand!—how these two opposing truths could exist in me simultaneously. "I don't think I could handle getting pregnant from this—" the very thought made me nauseous "—but something won't let me take that stupid pill."

"Is it because you've been praying for a baby for so long?" Lori asked.

"No, that's not it." I shook my head. "I want a baby with *Steve*. I don't want this …" I dropped my head into my hands. "It doesn't make sense."

Actually, nothing made sense. It didn't make sense that I had to make this decision. It didn't make sense that I was sitting in a sunlit room on a gorgeous fall day, broken and scared. It didn't make sense that I had been raped.

"Heather," Mark asked, "would you feel comfortable letting your Bible study group know about this? I'd like to ask them to pray for you." Lori was in the group. Maryann was in the group. The other three members were women I had grown to love and trust as well.

I groaned inwardly. *I'll kill you if you tell …* had clearly lost the battle, but its power clung to me with surprising tenacity. Of course I wanted the prayers and support and wisdom of my sisters. "Yes," I said in a voice much stronger than my spirit felt. "Please do call them."

Lori used my phone to make arrangements. They all promised to come that afternoon. When Mark and Lori left, I felt a little stronger.

The next person I called was my mother. Steve was still sleeping.

"Hi, Mom," I said as cheerily as I could.

"Heather!" she exclaimed in her soft Dutch accent. "Is anything wrong?" She was three hundred miles away, but I knew exactly where she stood—constrained by the telephone cord—and what her house smelled like and how her dusty blonde hair fell when she put her hand to her head. I wasn't surprised that she asked what was wrong. Still, I rolled my eyes and wanted to say, *Can't I call two days in a row without it being a big deal?* But I couldn't say that because what I would tell her *was* a big deal.

"Is anything wrong?" she asked again with a little too

much paranoia in her voice.

I was a teenager again who wanted none of my mother's protection. I wished I hadn't called. But it was a fair question, and it had only one answer. "Well, yeah." I sat down heavily on a kitchen chair and took a sip of my cold tea. "Something's wrong."

"Oh, no!" she cried anxiously. "Did Steve leave you?"

I rolled my eyes again. "No, Mom, Steve didn't leave me. We're happily married. The kids are all fine and nobody died."

"Oh." She must have heard the patronizing ooze in my voice. It wasn't a very good setup for what I was about to say.

"But it is serious." I prepared mental notes for my announcement and tried to leave adolescent behavior behind. "Maybe you should sit down."

"Oh, dear." I'm sure she didn't sit down. In my mind's eye I saw her walking from the kitchen into the hallway, as far as the cord would extend, and back through the kitchen toward the dining room, as far as the cord would extend. Back and forth. She wouldn't sit down in the face of trouble.

"Mom, listen." Hedging wouldn't work with her, so I didn't try. Besides, I wanted to get this out before she accidentally unplugged the phone or clicked it off in her agitation. "I was raped last night."

"No!" I doubt she noticed her own reversion, but she whispered a phrase in Dutch that meant something like *God help us.* I hated making my mom cry.

I told her the dilemma of the pill. It was the only thing I looked forward to in this conversation: getting some commiseration about the difficult decision before me. I thought she might be the only one who would understand the agony of my choice.

Instead I got "Why, take it! Of course!" When I paused she said, "Heather, pregnancy just isn't an option. It would be too much for you."

A part of me gratefully accepted her concern. I nearly swallowed the pill right then as I absorbed the realization of what her statement granted: guiltless freedom.

But another side of me felt threatened by her protective admonition. I knew she didn't want me to suffer any more than I had to. I knew she was willing to give up her own convictions for the sake of my mental health. I knew her mothering was natural and appropriate. But I also longed for someone to agree with my strange aversion to the pill, to make sense of it for me. If this strong woman who had taught me the importance of the sanctity of life didn't get it, then I must be crazy.

The conversation ended with a prayer. It was short, but it was enough. "May God strengthen you, Heather."

"Thanks, Mom. I need to go now."

The last time I heard my mom cry was the day before I got married. I was sitting at the kitchen table arranging flowers, and she was preparing dinner. I was surprised when she started giving me advice on how to make my husband happy; I was even more surprised when I saw her eyes watering. At first I thought it was due to the onions she was slicing. I was embarrassed then, too.

"I love you, *schatje*," she said.

"I love you, too, Mom. Bye." I turned the phone off and put my head in my arms.

The phone rang a few minutes later, and I thought it would be my mom.

"Hello," I said sullenly.

Only silence answered.

"Hello?"

Nothing.

I slammed down the phone and then ran upstairs to Steve. He was in the shower, so I walked slowly back to the kitchen and glared at the phone until my husband came downstairs.

Steve went to the pantry to grab some cereal and then sat at the table. I didn't really want him to kiss me, but I wondered why he didn't. He started eating without looking at me.

"Look at this stupid pill." I pointed at it without touching it.

He looked up and stopped crunching his Mini Wheats for a moment. I banged the table when I stood up, knocking over the cereal. A bunch of it fell to the floor, but neither of us moved to pick it up. Steve looked at the pill. "Are you going to take it?"

"I don't know," I groused, banging the kettle on the stove. Neither of us said anything until I sat down again, a little more composed. "Mark and Lori came over while you were sleeping. He and my Bible study group are coming over pretty soon to help us decide."

Steve must have noticed my choice of pronoun, but said nothing.

"My mom thinks I should take it."

"She does? What did she say?" I felt a twinge of gratification at his surprise. I was right: She wasn't supposed to want me to take it.

"I don't know …" I didn't want to talk about it. I didn't want to think about my mom crying to my dad. I didn't want to imagine her breaking the news to my brothers and sister. I should have just kept my mouth shut. I was alive, the kids were alive—life would go on without getting the whole world involved. I turned to the mundane: "Did you call work to say you weren't coming in today?"

"Yeah."

"When are the kids coming home?" I didn't know if I wanted to return to the routine of daily life yet. It seemed both impossible and heavenly.

"We can pick them up anytime. I told them it would probably be after supper."

I took my tea to the living room and watched the leaves blowing around until the doorbell rang. Steve answered the door.

Maryann's eyes were red and swollen. She took Steve by the hand and couldn't say a word. She sat beside me and cried. "I love you, Heather," she finally sputtered.

Each of the women in my Bible study group greeted us in a different way upon entering our home, and each one added her scent to the aroma of love that hovered over us. When Mark and Lori arrived, they embraced Steve with the same concern they had shown me. Somehow, I forgot the looming decision before me and simply rested in their care.

But no decision is still a decision, and so our group eventually stared at the little pink demon on the coffee table and worried together about what to do.

"Is there a real chance you could get pregnant?"

"How does the morning-after pill work?"

"How long do you have to decide?"

Maryann answered most of these questions. Everything she said echoed what Dr. Manz had said the night before. The word "abortion" was not used.

We prayed.

"Father, you promise to give us wisdom when we ask for it."

"Holy Spirit, let us know your will."

"Jesus, we need your comfort, your grace."

I had often spoken similar prayers, but this time I didn't believe any of these words would soothe my pain or ease my decision.

We talked.

"You have to do what your gut is telling you."

"Either decision is okay."

"Think beyond this moment and consider your situation a year from now."

Steve remained silent during this entire exchange. I felt the power of his silence: He wanted me to take the pill.

"Heather," my pastor said softly, "I think you should take the pill." It was the first direct suggestion. I looked up at him, waiting for an explanation. "I'm not sure if this is from God or from my own heart," he said, "but I feel like I need to tell you that nothing will be hurt if you take the pill. I don't think you're pregnant."

His words were true. I knew them to be true. It didn't matter that he had never in my presence resorted to "thus sayeth the Lord" language before. It didn't matter that logic would have directed Mark to suggest dumping the pill if he believed I wasn't pregnant. It didn't matter that I didn't want to take it. His words were true.

The horns and fangs on the pill disappeared. "Okay." I was scared and relieved. "I'll take it."

And I did.

I felt nothing.

"Good," Mark said with finality in his voice. "Now to the next issue." I dreaded the "next issue," but I listened. "It's good that we've dealt with the immediate problem, but we need to care for the unseen problem. We need to pray for cleansing for you, Heather—for healing." My friends murmured agreement. I wanted them to go home. "This is going to sound odd," he told us all, "so if any of you are uncomfortable with this, tell me." We nodded. "This is what I suggest: Heather, you go take a shower. We'll stay here and pray for cleansing for you. As the water is washing over you, we will pray that all effects of this trauma will be washed away. Are you comfortable with that?"

Mark's words hit a spot in me that I had been avoiding: I felt dirty. He was right again.

I took the shower, no matter how weird it seemed. That day, singing in the shower took on a whole new meaning.

When peace like a river
attendeth my way,
When sorrows like sea billows roll;
Whatever my lot,
Thou hast taught me to say,
"It is well, it is well
with my soul."

Though Satan should buffet,
though trials should come,
Let this blest assurance control,
that Christ has regarded
my helpless estate,
and has shed His own blood
for my soul.

My sin—oh, the bliss
of this glorious thought:
My sin not in part, but the whole
Is nailed to the cross
and I bear it no more,
Praise the Lord, praise the Lord,
O my soul!

And, Lord, haste the day
when my faith shall be sight,
The clouds be rolled back as a scroll;
the trump shall resound
and the Lord shall descend.
Even so, it is well
with my soul.

It is well with my soul,
It is well, it is well
with my soul.

Nobody was praying when I came back into the living room. I wasn't surprised. They never prayed beyond what needed to be said. Instead, they were laughing. I didn't know the joke, but I smiled. *I'll kill you if you tell ...* was impotent.

The lie had been exposed.

Before they left, Maryann asked if they could ask others to pray for us. The answer was not easy. I still hated letting so many know about this, but I needed support: I still had to tell my story one more time to the detective who was assigned to my case. I still had to take the HIV tests. I still had to overcome the emotional trauma that had been thrown at me. I looked at Steve and he shrugged. So I told her yes.

The house felt strange after they left. I didn't want to read a book or listen to the radio or go for a walk. Everything was clean, so I couldn't do housework. I wasn't ready to get the kids or to talk on the phone. Steve had immersed himself in a magazine and didn't look interested in conversation. I ended up staring out the window again at the red and golden leaves that I had piled up the day before. After a while, I could almost predict where a leaf would land after it was wisped into the air by the unseen breeze.

I didn't recognize their car at first when it pulled into our driveway; I wasn't expecting it. But when Mom stuck her head out before Dad could even park properly, I jumped up and ran to the door.

"Mom!"

"I'm sorry for not calling, Heather. But I had to come."

I sank into her hug without an adolescent thought.

"Heather," she said anxiously, voicing her main concern before we even reached the front porch. "Don't take that pill. I was wrong."

*Horatio G. Spafford, "It Is Well with My Soul."

120

CHAPTER EIGHT

WALKING ON WATER

With the telephone in
one hand and the pepper spray in the
other,
I crept through my home.

Where did you go? Were you watching me during those months afterward? Were you hating me for smiling at my neighbors and laughing with my kids? Were you hungry for the abundance I flaunted? I'll tell you the secret of my strength. And the weakness of my strength.

"Did they catch him?" It was the first question I asked the young detective who invited me to sit in the chair on the other side of her desk the day following the assault. Lori had come with me and now waited in the room where "wanted" posters of black men stared from the walls. I was glad that Steve and my parents were at home; I didn't want the memory of this place stuck in their minds.

"No, they didn't," the detective answered. "But maybe you can still help us do that."

"I thought the dogs were tracking him," I said.

"They were. They tracked his scent to a house down the street from you—"

"So they found him?"

"No. Unfortunately, they didn't have a warrant to go into the house. Besides, they weren't sure if he had taken off in a car parked in front of the house or if he had gone inside."

"So when will they get a warrant?"

"They did already. They checked it out this morning. The house was abandoned. No one was there."

"What will we do next?" I asked, as if simply naming the steps could put the rapist behind bars.

"Well, do you think you can describe the suspect to a profile artist?"

I shook my head. "No. I didn't see his face."

"You can't describe him at all?"

"He was taller than me—at least a head taller. He was big. He smelled like beer. I think he was wearing a leather jacket."

"Was he wearing gloves?"

"I don't know. I don't think so."

"All the prints we gathered from your house match your family's prints, except one set that belongs to a child. So that isn't going to help, either. Is there anything else you remember?"

"No." I put my face in my hands and groaned. If assumptions are untried, unproven beliefs, I had one that suddenly exposed itself as pathetically false: Bad guys always get caught. I was shocked to discover that someone who had done such a wicked thing was still running free. "I was such an idiot!" I whispered.

"What do you mean?"

It was hard even to admit. "I covered my face while he was looking for the knife he dropped."

"You passed up a chance to look at him?" I realized that

she was disappointed. Solving a case quickly wouldn't have looked bad on her still-green record. "Why?" she asked.

"I don't know. I guess I was being self-protective. If he knew I wouldn't be able to describe him, then maybe he wouldn't kill me. It was dumb." I didn't look at her, but from her silence I guessed she was trying not to swear at me.

A moment later she said my name very quietly and very slowly. "Heather." I looked up at her and saw, if not compassion, kindness. "Let's get one thing straight," she said in a schoolteacher voice. "You did nothing wrong. Keeping his face out of your mind might have been the best thing there was to do. Look, you're alive, right?" I nodded reluctantly. "Why don't you tell me what happened," she said. "Maybe some important memory will come back that will help us catch this guy."

I wasn't surprised that she asked this, but I still resisted. "I've told the story so many times already," I explained. "I don't think I can tell it again."

She nodded sympathetically. "It must be hard, but there are reasons to tell. Not only will it help us get this guy off the streets, it will free you up to heal more quickly. You'd be amazed at what a difference it makes just to talk."

The getting-the-guy-off-the-streets argument won me over. The idea of healing more quickly seemed remote, or perhaps unrealistic. But as I talked, my voice shook less than it had the time before, and my heart beat at a normal pace. Detective Boers took meticulous notes and made me repeat things she did not catch the first time or things she wanted clarified. She closed her book at the end of the conversation and leaned back in her chair. "Okay," she said with authority that didn't match her age. "You let me know if anything comes back to you. I'll keep you posted about what's happening on our end. Does that sound good?"

We stood up to shake hands, and then I went back to the small room stacked with metal chairs with plastic seats where Lori waited for me. She was studying the photographs on the wall and reading their descriptions. We walked to the car without saying anything and talked little on the way home.

"Let Mark and me know if you need anything," Lori called after me. "Otherwise, see you at church on Sunday."

She didn't see me Sunday. Going to church terrified me. "Everybody knows about this," I lamented to Steve on Sunday morning as I flung more and more unfit outfits on the bed. "No one will know what to say. I don't know how I'll be able to look at anyone."

"We can stay home," Steve offered.

"What will my parents think?" I asked. Mom and Dad were downstairs brewing coffee.

"Does it matter what they think?" Steve asked.

I went downstairs. "Mom, I don't really want to go to church today. Would you hate me if I stayed home?"

"Of course not, Heather," my mom answered quickly. "I think we should all stay home today."

"Yeah, I suppose it would be hard for you, too." But I needed affirmation from both of them. "What do you think, Dad? Should I deal with all the questions now, or is it okay to put it off until next week?" If I had asked him whether I should buy a Mac or a PC, or if I should read a certain book, or the best way to wallpaper a room—I would have received an answer that might have convinced even a professional of his expertise on the given subject.

To this question he shook his hand at me as if he were wiping away an awful stain on his windshield. "I don't know, Heather. I don't know." *Don't go* is what I heard. How could I handle church if he couldn't handle even a question about it?

And so we stayed home the first Sunday after the rape. But our absence from church did not stop people from being jarred by the news.

An emergency prayer meeting was called on our behalf. I didn't go, but I was told that Sherman Street's sanctuary was packed. The meeting was an informal mix of prayer and discussion. Pastor Mark allowed people to express their feelings to each other and to God without any expectation that they say the "right thing." Some wept openly. Some admitted their own fear. Some called out for justice. Maryann told me that her husband, Byron, whose anger wouldn't allow him to pray, stomped around the church basement punching things and flinging verbal attacks against the "jackass" who messed with his friend.

Someone bought us the watchdog we had always talked about getting: a beagle whose bite would have tickled a child, but whose bark could rally neighbors a block away.

Someone wrote a newspaper article in my defense against the word "alleged" in the original news report.

Someone anonymously sent us money, lamenting the fact that he or she was not close enough to us to offer emotional support.

Family, too, rallied around us.

A few days after the rape, Steve and I went to his parents' house, where all his siblings had gathered. I was nervous. But when I walked through the door and saw tears on the face of my stoic brother-in-law and felt his protective hug, when Steve and I were sheltered in the embraces of each member of the family, when my mother-in-law looked at me with as much compassion as if I were her own daughter, I wasn't nervous anymore. This was a safe place.

Tasha took over the job of mothering us when my parents had to return home. She accepted the meals people brought to us and answered the phone. (We had received two more anonymous calls, and I hated answering the phone.) She played with the kids when we wanted to be left alone. She brought a large basket from home to hold the cards that overflowed from our mailbox—and she told us to keep these "acknowledgments of love" forever.

Best of all, she trickled wisdom into my empty heart in measures I could handle. Once we were taking a walk through the neighborhood while Steve watched the boys, and she dumped a load of wisdom on me.

"You know, Tasha," I began tentatively. I figured my next words would sound warped if I spoke them out loud, but the thought had wrapped itself around my soul and needed release. "The rape really wasn't a big deal."

"What?" She nearly exploded, but I put my hand on her arm to stop her.

"Just listen," I begged her. "I want you to know that it wasn't so bad. Look, my kids are alive, and I'm alive, and there really are no negative consequences."

"Girl!" She tried to break in again.

"Wait, Tasha. Listen. I'm okay. I don't blame the guy who did this. He's some black guy who has been put in his place all his life by white people. If this is the only payback to whites for how we've mistreated blacks, then it's not bad at all." I was thinking of the time my heart had disintegrated while reading *Aunt Annie*. I couldn't comprehend how anyone could live through the trauma of screaming and grabbing at her three-year-old child through a gate that separated them, desperate not to lose the grip of his fingers, hearing his terrified screams and watching his stricken face, running and stumbling and bawling as the wagon increased the distance between them. And then to hear her master say that the boy would forget her in a couple days. Whites had raped blacks with wickedness that far surpassed the experience forced on me.

I was thinking of my friend—a young, black man—who had been pulled over and frisked too many times simply for being in a neighborhood where he supposedly didn't belong while politely responding to verbal abuse.

I was thinking of my realtor's stories of refusing to show houses to blacks in certain parts of town so that he could keep up his white clientele.

I was thinking of the black kid at my childhood school whom my friends and I had all mocked.

And so I sadly told Tasha, "I don't mind taking this slap in the face as payment for—"

But Tasha shut me up quick. "Girl, that's enough. You ain't no Jesus Christ, so you just get the idea out of your fool head that you can take on the sins of the world. What that creep did to you was wrong. I don't care what kind of hardships he been having and what all them uppity white folk did to him or no such thing like that. He ain't got no right to rape a woman. He done you wrong, and don't let me hear you making no small thing about it again. You hear me?"

I heard her.

"Besides, you just looking for an easy way out of forgiving him. If it weren't so bad, then you don't need to forgive much. He done you wrong, sister. And you need to forgive the whole awful thing."

Who could argue with wisdom like that? And so my warped thinking smoothed itself out, and healthy, painful questions settled in. *What had I lost? Could I forgive?*

A week and a half after the rape, we considered staying home from church again. "No," I said despite the terror wreaking havoc in my belly. "I promised Mark I would say something to the church. I might as well get it over with."

So we went. We arrived a couple minutes late and sat in the back. People looked down when they saw us. I glanced knowingly at Steve.

The familiar routine of the worship service became startlingly foreign to me as I sat there that morning. We sang songs that I had been singing since childhood, and we recited the Apostles' Creed as easily as we would have said the alphabet, but I looked around the sanctuary with the eyes of a stranger. It was expected, but still a surprise, when Mark introduced me. I walked down the aisle and felt every eye on me. I cleared my throat and stared at the notes I had carefully written down. It took all the courage I had to get my voice to speak the words in front of me.

"God knew what he was doing when he formed churches: I don't know how I would have survived the last week or so without the support of this church." I looked at Tasha in the fourth row—her usual seat; she briefly closed a burnt-orange lid over one large eye. "I know you have given this support out of a genuine love and concern for us. But I also know it is healing for you to help us, for each of you have experienced some of the pain that we have. The man who attacked me, attacked also Sherman Street Church."

I hesitated, considering if I should ignore the rest of the words on the page in front of me and find my seat again. I looked up and caught the eye of an older man, one of the first people to welcome me into this church, someone who had often listened to me. He had big ears; they seemed to stick out of the sides of his head—like the character in the *MAD* magazines—bending toward my spoken and unspoken message. He had a faint smile on his lips, as if he were proud of me, and his smile broadened when he caught my eye.

I continued. "Our vision for racial reconciliation and community development has been placed under attack, and I want to be the first to say that we cannot give up. We are far from perfect, and the task before us is difficult and scary, but I know that God can use us to show the world his power and love. All we have to do is love our neighbors as ourselves."

Steve had read my speech in advance and had approved my words. I looked at him now—alone in the pew, staring at the floor—and I wished that he had been willing to come with me to face the church. Even he would have been touched by the scene before me.

The pianist, a lovely woman with long, graying hair—someone who had experienced and shared significant pain of her own—closed her eyes and swayed slightly. She was praying for me, I knew. A college girl who occasionally baby-sat our kids and who usually attended the smaller evening services, wept openly. A young mom whose husband had recently died of cancer held me up with a quick nod of her head. Some close friends of ours, a loving couple who had been married eight years without being able to conceive, held each other's hands and looked ready to spring from their seats to join me if only I said the word. A middle-aged man, a professor of music, touched fingers to his bald forehead, as if he were in pain; he was. A woman whose newborn baby had recently died sat in the front row. She had been to our house numerous times in the last week, delivering food and cards and encouragement.

I saw the newsletter team I met with month after month scattered throughout the pews: a middle-aged single woman whose mischievousness was contagious; an intelligent and warm man who was my age and from my country—a kindred spirit; a high school teacher who kept us laughing. I saw the musicians and readers and actors and dancers I so often consulted as I planned worship services. I saw my children's Sunday school teachers and the parents of the children I taught. I saw the evangelism team that often met at my round table to discuss theology and strategies: a counselor, a widow, a teacher, a mom.

"Even if nothing else good comes from this experience," I concluded with sincerity, "I now know with conviction that God's grace *is* sufficient—and that his church is a family worth being part of."

When I sat down, after walking past all the encouraging smiles and tears and gentle touches, my body trembled.

Abundance: Rich, fervent prayers for me and my family every day. Deep love and concern expressed so freely. Wisdom imparted with such grace.

So I walked on water: I smiled at my neighbors and laughed with my kids. And I told Steve to go to the next council meeting. "I'll be fine," I insisted.

He didn't go.

But the next month I was still riding the wave of the prayers of my friends. "You might as well go," I told him.

Steve hesitated. We both knew it would be my first time home alone since the attack. "What if you get an anonymous call?"

"I won't answer the phone."

"Can't you find someone to stay with you while I'm gone?"

"I could, but we've got to start to live normally sometime." The anticipation of being home alone matched the anticipation I once had of getting my driver's license: I expected to be liberated. I believed that this action would throw off the last shackle that kept me a victim.

I locked the door behind Steve when he left. I went to the front door to make sure it was locked. Then I went upstairs to give the kids a bath. As they splashed each other, happy and oblivious, I ran downstairs to make sure I had locked the doors properly. I thought about grabbing a cookie—I was starving—but the floor squeaked. I stood motionless, prepared for the worst. Nothing happened. I ran up the stairs to help the kids get ready for bed. We read books for a long time. The phone rang a few times, but I ignored it.

After tucking them in and kissing them goodnight, I knew I had to go downstairs. *I will get something done tonight,* I told myself. Barely out of their room, I froze. *What was that noise?* Long moments passed, and I pressed my back against the wall as I slipped silently down the stairs. I saw the dishes piled in the sink, but the clanking of the glass would stop me from hearing any disruptions, so I left them. The washing machine ran too loud; I turned it off mid-cycle. The radio no longer comforted;

I shut it down.

With the telephone in one hand and pepper spray in the other, I crept through my home. When even that activity seemed to echo in my ears, I sat tensely on the couch, listening. Listening. The house did not give up its shuffling noises even when I sat perfectly still. The floorboards seemed to creak around every corner. I wasn't sure if they were noises I simply hadn't noticed before or if they were new noises.

Who should I call? Mark and Lori told me to call anytime. But what would I say? I'm scared? Come baby-sit me? I could call Tasha just to chat—but then I wouldn't be able to hear what was happening in the house. The creaking grew louder.

I couldn't stand it. I rushed upstairs and threw myself into the kids' bedroom. They slept peacefully while I cowered behind their door, staring through the crack at the steps. My stomach felt nauseous.

Someone was in my house! *I know someone is in my house!*

I did it: I dialed 9-1-1.

The telephone rang a few times before a woman's voice answered. I whispered when she prompted me for information. Less than two minutes later, I heard the siren. With the phone and pepper spray still in my hands, I ran downstairs to answer the door.

"Someone is in the house!" I told the officers frantically.

"Okay, ma'am. Why don't you step outside while we do a search."

"My kids! They're sleeping."

"Are they upstairs?"

"Yes."

"Have you checked on them recently?"

"Yes. I was just in their room when you came."

"Okay, we'll have someone stay there with them until everything is clear. You wait on the porch until then."

Five police cars were parked around my house. I stood with an officer on my porch as two others crept upstairs— guns extended—and two went down to the basement. I saw a couple more slinking around the outside of the house. I trembled as fear turned to relief and as relief turned to shame. The officers found no evidence of a stranger in my house.

No one chastised me for the false alarm. "Sometimes these old houses make some pretty creepy noises if you're not used to it," one kind officer told me.

Even Steve shrugged off my blunder. "No one blames you," he said after the police were gone and we were behind locked doors again—and that after he drove up Neland Avenue toward the flashing red and blue lights distorting our house. I had never seen him move so fast, whipping the car to the side of the road and running up the sidewalk. I had never seen him so scared as he ran toward me and held me tightly in his arms. Still, he didn't blame me.

But I felt sick. I knew I had plunged beneath the waves. "I shouldn't have been afraid," I whimpered.

Steve didn't agree. "That's not true," he said without a hint of irritation. "It wouldn't be normal if you weren't afraid."

But I was hardly listening. I had run to the bathroom to vomit.

CHAPTER NINE

DOOR
NUMBER
FOUR

I thought about

heartburn.

And throwing up.

And not fitting

in my clothes.

All this for a baby

I didn't want.

I used to wonder if you had been planning that notorious night for years or if your actions were based on impulse. Now I know that how carefully you planned it makes as much difference as how carefully I tried to discern whether or not to swallow that pill.

I missed my period," I told Maryann. "Again." We were sitting in her office: she, with her back to the sturdy oak desk built into the wall-to-wall bookshelves; me, slouched in an oversized chair with my feet on the coffee table between us. We often had our consultations in this room after an exam.

"I'm not surprised," she answered. "Your system is thrown off by the medication and the stress. It's only been a couple months since …" Her voice trailed off and she looked at me carefully, as if assessing how much I could handle.

"You can say it."

"Listen," continued Maryann. "Ovral works. I'm more worried that you're suppressing your feelings than about you getting pregnant. Nobody is expecting you to keep up this strong exterior, Heather."

I knew what she was talking about. I had learned quickly that people didn't seem content to leave me alone until I had shed a tear for them. And I hated doing that. Strong exterior?

I wished I *could* ignore the despair I felt. "Oh, Maryann, are people really saying that? I feel like I'm crying all the time. People are always praying for me, at church and Bible study and on the phone. And every time Steve leaves the house, I have to call someone over to baby-sit me; when I don't, I end up calling 9-1-1. I'm pathetic, Maryann. I wish I *were* strong."

"You are strong. You've made some great decisions. You're still doing the work of twenty people at church—which I don't think you should do, by the way. You seem to be happy. But I am concerned that you're not in touch with your feelings. Take the whole situation with the pill, for example. You had such a strong aversion to the very idea of abortion— even at that early stage, even under those circumstances. I know that's how Christians are 'supposed' to feel, but in this situation it seemed strange to me."

"You thought I was faking it?"

"No. I wondered if you felt so strongly about it because of some situation you've been keeping secret." She looked at me carefully, as if trying to discover something on my face. She must have found only confusion, because I didn't comprehend where she was going. Unless she was accusing me of having an affair and covering it up by crying rape. It was my turn to look at her suspiciously.

She broke the silence: "Okay," she said, "I'm just going to ask you. And I promise I won't judge you."

"What?"

"Did you have an abortion when you were younger? Because if you did, you really should get some counseling for that. Most women don't understand how traumatizing—"

"No."

"What?"

"No, I didn't have an abortion. You've been the one to confirm every pregnancy I've had."

"Then why were you so opposed to it?"

"Because killing innocent babies is wrong." I might have sounded a little patronizing.

"Is that all?"

"Yes." I didn't mind that she asked me such a personal question. I didn't even mind, too much, that she had considered the idea that I might have had an abortion. What bothered me was her incredulity of my motives: I felt confused enough about my irrational conviction without her doubt on top of it.

"Oh. You're sure you're not suppressing your feelings?"

"I'm sure. Do you want to know how I feel now? Lousy. I think I'm pregnant, and I expect to find out someday that I have AIDS."

She shook her head. "I can't even imagine the depth of your fear. I'd be terrified. But actually, Heather, neither of these situations is likely. Look, you took the Ovral—" she waited for me to acknowledge this, which I finally did with a shrug of my shoulders "—and the first HIV test already came back negative."

"Big deal," I answered with as much enthusiasm as a turkey might muster after being passed over for Thanksgiving in anticipation of Christmas. "I still have twenty tests to go before we know for sure I don't have AIDS."

"Four," she corrected me.

"Okay, four. But waiting two years is going to kill me."

"Yeah," she agreed. "That's going to be tough. By the way, you and Steve are still holding off, right?"

"Yeah. I don't want to have sex anyway."

"Are you talking to your counselor about that? I mean, you certainly have to wait until the six-month test proves clear—and even after that you should use a condom—but meanwhile you'd better be dealing with your emotions."

I shrugged. My sex drive—or lack of it—was not on my list of concerns. "I feel like I'm pregnant, Maryann."

"Well, you've said that before and you weren't. Sometimes I think you believe you're pregnant so much that your body starts to act like it is."

"I've never had it this bad. I've been eating like crazy and puking."

She sighed. "Would you like to take a test just to be sure?" Her voice was slightly patronizing, but I didn't blame her. I was slightly embarrassed to wonder if I was pregnant. We both knew it was impossible.

"Yeah, I'll take the test," I said. "Maybe then I can quit worrying about it." But I didn't move. I wanted to mope a bit longer. "Who was it who said, 'A woman is like tea; you know what she's made of when she's in hot water'?" I asked morosely.

Maryann stood up. I knew she was holding up other patients for me. "It was Eleanor Roosevelt," she said. "But you quoted her wrong." I grinned and she chuckled, adding, "Besides, you've still got a lot of steeping to do before you'll taste any good."

"Aw, go suck a lemon," I told her.

"Go pee in a cup," she retorted.

I laughed in spite of myself and went to the bathroom. After putting the cup on the little shelf in the wall, I went back to Maryann's office and curled up in the chair. A picture of John Perkins on the cover of a magazine caught my attention. I had heard him speak several times at various conferences. An amazing man. Though harshly beaten and abused just for being black, he still worked tenaciously for racial peace—and with such grace! His wisdom had clearly been refined in fires hotter than I had been through. I picked up the magazine to keep myself occupied while I waited for Maryann. A paper slid out of the magazine. I was surprised to see an article I had written for the church newsletter a month ago—before a stranger invaded my bedroom. I skimmed it and felt my face grow hot.

> One of the reasons our inner cities are deteriorating is because anyone who *can* moves out, leaving behind the poor and broken. The only way to heal the inner cities is to fill them with people who are willing to work for community development, not for just a day or a week, but for years of daily living. No matter what the consequences.

I was suddenly jealous of the innocent faith I had lost. It wasn't that I disagreed with the words I had written, it was that it didn't seem so easy anymore. *No matter what the consequences?* I thought of Dr. Martin Luther King, Jr., who struggled deeply with fear, aware of the constant threat on his life. He confessed to God that he wanted to quit. Still, he walked in step with the Spirit until God gave him the peace that passes understanding. And then he was murdered!

No matter what the consequences?

The man pictured on the magazine in my lap didn't seem to care about the consequences. He faced beatings and imprisonment to fight for reconciliation. He risked his children's security by allowing them to integrate a school when tolerance was not an American value. He persevered in difficult relationships so that unity could grow.

And my article lauded these men as heroes.

A distinguished professor, who happened to be my cousin and friend, had scoffed at my article. Always cynical about my living in the city, he tossed it back at me and said, "I don't know why you continue to believe that you or your church will ever succeed in achieving that crazy dream. An inner-city neighborhood cannot be peaceful."

But I had maintained my faith and told him so.

"Listen," he ranted, "if even one person from your church moves into the inner city in support of this vision, I will be very surprised. Perhaps I'll even reconsider faith. But it won't happen. People know deep down that there is no God and therefore there is no worthwhile cause for which to sacrifice so much."

Apparently my choice to live in the city didn't count.

After the rape, his cynicism had turned to anger. "You're not moving?" he raved. "Heather, it's irresponsible to stay. Who knows, next time it may be your kids."

"God can handle things," I told him confidently. I believed it then—I was still riding the wave of the prayers of my friends. But now I squirmed. I hated being afraid.

I stuck the copy of my article between the pages of the magazine and glanced into the hallway. I waved down a nurse I hadn't met before and asked her if she had the results of my test yet. I wanted to get home. She grinned mischievously. "You'll have to wait for Dr. DeHaan," she said, "but I think you're going to like what you hear." She disappeared with a cheery wink before I could ask any questions.

"Great," I muttered to myself.

Eventually Maryann went to the nurses' station. I watched her through the open door. She talked with her employees like she talked with me: straightforward but kind, precise but down-to-earth. She wasn't talking about me, and I didn't pay much attention to what she said. But I watched her expression when the cheery nurse handed her my file.

Maryann glanced at the paper and then immediately flung her wide eyes in my direction.

I swore under my breath and tossed the magazine on the coffee table.

"Heather," she said when she walked in the room a second later. Her voice trembled.

"I don't even want to hear it." I put my fingers in my ears and playfully sang "La, la, la" to drown out her voice.

"This is not a game, Heather," she said when I stopped. She was sitting on the coffee table.

I wanted us to laugh, but we didn't.

"I've changed my mind, Maryann. I don't want to take the test."

She shook her head, ignoring my inappropriate behavior. "The test was positive. I can't believe it's positive."

We were both silent. I thought about heartburn. And throwing up. And not fitting in my clothes. All this for a baby I didn't want.

"You'd better call Steve," she said at last.

I didn't say anything, but I was thinking like mad.

"Heather?"

"I'll bet I have AIDS, too," I finally said.

"Stop it, Heather."

147

I dropped my face into my hands. I didn't want to laugh anymore. "I can't do this, Maryann."

I felt her hand on my shoulder.

"Mark said I wasn't pregnant," I muttered. As if that accusation could remedy the situation.

"That's not exactly what he said. Anyway, you'll have to talk to Mark about it. Talk to God about it." She waved her hand. "But that's not your immediate concern. Whatever the reason, you are pregnant. You'd better call Steve."

"What am I going to tell him?"

"That you're pregnant."

I groaned. "I can't tell him that."

"You have to."

I held my head as if I could contain the explosion happening inside. "Why didn't the Ovral work?" I asked.

Maryann shook her head. "I don't know. But you're avoiding the issue. Call your husband."

"I know. I will. I'm going home and I'll call from there."

"I'll call Mark for you," she told me. "This is too big for you guys to handle alone."

As soon I got the boys home and occupied I called Steve's cell phone. I rarely called him at the job site, so I didn't need to say, "I've got some bad news." But I did anyway.

I heard him readjust his phone. "What is it?" I'm sure his mind must have gone back to the last time I called him with bad news. I wondered which news would be worse.

"I'm pregnant."

"You're pregnant?"

"Yeah. Maryann gave me a test."

"How can you be?"

"Don't ask me. Maryann told me to take it up with God."

"I'm coming home. I'll be there soon."

I hadn't yet dared to think about what we would do, but Steve launched right into it when he got home. "Did Maryann say anything about abortion?"

"Steve!"

"I'm serious, Heather. Even the most fundamental anti-abortion groups recognize that a situation like this is different."

"What about adoption?" Even as I said it, I knew it wasn't an option. How could I carry a baby, deliver it, and then give it away to someone else to raise? But what other choice was there? Keep it? That would be even harder. How could we raise the baby of the guy who raped me?

I wanted door number four to open up and to hear someone declare a new and better option with as much excitement as Monty Hall announces, "A new car!" But all I heard was my stomach rumbling.

"What are we going to do, Steve?"

"I don't know," he said. It sounded like a strangled cry from someone who was dying. He wrapped his arms around me, and I felt his body jerk with emotion he didn't even know how to feel. "Why is this happening to us?" he said quietly.

I didn't quote the poster I had seen hanging in the nurses' station at Maryann's office: *I know God gives me only what I can handle, but I wish he didn't trust me so much.*

I didn't insist on doing things my way.

I didn't make a dumb joke.

I didn't tell God he had picked the wrong people for this job.

I just cried. And as I held Steve's ringless hand, I knew I loved him. It didn't matter that he was not romantic. It didn't matter that he was not the spiritual leader I had always hoped for. He was my best friend. We were in this together.

And so his next words shocked me: "It's your decision, Heather. I knew that from the moment we sat here with your Bible study group. I'm out of it. But I can't be part of that baby. I just can't. I'm sorry." He got up from the couch and walked to the family room where he slouched between the boys in front of a video.

I called Tasha.

I hardly gave her time to grieve the fact that I was pregnant. "Do you think he would leave me?" I asked.

"He didn't say that."

"Maybe he's scared of saying it straight out because he's so used to being good. What else could he have meant?"

"Forget about Steve for a minute," Tasha told me.

"But—"

"Listen, sister. Do you think God wants you to have an abortion?"

"No. But what else can I do? And I certainly don't want to put my marriage in jeopardy."

"What matters more: keeping things straight with your man or with your God?"

"Yeah, but what about this whole submitting-to-your-husband thing?"

"Interesting that you start caring about that now. No, I'm sorry, Heather. If he wants you to do something against the will of God, I don't call that leadership worth listening to."

"Okay, so you're saying I should lose my marriage to have a baby that was conceived through rape. I don't even want the baby!"

"I'm saying you should obey God. Besides, Steve is too good a man to leave you."

I sobbed. I didn't want to be having a theological discussion on whether wives should submit to husbands. I hated that topic anyway.

"I don't know what to do, Tasha!" I walked to the window in the boys' room and saw Steve pushing the kids on the swings in the backyard. "I don't want to lose him. I don't want to have this baby."

"I think you do know what to do."

She was right, of course. "Sometimes I can't stand you, Tash."

"Girl, you love me. Now go ask your man to pray with you about this. I'll be praying that both of you can hear the voice of God." I agreed with her and was about to say good-bye when she broke in again: "I know this ain't easy, Heather. I'm sorry you have to go through it. You know I love you. I'll love you no matter what you do."

And so I went to join Steve and the boys in the backyard.

"It's Simon's bedtime." I spoke to my husband more carefully than I ever had before. "Do you mind if I put him to bed?"

Simon minded. It took me half an hour to settle him down. Or maybe it took me half an hour to settle myself down. When I finally moved away from his crib, he was already drooling on his bed sheets.

I sat beside Steve on the grass where he was watching Chad play in the sandbox. Steve didn't acknowledge my presence, and I didn't know what to say. He sat with one knee up and a piece of grass in his mouth. I sat with both knees pulled into my chest. Chad often played nicely by himself; I doubt he thought about his parents' quiet presence twenty feet away.

Finally I spoke softly. "I want to do the right thing. Will you pray with me about it?"

Steve didn't respond for several minutes. I had been married to him for nearly a decade but still wasn't used to his silences. Maybe I had spoken too softly and he hadn't heard me. Maybe he was so angry he didn't want to talk to me. Maybe he didn't think prayer would help. The only time we ever prayed together was at the dinner table where we asked God to bless our food. I assumed he had a private prayer life like I had, but I never asked.

He turned his head slowly to look at me before he spoke. I saw anger and scorn in his eyes. I suppose those emotions might not have been directed at me, but I didn't know how to deflect them. "I can't pray right now," he said. He didn't say why, but I didn't dare to press.

"Okay," I said. "I can't either. It was a dumb idea." I had never been so anxious to please. "I'm sorry." I think I was apologizing for mentioning such a crazy idea, but it might have been more: I might have been apologizing for causing us to be in such dire circumstances with no way out. I might have been apologizing for thinking we could ever make a difference in our neighborhood, for not locking the door, for making awful phone calls to him, for hesitating about taking the pill.

I might have been apologizing for sitting beside him. I might have been asking him to say it's okay. That everything would be okay. To have him take me in his arms and say he would always be with me, no matter what the consequences.

He looked toward Chad and said, fatalistically, "You're not going to have an abortion, are you?"

"I will." My own words surprised me. "I'll call Maryann and tell her not to tell anyone. I don't want anyone to know." I'd have to call Tasha, too, but I didn't tell Steve that.

He turned his head slowly again, but his expression had changed. I'm not sure if he looked suspicious or concerned or disappointed. "You will?"

"If you promise not to tell anyone."

"Okay." I was about to stand up—to take instant action on my decision—but he grabbed my arm. "Are you sure?"

"No," I said honestly. "But what else can I do?" I shrugged him off and got up. This time Pastor Mark's car stopped me. He got out of it and walked up the path to the backyard and waved when he saw us. I prayed that he wasn't here for the reason I expected.

"Hi," he said. "I couldn't get you by phone. I hope it's okay that I stopped by."

"No problem," Steve said. "What's up?"
Mark looked at him curiously and said, "Maryann told me the news. I thought you could use some encouragement."

CHAPTER TEN

COMPROMISE

"You're due for your

three-month HIV test."

*Hatred is not a strong enough word to describe what
I felt toward you. Loathing. Abhorrence. Repulsion.
It came on me in a flash, but it didn't end in one.
I stood trapped, condemned, ruined—all because of
your few moments of power.*

Mark sat down on the grass. I hadn't moved from where I stood except to turn my head toward my husband. Steve remained motionless as well. Chad, however, ran to our pastor and jumped on his back. "Hey, buddy," Mark chuckled.

Steve and I engaged in silent conversation. Steve turned his head to look at me—and saw my despair. He stared mercilessly at me for a moment and then gave in. He waved his hand in resignation and went back to chewing the grass. I let Chad play with Mark for a few more minutes before I offered crackers and a video to my carefree child. He had never sat in front of the tube so much in his life, and he was delighted by this recent change of policy. I held his hand as we walked to the house, and I tried to listen to his happy chatter about

Bambi, but my ears itched to hear the conversation beginning outside. I settled Chad down as quickly as possible.

"What can *I* do?" The resentment I heard in Steve's voice when I stepped outside contrasted with the resignation of his words. "It's her decision."

They both saw me coming. Mark smiled at me but continued talking to Steve. "I would think that this is a decision the two of you will have to make together."

Steve grunted.

"How could it not be, Steve?" Mark pressed. "It affects you as much as Heather."

Steve didn't look up when he answered. "I can't make her do something she doesn't want to do."

I thought he was complaining about my stubbornness, so I blurted, without thinking, "I said I would."

Steve looked up at me and shook his head. "I mean that I can't ask you to do it. I know you don't want to and that ultimately you won't be able to do it. And abortion probably is wrong." He shrugged and then turned to Mark. "But I can't stand to think that she's pregnant from this. I just can't stand it." I knew he felt as trapped as I did.

I was surprised to feel slightly disappointed that he was releasing me from abortion; if he insisted on abortion, my problem would be gone, and I could privately blame the crime on Steve. I shuddered at my wickedness. I wondered at the stability of my mind.

"Have you guys thought about giving the baby up for adoption?" Mark offered tentatively. That was door number two; I wanted door number four.

"I can't do that," I said.

"Do you want to keep the baby?" Mark asked,

surprised.

"No. I can't do that, either."

Steve looked irritated. "You have to do something," he said.

I kept looking at Mark. Waiting for another option. We were all silent for a moment.

"Jon and Barb Adams want a baby," Steve mentioned as casually as if he were noting the weather. But the effect was not casual: I was propelled into envisioning the reality of this possibility. I thought of the late-night conversations we had with our friends, agonizing with them over the pain of being barren. They loved children. We loved them for loving our children.

Mark and Steve both watched me as the freedom of choice choked me. I knew I had to do something, but I wanted to stall. "Do I have to decide right now?" I asked. Maybe in time I would feel comfortable with someone else raising the child of my womb. Especially when I knew how terrific the potential parents would be. But not yet.

"Take all the time you need," Mark answered. "This is no small thing."

Steve glowered. I didn't blame him. The answer seemed obvious now.

"I encourage the two of you to talk and pray about this until you both feel comfortable with the decision," Mark told us.

Yeah, right. I thought. *Talk. Pray. Comfortable.* My silent sarcasm was not directed at Mark. And my anger was not directed only at Steve.

But my real anger had no one to receive it. So I turned to Steve when Mark left: "Why don't you just tell me what to do? Don't give me this it's-all-up-to-you crap. We have to decide together." He looked about to say something, but I intercepted his words. "No, I'm not going to have an abortion." Steve looked at me with agonizingly patient eyes. He remained silent, and I recognized the illogic of my outburst. "Oh, be quiet," I told his silence, and stormed into the house.

He didn't follow me immediately, and I was mad about that, too. When he finally came in the house and tried to kiss me, I shouted at him again. "Leave me alone!" When he left me alone, I cried that he didn't hold me.

It took the rest of the evening and the quietness of the house after the kids were in bed for me to settle down. My anger, like the glowing coals of the sunset, cooled into deep blue sadness and then desperate blackness. So I went quietly to Steve. I sat beside him on the couch and laid my head in his lap. He set down his magazine and stroked my hair. I waited a long time before I spoke. "I can't have an abortion, Steve. But maybe I can give the baby up for adoption."

He said nothing but continued to stroke my hair.

"Maybe it would be good to give the baby to Jon and Barb. What a gift that would be for them."

He remained quiet.

"I don't think I would mind seeing the baby around."

He rubbed my shoulders.

"I know they would be good parents."

I rested on his lap, imagining how happy our friends would be to have a child—an infant. They could come to doctor appointments with me. Maybe they could even be there for the birth. They could name the baby. I pictured the joy on their faces as they embraced a newborn.

Steve picked up the magazine, leaving one hand to rest on my back, but I remained as still as the emotions inside me.

"It's the right thing to do," I finally concluded, as if he had shared in my silent conversation.

But that night I dreamed of nearly dying in childbirth and then not knowing the name or gender of the baby I delivered.

I didn't call Jon and Barb the next day. Or the next week. Neither did I keep the pregnancy a secret. I told people my news as calmly as I told them that Chad had chicken pox. Just one of those things. I was aware that people probably thought I was "suppressing" emotions, to use Maryann's analysis —and maybe this time I was. I certainly didn't want to think about what was happening to my body or how I would deal with the child within. I ignored Maryann's pleas to set up prenatal visits.

One card I received read, *We're holding out hope that the baby is Steve's.* I had no such hope.

Another card read, *We are delighted that you have decided to keep the child.* I didn't know what we had decided.

I didn't take out the Christmas decorations. Neither did Steve.

Sipping coffee after church one Sunday, someone said to me, "People in this church just tell each other too much. Aren't there any secrets anymore?" Maybe she wanted to offend me since I was not crying on her shoulder about my pain.

Instead, I agreed with her. "Yeah, I shouldn't have told

anyone," I said. She looked embarrassed and mumbled something about needing more coffee before she rambled off. I left the kids in the nursery and waited for Steve in the snow-covered car.

Maryann confronted me in Bible study one morning. We were at her house. Christmas music played in the background. Her grand tree was decorated with red and white lights and tiny silk bows. We nibbled home-baked cookies sprinkled with green and red candy. "I can see that you won't take care of yourself, Heather," she said, "but please take care of that baby."

It surprised and scared me how I could jump from flat-line emotions to flaring anger. I wanted to lash out at her, to accuse her of giving me the wrong medicine or of misleading me to believe Ovral could solve all my problems. But then she would do something sick like congratulate me for expressing my feelings. So I shrugged.

"You're due for your three-month HIV test, too," she told me.

I knew that. I didn't have the day circled on my calendar, but I saw it approaching like a steam-engine locomotive chugging toward me on the tracks I was tied to. I shrugged again and let the conversation change its course. At the close of the meeting I told the ladies I needed a little break from the group. "Just meet without me for a while," I told them when they asked why. I gathered up Chad and Simon from the playroom, stuffed them in their snowsuits so their arms stuck out like snowmen's, and squinted my eyes against the glare of the white and shapeless landscape. "See you," I called out calmly as we all disappeared into our Hondas and Volvos and Jeeps. But my anger against Maryann's mothering had already formed a plan.

I dropped the kids off at a sitter later that week and drove the precarious roads to the County Health Department. The bite of the wind chased me into the building I wanted to avoid. Once inside, I pulled off my dress jacket and swung it over my suited sleeve. *No one will look at me with disdain,* I assured myself as I walked briskly to the information desk.

"Where do I go for HIV testing?" I asked as indifferently as possible. Perhaps if I had belted out, "I have confidence in me," like Julie Andrews did in *The Sound of Music,* I would have felt better.

I ignored what the young woman's face revealed and followed her finger to a small room down the hall on the right. I pushed the heavy door open and briefly endured the glances of the constituents. A glass window at the far end of the room separated the clients from the staff. I scribbled my first name on the sign-up sheet and checked the box in front of *HIV Test.* Then I sat in one of the plastic chairs surrounding a television screen bolted to the ceiling; I craned my neck uncomfortably to watch it.

On screen, a terribly sad-looking teenager hung her head and held her very pregnant stomach. Her face was replaced with the image of a patient dying of AIDS. "This could be you," the unspoken message shouted. "Don't sleep around without protection," the actors told us. "Don't share needles." I consoled myself with arrogant disinterest. I was neither a whore nor a drug addict.

Eventually I dared to look around the room at the whores and drug addicts. They stared at the monitor or buried their heads in magazines. One young mom—she must have been sixteen—slapped her two-year-old's hand every couple minutes and whispered a harsh reprimand. She was lovely, but she looked tired. A man wearing a do-rag was rocking to the rap that beat into his ears, looking nowhere. A woman who looked about my age seemed to be ten months pregnant; she leaned back in the chair and rested her hand on her belly.

I smoothed my suit coat and touched my hair. I was overdressed and I felt silly.

When my name was called, I thought about bolting; but I stood up with grace and confidence. I breezed toward the waiting nurse, smiling. "Hi," I said to her in the tone of voice I used with my Sunday school students. She brought me to a small room privatized with a curtain.

"Did you get a chance to watch the film, dear?" she said to me in the same patronizing tone I had used on her. I half nodded, half shrugged. "It's okay if you didn't," she said. "I have the same film right here for you to watch if you were distracted out there."

"I watched it," I said quickly.

"Good. I need for you to fill out the little form to be sure you have a proper understanding of HIV." She handed me a multiple-choice test. "If you need to watch the film again to help answer some questions, let me know. Otherwise, just give me a little shout when you're finished."

"Okay." I answered the questions in five minutes. The nurse sat down, crossed her legs, and held the sheet in front of her so we could both see it. She proceeded to read each question and each answer out loud. She copiously praised me when I got answers right and gently added information when my answers were vague. This went on for five minutes before I finally interrupted. "Excuse me," I said, crossing my manicured nails in front of me. "I think it's wonderful that you educate all your clients so well, but this information just doesn't pertain to me. Could we go ahead and run the test?"

She touched my knee and smiled. "Those statements seem a little inconsistent, dear. You want to be tested for HIV, but how the virus is contracted does not pertain to you?"

I nodded my head. "That's right. My husband is my only sexual partner and I do not do drugs. May we please run the test?"

She raised her eyebrows.

I sighed deeply and looked out the window. "I was raped, okay? Please can we just get this over with?"

She didn't talk until I looked at her again. "I am not here to judge you, dear," she oozed. I knew she didn't believe me. "I am here to help. Now, I am required by the state to go over this quiz with you. We're nearly done, and then I can get the blood test."

I listened sullenly to the rest of her lecture. She maintained her sugar-sweet demeanor.

I signed the papers she handed me. She coolly drew my blood.

"The test results will be available in a week—"

"A week?"

"Yes. Please make an appointment for next Tuesday to get the results."

"Can't I just call?"

"No. It is our policy to share the results with you in

person. I recommend that you bring your husband or a good girlfriend. If the results are positive, you'll need some emotional support."

I nodded.

"It's humbling, isn't it—" she said as we both stood up and moved toward the door, "—humbling to know how frail each of us is, no matter who we are."

I walked out of the waiting room, past the whores and drug addicts. The pretty young mom smiled at me. A week later I would be sitting with them again, one of them again, frail with them again.

That night I told Steve I had gone for the test. He didn't ask why I hadn't gone to Maryann's office. He did ask me when I planned to talk to the Adamses. When I shrugged, he said, "You can go alone to the County Health Department to get tested for AIDS, but you can't call the Adamses?" I shrugged again. "You can face a church full of people and tell them what happened, but you can't call your best friends?"

When have I ever claimed to be logical? I wanted to say to him.

But the next day I asked Steve to make the call. "Ask them if they're willing to *consider* this," I said. "Don't make anything definite. Who knows if they'll think it's too weird to be friends with the birth mom of their kid. I wouldn't want this to ruin our friendship. And who knows what *we'll* decide."

I listened to Steve's side of the conversation and couldn't tell how Jon responded to his invitation to "talk with you guys about maybe adopting the baby." When I asked him how they sounded, he said, "Probably excited."

Before they came, I cleaned the house with meticulousness. I emptied cupboards and wiped down coasters; I rearranged furniture and washed couch pillows; I aired out bedspreads and organized closets. As I worked, I knew the state of our closets was not an issue to our friends—they had seen our dirty dishes, they had teased me about the mounds of laundry, they had discovered our moldy sour cream. But if the pope were planning to stop by, I would have been no less nervous.

I saw the thrill on Barb's face when she walked in the door—though she tried to subdue it. She looked like I often felt on the racquetball court: Don't show the joy of victory because it is gained at the other person's expense. I saw her controlled elation, and my heart lurched. At that moment, I wanted to give Barb whatever it was that would free her to express the suppressed joy that must have been making her skin itch. I knew her deepest longing, and I had the power to let this dear friend realize her most precious dream. We hugged as if we hadn't seen each other in years, though just the weekend before we had been playing dominoes around their dining room table.

And so I didn't protest when Jon followed our hugs with "Guys, I have no doubt that this is an answer to prayer. You can't imagine how thankful we are for this."

And neither did I amend Steve's reply: "This just might be the answer to both our problems."

My cheeks ached as I smiled my way through the evening. I sat mesmerized, as if I were watching a family of deer frolic in a meadow. For fear of sending the nearly tangible joy that danced in my living room back into hidden places, I dared not speak of my growing awareness of loss.

But, hours later, when the laughter trickled down our

front step and disappeared into a warmed-up car, when I pushed the door closed and heard the quiet *poof* of the air settling in the frame, when my strained cheeks were released from contrived happiness—I leaned heavily against the wall beside the front door and gazed out the window.

I saw gorgeous icicles glittering from the porch railings, and I saw my friends' footprints in the newly fallen snow as I stood there willing myself not to cry. And, just as clearly, I saw my child nestling in their arms. I saw my child being carried far away from me.

Emptiness had searched until it found me once again.

Chapter Eleven

Connection

It was our first real kiss

since the rape.

Pregnancy provided one solace: distraction. You consumed my thoughts no more than a buzzing mosquito would bother a soldier in the midst of battle.

The simple act of standing, as the red taillights of the Adamses' car disappeared around the corner, overwhelmed me. I sank to the floor.

Steve was walking toward the kitchen with the dishes we had used that night and caught sight of my descent in his peripheral vision. "Past your bedtime, old lady?" he called out to me. "You'd never survive the party next door."

I didn't answer.

"Heather, you okay?" his voice still held a hint of laughter. I heard the clatter of dishes being put in the dishwasher.

I knew my husband had not been so happy since my panicked phone call six months earlier. I looked up and smiled when he came out of the kitchen. It was a weak smile, and Steve saw right through it.

"Oh, babe," he said softly. He came over and sat on the

floor beside me. I accepted his strong embrace, trying to be strong myself. "Have I ever told you what an amazing person you are?" he whispered, smiling.

I pushed my face into his chest and thought back to the day I met this good man who was willingly walking this difficult journey with me.

I was a freshman in college. My sophomore suitemate, Bonnie, had just taken me shopping. "You've got this perfect bod, but you hide it under those frumpy clothes," she said one day as I stood in front of the mirror, grumbling about having nothing to wear. "Get your money and come on."

She had a car, so we went to the GAP and Express and then back to our dorm. "Wear the jeans," she said. "I want to show you off."

I felt gorgeous and so laughed loudly all the way over to another dorm where some of Bonnie's friends lived. But I got quiet when I saw the beautiful young man working behind the dorm lobby desk whose huge brown eyes smiled at me.

Bonnie noticed the attraction. "Hey, Steve," she called out to him. "Take care of this little girl while I run up to get a CD from Bob." She squeezed my arm and whispered between her teeth, "Go talk to him. He's really sweet." She disappeared into the stairwell, but stuck her head back out to say with a wink, "She just got new clothes. Don't they look great?"

And so, before he knew my name, Steve had me twirling in front of him, showing off my new outfit. I blushed, and our courtship began.

The conversation that began in the dorm lobby continued long into the night in Bonnie's room. A bunch of us college students sprawled on the floor or on Bonnie's horrible flowered couch, gorging on pizza and pop and philosophical debate. Bonnie was there and a few of my other friends, but I noticed only Steve. We discussed everything from politics to legalizing drugs to Kierkegaard's view of education. We flirted a bit as Steve tried to convince me (as if I had to decide anytime soon) to remain in the great U.S. of A. after graduation rather than return to my home and native land. We threw food and pillows at each other occasionally, but resisted touching each other.

It was way past curfew when Steve finally stood up to leave. He said good-bye to Bonnie first: "Here comes another great year, Bon. I'm glad to see your excellent taste in friends hasn't diminished." He looked appreciatively at me. "Freshmen aren't usually as sophisticated as this Canuck you've discovered."

He winked at me and left.

"He's in love with you, Heather," Bonnie said.

"No, he's not," I giggled. "Is he?"

"Definitely. All conversations combined, that boy didn't say as much last year as he did tonight in one conversation. He's flipped over you."

The next day there was a note on my door: *I heard you were calling out my name in your sleep. SG*

The day after that we saw each other in the cafeteria, and he asked me out on a date.

Bonnie made me go shopping again. "He's a *junior*, Heather." As if for that reason alone I should give up the rest of my tiny savings. "He's gorgeous." I still hesitated. "It worked last time …" She had a point.

Steve held my hand during the movie, and I enjoyed the

175

way our intertwined fingers communicated. We discovered many affinities during dinner at a quaint diner in Easttown and laughed easily during dessert at an ice cream parlor a few blocks down. Dating wasn't a new thing for me, so when he turned off the car back at my dorm, I knew that he wanted our good-bye to linger. Steaming up car windows was an activity I had often enjoyed in my high school days, so it couldn't have been good Christian purity that made me bolt from that car without even saying good-bye. I ran because I knew that I had found the man I wanted to marry. I was terrified of messing things up.

I called him the next day to thank him for the lovely evening and to apologize for running off so quickly—and he asked me out again.

At the close of our second date, I didn't run.

Steve and I spent all our time together after that. We studied together in my dorm basement where other kids played Ping-Pong or watched TV. We watched quality movies like *Dr. Zhivago*, presented by the Student Activities office, and we stayed for the discussions afterward. We met in the cafeteria for meals and in the library for homework. We went to the on-campus church service every Sunday and drank tea afterward. And we lounged in his apartment where his roommates fought over room temperature and chores and food ownership and television shows.

"I hate math!" I passionately declared one sunny winter day as we walked back from Hieminga Hall after my algebra class. I felt like breaking something. "I just can't do it!" I was used to being able to accomplish whatever I set my mind to.

Steve, the math major, my math tutor, nodded in agreement. "Math is tough."

"What am I going to do when you're gone?" I said with as much accusation in my voice as grief. He had signed up for a semester in Spain long before he had met me, but I still resented his going.

"You'll be done with this class before I leave," he said, pulling me into a sideways hug, "and you won't sign up for another math course as long as you live."

"And you'll write me letters every day and you'll send me pictures of yourself and you'll stay far away from all those gorgeous Spanish girls who will try to convince you to never return home to your one true love."

"Oh, babe," he said with a grin. "Of course I'll send you letters and pictures."

I socked him.

Steve's birthday was two days before he left for Spain. I created a lavish treasure hunt for him—making him retrieve notes from professors he hated and from musty old library books most people didn't even know existed and from cute girls he never dared to talk to—until he finally ended up in our friend's cabin on the river, where I was creating a scintillating dinner.

Steve and I had previously agreed that we wanted to resist "going all the way." We also both knew that if we stayed in the cabin after dinner, our resistance would crumble. "Flee temptation," the Bible says. It doesn't say to merely resist.

But time together was running out. We stayed.

I wonder now how different our lives would have been if we hadn't stayed. I wouldn't have gone through the secret terror of researching cancer and other diseases to try to discover why my breasts hurt so much. I wouldn't have wept at the on-campus med center when the young female doctor, who eventually became my mentor and friend, gently told me I was pregnant. I wouldn't have had to call Steve on the other side of the world to tell him he was going to be a dad. I wouldn't have become engaged over the phone. I wouldn't have had to break my parents' hearts by telling them that their good little girl had messed up. I wouldn't have had to sit in my future in-laws' living room alone and guilty while they tried to balance grace and justice.

But then Steve might have noticed the gorgeous Spanish girls rather than baby strollers. ("I can't believe how many babies there are," he said in a long-distance phone conversation to me. "They're everywhere.") We might never have talked about how many kids we wanted, how we spend our money, how our faith plays out in our lives, what our parenting style should be, what kind of wedding we wanted. We wouldn't have held in our arms the baby—the perfect, gorgeous, beautiful child—who transformed us from careless college students into devoted parents.

And I wouldn't have discovered, as I sat on our living room floor clinging to my husband, how deep love goes when tragedy binds you together.

You looked happy tonight," my husband said. "Aren't you happy?"

I sighed. "I don't know how to feel. I want to help Jon and Barb, and I want our problem to go away. I really thought this would work."

"But you can't do it, can you?"

"I'm sorry for being so mixed up."

"You want to keep the baby, don't you?"

"I don't know." I nodded my head toward the door. "All I

know is that when I watched Jon and Barb leave this house, I knew what it felt like to see someone walk off with my baby." I sobbed.

Steve remained silent for a moment, but I felt his strong fingers massaging my neck. "Our baby," Steve said quietly.

I looked up at him.

"It's *our* baby," he said. "If we're keeping it, we have to start talking that way."

"What are you saying?" I asked carefully.

"I was thinking about how much pain came out of this—for you, for me, for others. And then I realized that the baby has nothing to do with the crime. The baby is innocent. Why cause pain for her by taking her away from her mother?"

"Or him."

Steve put his hand on my tummy that was just starting to protrude. "Do you think you can love this baby, Heather?"

I nodded my head. "I think I already do." My hand met his, and I liked how our intertwined fingers communicated. "Can you?" I asked.

"If she's anything like you," Steve said, pulling my lips to his, "then, yes."

It was our first real kiss since the rape, and we were both hungry for it. I welcomed his mouth on mine without thinking of the poisonous touches of my rapist, without mistrusting my husband's intentions, without even worrying about passing on a disease. And Steve welcomed my renewed enthusiasm.

We were just getting to the point of giggles when Simon's shrill cry beckoned. "Ahh," said Steve when I got up to tend to our demanding toddler. "It feels like everything's back to normal."

I grinned because, to me, normalcy was even better than sex.

The next day, Steve called the Adamses. "Uh, Jon," he said reluctantly. I was sitting beside him at the kitchen table, cringing behind my hands. "Listen, have you got a minute?... Actually, that's what I want to talk about. I don't think you should call that adoption lawyer yet.... No. That's not it. Heather and I have been talking. Listen, we've decided to keep the baby.... I know. We shouldn't have—" Steve looked at me and shook his head. It wasn't going well. "I know. We feel awful. But it's the only thing we can do.... Okay. I understand. Please call us when you can."

"Do you think they'll ever forgive us?" I asked when Steve set down the phone.

"I don't know." He looked miserable. Jon was his best friend.

"We didn't mean to hurt them."

"I know. It sure seemed like the right thing to do at the time."

Tough decisions can still feel good when you know you are doing the right thing. We didn't feel good at all: Door number three was ours by default only.

We didn't understand the depth of the blow to our friends until we found out the next Sunday that Jon and Barb had decided to leave the church. They couldn't bear to be around us; they didn't have the strength to watch us raise the child they had mentally adopted. "It was your church before it was ours," I told Barb in a telephone conversation she didn't want to have. "We'll leave so you can stay."

It was an agonizing offer to make—the people of the church had been our lifeline, and losing them was almost beyond comprehension. But the pain of betrayal we caused our friends was not something to be taken lightly. I wanted to, and couldn't, make amends. Besides, I knew that their current pain needed the body of Christ as much as our recent pain had.

But my offer seemed to make Barb even angrier. "No," she snarled. "You stay. Everyone would be mad at us if we drove you away." Resentment dripped from her voice.

"That's not the way it is, Barb," I answered. But she repelled my words as strongly as one north end of a magnet would repel another. I was sad, remembering a recent Friday evening at their house when they had insisted we take back the money we had dropped on their counter to help cover the pizza bill. I knew that, like that twenty-dollar bill sitting untouched between us, Sherman Street Church would remain ineffective to both of us: Steve and I would have to leave the church along with them.

Pastor Mark did his best to reconcile us, trying desperately to care for both our needs, to keep both families in the church. But it was no use: The Adamses had risked revealing to us their one vulnerable spot, and we had deepened the wound. Only forgiveness could return both families to the fold.

So we left the church.

But the church did not leave us.

Maryann was one of the first to call. "You made a public statement, Heather," she told me angrily. "You said that this attack was not on you alone, but on the whole church. You'd better not forget that."

"I remember," I told her.

"Then why are you leaving us? You don't have the right to leave the church—and certainly not our Bible study—not after all we've been through together."

"I can't leave?" Her words were rushing into me like helium into a balloon, but she mistook my buoyancy for rebellion.

"No, Heather, you can't. And you certainly can't continue to neglect that baby. You may think that I'm being—"

"Maryann," I interrupted, "I called your office yesterday to make an appointment to see you."

"What?"

"I'll be in first thing next week."

"What?"

"I'm coming for a prenatal visit."

"You're kidding! I mean, I'm glad. How—?"

"We're keeping the baby, you know."

She laughed a little. "Everyone knows, Heather. And we're all proud of you."

"Everyone knows?" A healthy church is like a small town: There are no secrets.

"Of course," said Maryann. "We were all in agony with you as you were deciding. I think you've made a wonderfully brave choice, and I think Jon and Barb will get over it."

"Oh."

"You also need to get the next HIV test done."

"No. I don't know why I did this, but I ended up going to the Health Department for the test. I'm sorry for being so dumb."

Apologies were coming out of me unbeckoned on every front.

"And?" Maryann asked.

"I was supposed to go back to get the results weeks ago."

"You didn't?"

"Oh, Maryann! I just can't get myself to go back."

"I don't blame you. That's a tough thing to do alone. Let's have them forward the results here. Can you come to my office today to sign a release form? We can fax it to them."

She couldn't have known how good it felt for me to be back in her capable hands. "That would be great," I said. "I'll have to come with the kids, though. I won't stay for the answer."

"It'll be fine, Heather. It'll be fine."

I almost believed her.

Tasha was another friend who wouldn't let me escape from the fellowship so easily. "Girl," she told me that same afternoon, "I think you just using those friends of yours as an excuse to get away from the church."

"Why would I want to get away?"

"Because everyone know your story."

"So?"

"So you don't want to deal with it anymore."

"No," I told her. "You're usually right. But not this time. I have to deal with it whether I'm at Sherman Street or not."

"Well, I just hope you all get over this whole thing before the baby is born. You know that the baptism has to be with us. This is everybody's baby."

"Yeah. Besides, if we're not at Sherman Street, how are we going to explain a mixed-race baby?"

"You gonna be explaining that for the rest of your life,

girl. But you can hold your head up high when you do. And don't you ever forget that."

Not everyone's opinion was as encouraging as Maryann's and Tasha's, though.

"What if it's a boy?" someone asked me. "He'll grow up to be a black man." The person expressing this profound truth had heard that we had decided to leave the church and wanted to make sure we were okay. She talked more than she listened.

"Jon and Barb would have been wonderful parents," another person commented. "Why'd you change your mind?"

"You know this child will be naughty, Heather. Are you sure you want that responsibility?"

These questions from acquaintances and loved ones baffled me. "Doesn't she realize that she was talking about a baby who is as much a part of me as Chad and Simon are?" I asked Steve after we had tucked the boys in bed and settled in the living room for the evening. "Why does she think this baby will be naughty?"

"It doesn't seem like anyone gets how racist and patronizing and insensitive their words are," he answered. "It makes me wonder what I've said to people before that I shouldn't have."

"Yeah. Well, I'm just glad that I've got Tasha and Maryann to keep me sane," I mused. "I feel bad for you. Who do you go to when your best friend is the very issue you need to talk about?"

Steve nodded. "I could sure use a game of pool with Jon right now," he said.

The telephone interrupted our conversation.

"Heather," said Maryann's gentle voice, "I have the results of your test. I didn't want to wait until tomorrow to call you."

DESTINY

"Do you really

still believe God wanted us to live here?

So you could get raped?

If that's the case,

then God is a jerk."

Sometimes I wonder if you've ever been caught for some other crime you must have committed. Perhaps you, like I, know what it's like to wait six months to find out whether you're going to be on death row.

I hung up the phone and smiled at my husband. With calm in my voice that didn't betray the whirlwind in my heart, I said, "That was Maryann with good news."

It took Steve a moment to catch on. But when he did, he rushed over and pulled me to his chest. "Oh, Heather! Oh, Heather. Thank God!"

I just laughed. I put my head back and laughed until my stomach hurt. I was free. I was alive. My deepest fear proved void. *Thank God* was not adequate.

Steve laughed with me until our mouths found each other.

"So all our waiting was for nothing!" he murmured happily.

We didn't stop kissing as we moved upstairs. We were like newlyweds who didn't have to wait a moment more.

No toddler's cry, no doctor's orders interrupted our giggles this time.

The memory of beer breath did.

I pulled away from my husband. He opened his eyes, surprised.

"I'm sorry, Steve," I said. I really was sorry. "I want to. I love you. I just can't."

Steve nodded his head and then rolled over to rest beside me. "I understand," he said. He even squeezed my hand. But he couldn't have understood. He had waited without complaint for six months only to find out that he needed to wait longer.

I turned from him and closed my eyes. He got up and went back downstairs.

God, I said silently, *I'm off death row, but I'm not yet free. Please, please make me better.*

I woke up the next morning to the sound of the doorbell. Steve was asleep beside me.

I threw on my housecoat and went downstairs. Deshawn was at the front door with his nose and hands pressed against the glass. I opened the door and glared at him. "It's six thirty in the morning, Deshawn. I told you to wait until eight before you come."

"I don't know how to tell time, and my mom is sleeping."

"Couldn't you just watch TV or something?"

"No. There are people sleeping in the living room. And I'm hungry."

I could feel the freshness of the cool air on my face. The city on a Saturday morning is wonderfully peaceful, especially when compared to the nighttime activities of a few hours earlier. But Deshawn didn't care that the clean, morning air offered to wash away the evils of the night. He just shivered in the cold.

I opened the door wider. "Okay. Come in. You can have something to eat, but I'm going back to bed. It's too early for a Saturday."

"Thanks, Miss Heather. I'll be real good."

I gave him a quick hug. "Ringing my doorbell at the crack of dawn isn't being good, but I love you anyway. Grab a bowl of cereal and then watch a video until the boys wake up, okay?"

Deshawn headed for the kitchen, and I went back upstairs.

"Who was that?" Steve asked without even raising his head from the pillow.

"Guess." I sank into bed, glad to discover my spot was still warm.

"I thought you told him not to come before eight."

"Well, he's hungry." I pulled the blankets up past my ears.

"No leftover food from the party last night?"

"I doubt it. Not with all those people who had the munchies. Dolores's cupboards are probably cleared out again."

"Stupid."

"She is, yeah. But why should Deshawn have to suffer for it?"

We were quiet for a moment, and I hovered between sleep and consciousness.

"I hate living here," Steve said just before I lost

awareness.

"You do?" I managed to say.

Steve lifted his head from the pillow. I didn't open my eyes. "Yes, I do," he said. "We were dumb to stay."

"No, we weren't," I mumbled.

"Yes, we were. I'm sick of having to save kids from the crimes of their parents."

My hand slid to my stomach, and I opened my eyes. "What are you saying?"

"I'm not saying anything except that I hate being kept up late at night by loud music and waking up early in the morning to bratty kids."

"Deshawn's not a brat." I closed my eyes again.

"I don't know why I believed all that God-wants-us-here stuff."

"Because it's true?"

"It's stupid," Steve said. "God doesn't care whether we stay in the neighborhood worrying about community development. He doesn't care about anything we do."

"Oh, brother," I said. "The doorbell wakes you up and suddenly God doesn't exist."

"Well, think about it."

"No. You're acting crazy. Go back to sleep."

I rolled over. Steve sat up.

"I'm not crazy," he said. "Maybe I'm finally sane."

I didn't say anything.

"Heather, think about this for just a minute."

"It's too early, Steve."

"You're so content to just accept all this crap that has been happening to us. Do you really still believe that God wanted us to live here? Why? So you could get raped? If that's

192

the case, then God is a jerk."

I sighed and pulled my pillow up against the headboard so I could sit beside my husband. "Yes, I still believe we are called to live here."

"So, you believe God is a jerk."

"Steve—"

"*I* don't think God is a jerk," Steve said. "I don't think he would cause you to be raped. I think he just doesn't pay much attention to what's going on here on earth."

"So, you're suddenly a deist." I shook my head in amazement. I could hardly believe this conversation was happening. Steve is the rock; I am the bird. He keeps me grounded; I keep him interesting. And now I was the one protecting our traditional faith.

"I'm not 'suddenly a deist.' I'm just trying to make sense of things. Listen, it's a joke when people pray for God to intervene. People ask Jesus for a parking spot. If a spot opens up, they thank Jesus. If it doesn't, they say that Jesus knew they needed the exercise. Really, he just doesn't bother himself with that stuff. God made the world self-sufficient, and then he sat back and let us take care of ourselves."

"Okay. So what about Easter? Did it ever happen?"

"Yes. I think Jesus came to die for us. That's the one thing we couldn't do our own."

"Are you serious about this, Steve?"

He was quiet.

"If you are, then you're saying that everything that has happened has been for nothing."

I heard a video playing downstairs. I hoped the boys wouldn't wake up.

"Is that the only reason you believe?" Steve challenged.

"So that this will have meaning?"

"No. Come on, Steve. You know the answer to that question."

"Well, then, we're back to God as jerk."

"No. We're back to God intended for us to live here, to get over our racism, to get to know our neighbors, to get to know Deshawn, to help make this community a little nicer place to live ..."

"And to be raped."

"I don't think God had anything to do with that part."

"Well, which is it? He's either involved or he's not."

"He's involved up to the point that we let him be. He directs us, but he doesn't force us to do anything. He lets us know what we should do, but we decide whether to do it. And that goes for everyone. God didn't rape me; the guy who raped me raped me."

"You believe that, don't you?" Steve said.

"Of course. It's nothing new. You used to believe it, too."

"I know." Steve sighed deeply. "I still do. But don't you ever wonder if we're wrong?"

I saw my leather-bound Bible on the bedside table with its torn-up cover and its numerous bookmarks. I thought about how no matter when I read it or where in the Book I start reading, some truth slaps me when I need to be slapped or comforts me when I'm in despair or strengthens me when I want to give up or surprises me when I'm bored. I thought about all the people —from in-laws to best friends to acquaintances—who believed God's promises for us when we couldn't believe ourselves. I thought about the startling beauty of God's grace.

"No, I don't wonder if we're wrong. But I do sometimes wonder if I dare to keep being a Christian," I said.

"What do you mean?"

"Well, I'll bet Satan would do whatever it takes to stop us from doing what God wants us to. So I can't help wondering if something like this will happen again."

Steve nodded. "It could."

"But can we live with that?"

"I don't know. I do know that we'd be kind of stupid to stay in this house if we're going to keep this baby."

"You really want to move?"

"Yeah, I do."

"Me, too," I said with a sigh. "Sometimes I scare myself at how badly I want to leave."

"Really? I didn't think you'd ever want to leave."

"Sometimes I scare myself at how inconsistent I am." I laughed. Steve didn't. "No, I don't want to leave. I love being where I know God wants us to be. I love this house. I love these neighbors. I don't want to leave. No matter what the consequences."

"Well, which is it? Either you want to leave or you don't."

"That's not true. I want both at the same time."

"Well, if we're going to keep this baby, we need more space. I think we should put the house up for sale again."

This time I dared to pursue the greater of the two issues Steve presented. "*If* we're going to keep this baby? Is there a chance we won't?"

Steve was quiet a moment. He sighed when he finally answered. "We'll keep the baby. We don't really have another choice left."

195

I pushed my pillow back down and told Steve I was going back to sleep. I was sick of this conversation. "I need to get a few more winks in before I get ready for the party tonight," I said. "You didn't forget about it, did you? Everyone's coming."

"Who's everyone?"

"You know. Byron and Maryann, Pam and Alex, Jeff and Dee, Dirk and Mel. Everyone."

"Not Jon and Barb."

"No. But everyone else. We're having a Saint Patrick's Day party. You have to wear something green." I bunched the pillow around my head and hoped sleep would come back to me before the kids woke up.

"No one will wear green."

I didn't answer, but I wanted to say, *You won't. Everyone else will.*

"So, I think I'll call the realtor today," he said casually.

"I'm sleeping."

Steve got out of bed and went downstairs.

I lay still for a while, and then I felt the baby move. It was the first time I let myself acknowledge the fluttering, but I didn't call Steve. It really was fluttering—it was not just a little arm pressed up against my belly with no way of moving away. It was a living child.

I wish it were dead. I blushed at the thought—even though no one could know what I was thinking. *I wish it were dead and it was Casey fluttering inside me instead.*

But even as I thought it, my hand moved to my belly and I held my breath so as to keep perfectly still. When I finally dared to breathe again, the fluttering continued. I kept my hand glued to the motion inside me until it stopped several minutes later.

And my fleeting thought of moments before was obliterated.

"Good morning, darling," I whispered. I got out of bed and dug in the back of my closet until I found my maternity clothes.

"You look great," Steve said when I came downstairs with Simon in tow. I was probably glowing. "I was wondering when you would give up trying to fit in your other clothes." He winked at me, and I smiled back.

As I cleaned the house and cooked up corned beef and sauerkraut for everyone else—plus all the edible food for me—I occasionally glanced in the mirror to look at my expanding profile or rested my hand on my rounding stomach.

It took most of the day to prepare for the party while also caring for the kids and getting a bit of laundry done. A half hour before everyone was to arrive, I rushed upstairs to get myself cleaned up.

"What should I wear?" I asked Steve.

"Green," he said as he pulled a black turtleneck over his head.

"It felt kind of good to wear maternity clothes today, but I don't know if I want to wear them when everyone's here."

"Do you have any green maternity clothes?"

"Yeah," I held up a forest green blouse. "But should I wear it?"

"I hate to break it to you, babe," my husband said as he brushed a kiss over my cheek, "but you ain't getting any skinnier. You'd better wear it."

I held the shirt in front of me. "But it would be so … I don't know … bold."

Steve raised his eyebrows but didn't comment.

"I mean," I tried to explain, "it would be sort of like telling everyone I'm glad to be pregnant."

"Or that you're getting too big for normal clothes," my logical husband answered.

The phone rang and I dropped the blouse over my head. "I'm going to wear it," I said with conviction as I headed for the phone.

It was Tasha.

"Oh, Tash! I'm glad it's you," I blurted. "Guess what! I'm going to wear maternity clothes tonight!"

I don't know why I thought she would instantly understand the symbolism of my announcement. Neither do I understand why I didn't stop to listen to her before I spouted my own news. She answered with some polite acknowledgment and then I continued.

"Listen, Tash. I can't talk right now because some friends are coming over in a few minutes, and I look horrible. I need to do my hair and makeup. Can I call you tomorrow?"

I hardly noticed the pause between us, and I hung up the phone mere seconds after she told me, "Yeah, that'd be fine."

I wore my green blouse with pride and talked about heartburn and babies with my other girlfriends most of the night.

"It's good to see you so happy, Heather," Maryann whispered to me when we happened to have the kitchen to ourselves.

"It's good to be happy," I told her. "I just hope nobody is

mad at me for being in love with this baby."

"Why would they be?"

"I don't know. Sometimes it seems like people think I should be depressed. Maybe if they hear me getting all excited about having this baby, they'll think I'm not taking seriously what happened."

"Nah. You're reading into things too much."

"Maybe." I shrugged and grabbed a bowl of pretzels that had been dipped in green-colored chocolate. "But even if it's true, I don't care. There is no way I want to stay in a place of despair. What's the point? I like being happy better."

"I agree."

I paused outside the door. "I have to admit, though, that a little bit of me worries that being happy about the baby minimizes the pain of what I went through." I looked at my friend's face to see how she would respond to that.

She looked vindicated. "Aha!" she said. "See, you're projecting your feelings onto everyone else. No one wants you to be depressed. You're doing it to yourself."

"Maybe. Or maybe it's a little bit of both. Either way, I'm not giving in to it. I have so many good things in my life. I'm going to enjoy it all."

"Me, too. Now give me one of those pretzels before everyone else devours them."

The next day after lunch, I called Tasha. I wanted to ask how the service at Sherman Street had been that morning and to tell her how frustrated I was that we couldn't find another church we liked. She picked up on the last ring.

"Heather, listen," she said in response to my initial greeting. "I don't feel like talking to you."

"What's wrong?" I didn't notice the emphasis on her last two words.

"What's wrong? Girl, don't you know?"

"No, what is it?"

"Heather, you don't need me."

I started to notice a coldness on my neck. "What do you mean?"

"Girl, you so into your white friends. You drop me as soon as they come in the picture."

"I do not!"

"Yeah, you do. And it hurts. I'm not going to let you hurt me anymore."

"Tasha, last night's phone call was just at a bad time."

"Think about it, Heather." She didn't have to tell me that—my mind was racing. "Personally, I've thought about it enough. And I've decided that it's time for us to part ways. At least for a while."

I didn't say anything. The coldness that had settled on my neck was moving deep into my bones. *Part ways?*

"Good-bye, Heather."

"Tasha, wait—"

But she was gone.

I didn't hang up the phone until the silence turned to beeping and the beeping to silence again.

After some time had passed, I wandered outside to where Steve was playing catch with the boys. Simon giggled with two-year-old glee when I joined the game, and I welcomed his affection with renewed appreciation. When the sun started to sink and the boys got chilly, we moved back indoors where blocks and Legos consumed them.

"Don't ever leave me, okay?" I said quietly to my husband who was deep into a golf magazine.

"I've never even considered it," he said without looking up.

I cuddled up to him without saying anything. He kept reading.

He made it through about four more pages before I talked again. "How can I handle big things when I'm such a pathetic baby over smaller things?"

"Hmmm?"

I knew he wanted to keep reading. I restrained myself for a few more pages until I finally had to say, "Actually, I don't think rejection is a small thing."

Steve turned the page.

"Tasha told me she wants to 'part ways.'" A tear escaped.

Steve looked at me.

"She says that I drop her whenever my other friends come around."

"That's not true. Anyone can see that you like Tasha better than them." He looked back down at the magazine.

I shrugged. "In some ways. Really, I like her different than I like them."

"Maybe she can tell it's different and that's why she's offended."

"It's different just because they're part of a big group. They're *our* friends. Tasha's *my* friend."

"That's what I mean. She's your best friend. Don't worry. She'll get over it."

Steve went back to reading. I went back to thinking.

"No," I finally said. Steve had probably already forgotten

what we were talking about. "Maybe I do pay too much attention to them. I really do love Tasha best, but I have more fun with them. And I never invite her to join our parties."

"Mm."

"And maybe I take too much from her. I talk about me all the time, and I never listen to her."

"Mm."

"She said I'm racist."

"She did?"

"Well, she said I care about my white friends more than her."

Steve finally put down his magazine. "Oh, brother. I didn't think Tasha would ever use the racism line."

"What do you mean?"

"I don't know. It just seems like white people can't do anything right. No matter what we do, it's because we're white and we don't understand what it's like to be black. I didn't think Tasha would ever believe that junk."

"In some ways it's true."

"Okay. It's true that we don't know what it's like to be black, but that doesn't mean our every motive is to demean black people. I don't even think about whether people are black or white when I'm talking to them."

"We're supposed to notice. If we don't see color, we're not valuing them for who they are."

"Supposed to. What bull. Listen, I don't want to waste my life in the ghetto when the game we're playing is meaningless. We're not helping anyone by living here."

I didn't know what to say. His logic made sense, but it still felt wrong. "I don't know how we're helping, but for some reason God wanted us to live here."

"Wanted."

"And wants."

"It's meaningless, Heather. And we're both scared here."

It was true. Steve was as jumpy as I was, especially at night. And every time the phone rang.

"Remember," I said, "they might have caught the guy. Detective Boers said she would call this weekend to confirm."

"I doubt they caught him. They couldn't even trace those phone calls. And even if it is him, would you stop being scared?"

I shrugged. "It would help." We were silent for a moment. "Okay, maybe it wouldn't help," I admitted. "A part of me would still worry that someone else would do the same thing. But even now, with him still out there, I'm not really afraid."

Steve looked at me skeptically.

"Really. I'm jumpy. I'm cautious. And I definitely don't want anyone to break into our house again. But when it comes down to it, I'm sure we're going to be okay."

"I'm not buying it. This morning you were worrying that the results of the test were wrong. You're still scared about a lot of things."

"Oh, I was just being stupid. I know the tests are fine. But even if I had AIDS, I think we would be okay."

"Having AIDS would not be okay."

"Think about it, Steve: Walking with God with AIDS is better than walking away from God healthy. God wants us here and so we're going to be okay. I believe that with my entire self ... except when I'm being stupid like I was this morning."

No one said anything for a moment.

"And I still don't want AIDS," I said quietly. "God, did you hear that? I don't want AIDS!"

The phone rang. I jumped up to answer it. "I'll get it. Can you put the boys to bed?"

I heard the kids squealing with delight as Steve began the bedtime ritual—which I hated but had to admit worked—of chasing the boys up to their rooms.

"I hope it's okay I'm calling on the weekend," Detective Boers said to me. "I have news."

"Of course it's okay." I twirled my hair nervously.

"Listen, it wasn't him," she said. "The DNA didn't match."

I didn't say anything. I didn't dare use my voice. And I didn't know how to feel: disappointed or relieved.

"Sorry, Heather. We'll keep trying."

"That's okay." I was glad my voice wasn't quavering. "I guess I'm not surprised. Thanks for checking anyway."

After I hung up the phone, I sat on the couch and waited for Steve to come downstairs. A few minutes later I got up, not to call Tasha with the news, but to adjust the curtain I had recently made for the bay window. I wanted to be sure it was tightly closed.

"It wasn't him," I said to Steve before he sat down a little while later. "The DNA didn't match."

Steve shook his head. "We're out of here, Heather," he said quietly.

"Why, Steve?" I whispered in sudden anger, careful not to bother the kids. "Why do we have to leave? I'm the one who just lost a best friend. I'm the one who was raped. If anyone wanted to run from here, it should be me. Why—"

"It's not all about you, Heather. This has been hard for me, too." Steve's voice was quiet, but the tension between us was loud and clear.

"Of course it has. But I still don't see why you have to give up on this neighborhood. We belong here. We're part of the neighborhood. And that doesn't come after just a few weeks of living here. We've invested ourselves. And it's paid off. There are people here who love us and count on us."

"We would have the same thing in another neighborhood. Why not invest ourselves where we're safe?"

I flung my hands up in the air. "Because this is where we've been called! I'm so sick of this fight." I didn't say the next words that flitted through my mind: *Why don't you just go and I'll stay.*

Steve didn't say what was going on in his mind, either. And neither of us looked at the other.

I was surprised to feel Steve's fingers on my shoulders a few moments later. He pulled my hair into a ponytail and kissed my neck. "I love you, babe," he said.

I turned and looked at him.

"I love you even when you're mad," he said.

He kissed my fingers. I offered a doubtful look.

"I love you even when you're right," he said.

He kissed my eyelids.

I held up a hand in mock disinterest, but I had already forgiven him for all his real and imagined faults.

"I love you madly, Heather," Steve said with an unusually playful smile. He kissed my arm again and again, moving his mouth closer to my neck. "You make me come alive."

I finally laughed out loud and returned his embrace. "I love you, too, crazy man."

This time there was no memory of beer breath to stop the expression of love between us. We were one again. I fell asleep in my bed that night safe in my husband's arms, thinking of nothing but this incredible man who loved me despite everything.

When I woke a few hours later, I smiled on the way to the bathroom.

But my smile faded when I discovered blood staining my legs and panties. I instinctively put my hand on my stomach; I felt no movement.

"Steve," I called weakly from the bathroom, "something's wrong." And then I whispered to myself, "Something's wrong again."

CHAPTER THIRTEEN

BABY

"We're not going to lose our baby,"

Steve said again.

And then he went down on his knees

and put both hands on my stomach.

"We're right here, Baby," he said. "You're

going to be okay."

Faith is a journey, but there are definite moments along the way when truth propels a person from one state of being to another. I can name several defining moments in my life. I wonder if you can do the same.

I s this normal?" Steve whispered frantically in the bathroom with midnight silence all around us.

"No." I shook my head. "No, I don't think so." We stared at each other for a moment. I thought about Casey's perfect little fingers that had rested on mine. "What if we lose the baby?" I croaked. I thought of a foster brother I had so many years ago. He was black, and I used to love to run my fingers through his hair. I thought of the little yellow pajamas I had seen at the store the other day, and I imagined how stunning they would look against the skin of my olive-skinned child. I thought of the fluttering against my belly only the day before.

Steve took my hands in his. "That's not going to happen." He brushed my cheek as he put a lock of hair behind my ear. "We're not going to lose this baby, okay?"

I nodded. "Okay."

"We're not going to lose *our* baby," Steve said again. And then he went down on his knees and put both hands on my stomach. "We're right here, Baby," he said. "You're going to be okay."

I laughed through my tears. "I'm glad you say so, but I'd really rather hear those words from Maryann." I squeezed his hand and added, "I really don't want to lose this baby."

"You'd better go to the ER," Maryann advised over the phone a few minutes later. "Everything is probably okay, but I'd feel more comfortable if you had things checked out. Call me as soon as you find anything out."

On the way to the hospital, after Steve's parents arrived to watch the kids, Steve and I talked about what name to give our baby.

"Let's name her Andrea," I said.

"It's going to be a boy," Steve said. "But I don't think there are any good boy names left."

"How about Ollie after my dad?"

"How about Harvis after mine?"

We both laughed.

"If it's a girl, let's name her Willie after my mom," I said.

"No, let's name her Eunice after mine."

We laughed again and then rested in the silence.

"Are you scared?" Steve asked.

"Yeah."

"So am I. But you know what's really cool?"

"What?"

"It's cool to know that this baby is ours. It's cool to know that I don't want to lose this baby as much as I didn't want to lose Casey."

"It doesn't feel very cool to me." Knowing how much I loved the child within me was wonderful; knowing the child might die was not.

"It's going to be okay, Heather. I really believe that."

I let him hold the hope.

Steve dropped me off by the emergency room entrance, promising to catch up with me in a second. It was not the same hospital we had been at six months earlier. Neither of us had talked about it, but we both knew we would never go there again. This hospital was smaller, but it held no memories. I gave the facts to the triage nurse—six months pregnant, vaginal bleeding, last child born dead—and I was called into a room mere moments after Steve joined me.

"It must be bad," I said to Steve.

Before I had been in the hospital a half hour, I was wheeled into an ultrasound room. I anxiously watched the screen, looking for my baby's heart.

"There it is," the technician said happily. "Beating strongly. Can you feel all the kicking going on? This baby is active."

Steve grinned. "Told you," he said to me.

"Did you want to know if it's a boy or girl?" the technician asked. "I could easily check for you."

Steve and I looked at each other. We hadn't known in advance for the other kids.

"I want to know," I whispered with renewed excitement.

"Yeah, I do, too." Steve was grinning. "Okay, prove me right again. It's a boy."

"Wrong," he answered a few moments later. "It's a girl. She's definitely a girl."

213

"A girl! Wow! We're going to have a little girl!" I could hardly believe it.

"Wow. A girl," my husband answered with the same amazed tone.

She had no name yet, but she was ours.

"So then why was I bleeding?" I asked the doctor a little while later, after the heart rate monitor hooked up to my belly continued to indicate the vitality of the child playing inside me.

"It's hard to say. That could have been caused by several factors: mental stress, physical activity, sexual intercourse … among other things. Do any of those sound like possibilities?"

"All three. But it was probably the last thing. Last night was the first time in six months I had sexual intercourse." I didn't want to explain why.

"Ah, well. That explains it." He didn't seem even vaguely interested in the reasoning for my abstinence. "During pregnancy there is increased vasculature in the cervix. The minor trauma of sexual intercourse causes the little blood vessels to break, and vaginal bleeding results."

"So, everything is okay?"

"Everything is okay. However, it's good you came in. When bleeding occurs in a second or third trimester, it's wise to rule out more ominous causes like placenta abruptio or placenta previa."

I nodded. "So, we can go now?" I asked.

"I'm going to ask you to stay for another hour or so to make sure the stress tests remain stable, but then you can go back home and resume normal activity."

"Except sex," Steve said.

"No, even that should be okay. I don't expect to see you folks back in here for about three more months. And that will be to receive your daughter."

We got home at dawn. I went straight to bed and didn't wake up until Simon climbed on me a few hours later.

I held Simon's hand as we worked our way downstairs and then picked up the phone to call Maryann.

"I hope I'm not waking you—" I started.

"What are you talking about?" Maryann interrupted. "I've been waiting by the phone. Is everything okay?"

I looked toward Simon who was crawling toward a pile of magazines. The bright morning sun beat through the windows, and I suddenly saw a glitter between the bookshelf and the wall. I ignored Maryann for a moment and went over to it.

"What is it, Heather?" she said through the receiver.

I laughed. For some reason, I wasn't surprised at what I found: Steve's wedding ring. "Yeah, everything's okay, Maryann. In a few months a beautiful baby girl will join this family."

It was three months to the day.

Steve came home from work and found me curled up on the couch. Even at nine months pregnant, I wasn't often caught snoozing.

"Uh-oh," he said with his eyes on me while welcoming the hugs of his boys. He was smiling.

"Yep," I answered without the smile. "It's starting."

"How far apart are the contractions?"

"Far. Right now I just feel lousy, not agonized. But I

think we'll be calling your parents in the morning."

"Come on, let's go run around the block so we can call them sooner," he said with a grin.

"Don't play with me, Steve. I'll kill you with this pillow if I have to. I could easily claim temporary insanity."

"Not self-defense?"

"That too." And then I groaned. "Oh, I hate this."

"Why don't we just call my folks now?" Steve asked.

"Because this might not be the real thing. I don't want to go in with false labor."

"It's the real thing."

"How do you know?"

"Because I've never seen you lounge on the couch with such a sorry expression on your face before. And because you're a day overdue. And because you were dilated to five at yesterday's doctor appointment."

"Okay, but let's still wait a bit."

"It's supposed to go quicker every time, and the other times went pretty quick."

"For you, maybe," I retorted. "I don't want to do this again, Steve."

"You've done this three times already, babe. You can do it again." He gave me a sloppy kiss on the forehead and went to the telephone, whistling. "I'll just tell them to stay near the phone." Each boy clung to one of his legs, and, to their great delight, Steve swung them along as he walked.

I liked Steve's enthusiasm, but I couldn't muster up the strength to join him in it. Instead, I closed my eyes and tried to deny the inevitable.

I made it through the night. Steve woke up every hour or so and asked me if it was time to go. I didn't use my energy to answer. I simply walked from room to room, looking in vain for comfort. At about five in the morning I finally nodded my head to Steve when he asked the question. "Yeah. You'd better call them."

"How far apart are the contractions?"

"Two or three minutes."

"Yikes. Why'd you wait so long to wake me?"

"I wanted to be sure."

Steve called his parents. I called Maryann.

"Don't go over so many bumps," I bellowed to Steve as we sped to the hospital a half hour later.

"I'm not," he said.

I groaned. "I can't even blame this on you this time, can I?"

"You can if it helps." He was grinning at me, but I knew he meant it.

"Why do you always act so happy when I'm in labor?"

"I can't help it. We're going to have a baby today." He was almost giddy.

After another labor pain passed, I looked at Steve and dared to speak my deep longing. "Do you think there is a chance this is your baby?"

"No, not physically." The sun was creeping over the horizon, and Steve's face reflected the melon-colored glow. He looked at me. "But don't even think about that, Heather. We're having a baby. That's all that matters."

"What will the hospital staff think?"

"What do you mean?"

"Here we are, a white couple, and out comes a biracial baby. You'll be all excited, anyway. Will they think you're stupid to not notice or what?"

"Who cares what they think?"

"Well, it will be kind of weird."

"Maybe Maryann will tell them."

I nodded. "Yeah. I should tell her it's okay to tell them. I don't want anyone acting weird when she's born."

"Don't worry about how they'll act. They'll act weird if they know, and they'll act weird if they don't know. Who cares? It's none of their business."

I didn't answer. I was trying to breathe—hooooo-hoo-hoo-hoo—in such a way that my body would relax and could operate at optimal performance. It didn't work. I just hurt. "Never again let me say that giving birth is an amazing experience. I would rather face all the obstacles that confronted Voltaire's Candide than to go through labor and delivery one more time."

"We're almost there," Steve said. "Keep doing that breathing thing."

He tried to drop me off at the emergency entrance we had been at three months ago. "No, I can walk," I said. I suppose the pain was stopping my mind from grasping the truth that procrastination is sometimes impossible.

"Heather, your contractions are just minutes apart. Go in."

"I know. Hurry up and park the dumb car."

Steve had learned by now never to argue with a woman in labor. He parked the car. And he didn't say "I told you so" when he had to practically carry me through the parking lot.

"She's having a baby!" Steve said frantically to the first person he saw when we walked through the doors. "Hurry! She's having a baby!"

I was on a stretcher trying to hoooo-hoo-hoo my way through the pain while the nurse who wheeled us down the hallway chatted happily. "I see that you're Christian Reformed," she said. I was hoping she was going by our paperwork and not our panicked faces. "I am, too," she told us, and then she pointed to a speaker. "Listen to the radio." She laughed softly in the momentary hush. "It was so quiet on the floor tonight, I thought I could get away with putting a Christian station on. Nobody's said a word."

"That's great," Steve said. I suppose there was nothing else to say.

I wiped away a drop of sweat before it slipped into my eye. "Is Dr. DeHaan here yet?" I asked.

"Not yet, sweetie. I'll be taking care of you until you're close to delivery. But don't worry: You'll be getting my full attention. You've pretty much got the floor to yourself."

"Okay. I need to tell you something then." I was able to talk only because I was between contractions. "We've kind of got a unique situation here."

I looked at Steve so he could take over. The nurse looked from me to him.

Steve looked uncomfortable, and I regretted putting him on the spot. My regret passed immediately because another contraction attacked me. When it passed, I continued. "Listen, I need to say this because otherwise I'll be thinking about it when the baby is born, and I don't want anything to taint that moment." I paused only briefly. I had to say it before another contraction struck. "We expect our baby to be biracial. I was raped by a black guy."

"Oh, honey," she started to ooze.

"No," I said quickly. "It's okay. We're excited about

having this baby. Just please make sure no one makes a big deal of the baby's race."

She looked like she wanted to stroke me. "I promise you that will be taken care of." We had slowed down and were starting to turn into a room. She stopped and returned me to the hallway with sudden confidence. "No, I'm not putting you in here. You get the VIP room. No one deserves it more than you."

I never thought about the concerns of the staff again.

"You're dilated to 9.5, Heather," Maryann told me moments later. She hadn't waited for the call from the hospital. "What were you trying to do, have the baby in the car?" There was no hint of humor in her voice.

I wanted to cry. "I can't do this again, Maryann."

"Yes, you can," she answered simply as she went about her business calmly. "You're going to do just fine."

Steve laid a blanket over my shivering body. I whipped it off a moment later and moaned. The despair in my voice might have convinced even a bitter enemy to pity me.

"Do you want drugs this time?" Steve asked.

"No. It's almost over anyway, isn't it?" I looked at Maryann imploringly.

Maryann nodded slightly. "I don't think you need an epidural, but I'm definitely going to give you some Demerol. You're shaking uncontrollably." She put a hand on my forehead and smiled softly at me. "Relax, Heather.... Breathe.... You're going to do just fine.... You're strong.... You're going to do just fine."

I hardly noticed the IV the nurse gave me, but my body soon stopped shaking.

Steve held my hand, and I nearly maimed his fingers in

response. "I'm cold," I said. But I furiously threw off the blanket he once again gave me. "Maryann," I shouted, "I need to push!"

And then Maryann said what every obstetrician must fear saying to a woman whose labor pains have ripped from her every inhibition, from manners to modesty. A woman gentle in her usual state might turn violent in this one. Maryann said, "Wait."

"Aaahhh!" I wailed. "I need to push!"

Moments—or perhaps years—later I heard my doctor say to her staff, "Alright. I think she's ready. Heather, you may push."

Steve put his mouth to my ear. "Heather, I want you to watch." He pointed to the mirror that the nurse had set up for just that purpose. I hadn't watched any of my other babies being born. "I want you to see this." His words were so soft that I might have ignored them in the midst of my pain, but his uncharacteristic passion caught me. I looked at his face close to mine and saw his moist eyes. "Please."

I pushed, and I saw the crown of my daughter's head. A rush of passion charged through my body. "There she is," I whispered. The next fifteen minutes of my life were filled with laughter and tears as my husband and I watched the miracle playing out before our eyes: a head, eyes, a mouth, shoulders, and the rest of the tiny perfect, wriggling body.

"She's here," Maryann announced, smiling crazily as she held my baby out to me.

"A girl!" Steve said through tears. "She really is a girl. Heather, we have a baby girl!"

"Rachael Maria Gemmen," I crooned to the child in my arms, exhaustion forgotten. "I'm glad to finally meet you."

A
LITTLE
DUTCH
GIRL

*If the first Sunday
back in church after the rape was
emotionally brutal for me,
this first Sunday
back after the birth of our child was
dazzling.*

My fantasies about you bounced between watching your face on the stand as the judge sentenced you to the chair and watching your face through a heavy glass as you absorbed the truth of God's infinite grace. One way or the other, I wanted your life to be changed radically.

What if he comes back and kidnaps her?" I asked Steve in our living room the next week. As I stared down into the face of the little person in my arms, I did not doubt that a biological parent of Rachael would want her desperately.

"He won't. He's long gone."

Rachael yawned and I smiled. "She's got my sister's nose, don't you think?" I said.

"I think she looks like you."

"You do?" I was delighted. I searched my daughter's face, looking for parentage. I saw only beauty in her soft, brown skin and deep, dark eyes. "I'm glad I didn't see his face. I don't know if she looks like him or not. I don't want to know."

"Quit talking about him, okay? He's not part of this."

I heard the *vroom-vroom* noises of the boys from the playroom and the cooing of the little girl in my arms. Noises of abundance. I shrugged my shoulders. I didn't mind talking or not talking about the man who had become, in my mind, merely a sperm provider for the most beautiful baby on earth.

"Hand me that blanket, would you?" I said to my husband.

"Are you going to be feeling well enough to go to church tomorrow?" he asked as he tucked the softness around Rachael's little body.

"Are you kidding? I can't wait to show her off. I don't care if I'm half dead."

We were back at Sherman Street. The person who had most influenced Steve and me to return after our two-month sabbatical was a sixty-five-year-old Jamaican man. Financial stress had forced him to leave home more than a decade ago; he missed his family intensely. Every Sunday for several years this grandfather had greeted us with a kiss, pushed candy into the hands of our kids, and reminded us of some good reason to praise God. He had often joined us at our home for a meal after church, bringing with him apples or cider from the farm where he worked. Every Sunday we were gone, he called us at home and told us how tremendous the sermon had been and how much he had missed our presence there. One day he said, in broken English, "Have you call Jon and Barb yet? God not wanting to see the body broken. Yous need to figure things out and then come worship the Lord together."

We wrote a letter to Jon and Barb, apologizing for hurting them and asking them to please forgive us. We didn't get a response, but we went back to our church family.

If the first Sunday back in church after the rape was emotionally brutal for me, this first Sunday back after the birth of our child was dazzling. We showed up early because I had anticipated some enthusiasm over our newborn, but there was no way I could have prepared myself for the passionate expressions of welcome that bombarded this youngest and most famous member of the congregation.

"My granddaughter," said our Jamaican friend with tears in his eyes. He has called her by no other name since.

"A little Heather," said another friend, one who had often enjoyed late-night conversations at our house and so knew what he was talking about. "Look out, world!"

"She is a miracle," said an older, Dutch gentleman whose frequent words of encouragement had often nurtured my soul. He took Rachael from my arms and paraded her through the church, beaming as joyously as would a young boy with a remote-controlled airplane.

Amidst all the gushing over my baby's soft curls and tiny newness, I heard a word of hope: "Heather," said a middle-aged woman whose husband a few years previously had fallen from a ladder to his death. Her compassion for others had not been diminished by her loss. "I know of some kids who need a home. Do you think the Adamses would be interested in adopting a sibling group?" Two girls and a boy, ages one, two, and three. Available immediately.

"It's sure worth asking them," I said with enthusiasm.

"I didn't even know they were looking to adopt," she said. "Gosh, there are so many kids needing a home, I'm sure something will work out for them."

"I hope so. Please do call them. I know it would mean a lot to them."

The music in the sanctuary increased in volume, and the stragglers sneaked in. I stayed in the quiet foyer to nurse Rachael and then joined Steve and the boys.

My Dutch friend preached that Sunday with an accent that made me nostalgic for home. He read the story about Jacob wrestling with an angel. "Don't go unless you bless me," Jacob had said to the angel after an all-night struggle. "Don't let your pain be for nothing," my friend interpreted. "Ask God to bless you in your struggles, to let you grow from them." I felt conspicuous, like this sermon was preached specifically to me—until I looked around and saw the people who surrounded me: men and women strong by the grace of God through their trials.

How are you feeling, Heather?" asked one of my girl-friends after church. "Are you still up for dinner at my in-laws'?"

Steve had thought the invitation odd at first. "Why would we want to hang out at their parents' house? We don't even know them."

But I loved the idea of getting to know our friends on another level. We would get to see the house our friend grew up in and meet the people who raised him. "Besides," I said, "I hear that Mrs. Vaandering cooks a mean dinner. I bet it'll be as good as my oma's Christmas dinner."

It was. We crowded around a cozy dining room table with placemats and cloth napkins and lovely china, eating mashed potatoes with thick brown gravy, buttery green beans, and tender roast beef cooked to perfection.

"A preacher with a Dutch accent and then a meal like only the Dutch can make," I said appreciatively.

"Ah, *schatje*," Mrs. Vaandering said, "you are Dutch, then, too?"

"My parents are both immigrants." I knew it would impress them. I intended to inspire them with my knowledge of all things Dutch, but Rachael woke up and demanded to be fed. I retired into the living room where the couch and straight-backed chairs had doilies over the armrests. I looked around at the family pictures hanging on the walls and at the knickknacks on the dusted piano as I listened to the humorous stories Mr. Vaandering told about his son. I made it back to the table just as dessert was being passed around.

"Let me burp her while you enjoy a little something, eh?" Mrs. Vaandering said, taking Rachael from my arms. I happily complied and dove into my warm apple crisp topped with a generous amount of ice cream. "Less than a week old, eh?" she said, crooning at our baby. "Beautiful. But I see she has some jaundice."

Rachael had no jaundice. I didn't say anything.

"Yes, you'll want to keep an eye on that. Her skin is so dark," Mrs. Vaandering said, gently touching Rachael's perfect cheek.

"Mmm-hmmm," I murmured. I glanced at our friend. He cringed. I could see he hadn't told her.

"I mean, she just doesn't look like a little Dutch girl, does she?" Mrs. Vaandering looked up at me. I saw her eyes move over to Steve and then fall back on the face of the baby she held. "No, not a little Dutch girl at all." She looked up at the boys who had devoured their food, and I saw her watching their faces as she offered the backyard to them. They ran out happily.

I wondered for a moment if I should tell her why the daughter of my womb didn't look the same as her brothers. But I quickly dismissed the idea. It wasn't exactly dinner-table talk, and I hated the idea of her thinking of me always as "that girl who was raped." Secretly, I was pleased my friends hadn't considered the point worth telling their parents. I was simply their friend, not "that girl."

I got a phone call from Mrs. Vaandering that evening. "Oh, my dear," she said, "I am mortified over my blunder of this afternoon. Please, please forgive me if I embarrassed you."

I laughed, genuinely humored by the memory of the confusion. "I was embarrassed, but you don't need to apologize. You had no idea. I guess I'm going to have to prepare myself for those kinds of situations. No one is going to walk around in front of me all my life, cueing people in to what they should say to me."

I didn't know how true my words were.

In the diaper section of the grocery store a woman gushed over Rachael and asked me which country she was from. "From here," I answered stupidly.

"Wow. Good for you. We had to go with foreign adoption because we were tired of waiting so long. What agency did you use?"

I wanted to turn around and walk away. What could I say? Should I say she's not adopted and open myself up for further questions … or silent suspicions? Should I let this stranger continue to believe my baby was adopted and so lie in front of my kids … and rob myself of hard-earned motherhood?

"Listen," I said, "I'd love to talk, but I'm kind of in a rush."

Our family was eating pizza at a restaurant near our home when Rachael was just a month old. Deshawn was with us. "Wow!" said the waitress. "Are these all your kids?" I didn't blame her for asking: We were an eclectic group. But I still cringed.

"It's a long story," I told her and then ordered our meal.

I nursed Rachael in the club nursery before taking off for a game of racquetball with Steve. "Don't ask!" my aura screamed, in vain, to the older woman who hovered in to ask, in a hushed voice, if my *husband* would be picking her up or not. "He is your husband, isn't he?" she whispered conspiratorially.

Rachael was sleeping in the stroller by the time I reached the playground with the boys, and her sweet face attracted the attention of some of the moms who were there. "What a doll," a thirty-something black woman said to me. "Are you watching her for someone?"

"No," I said, reaching down to adjust the visor over my daughter. "She's mine." Inwardly, I wondered why I had to answer all these questions to every stranger I met. Outwardly, I smiled graciously.

"Sister," the woman answered, "what you got one of our babies for?" She laughed and touched my arm kindly. I laughed, too. I didn't know what else to do.

"That's obvious, ain't it?" another mom answered. "She got one of our men." Before I could respond—more accurately, before I could think of a response—she said, "And them boys are yours, too?"

231

"Not the oldest," I said in reference to Deshawn. "He's our neighbor."

"Mmmm-hmmm," the second woman said, laughing, she thought, knowingly.

I wanted Tasha around to protect me.

"That's alright, sister," the first woman said to me. "I don't blame you for wanting some black magic."

I suppose I should have just told some of these people the truth. Maybe "I was raped" would have given them reason to pause in the future before they blurted out their thoughts and questions. But so many people knew already. Having every acquaintance know my most personal story was hard enough; telling every stranger I met was beyond my strength.

The one person who had the right to question Rachael's presence, didn't. "Let me take her," Steve said one night after I had finished a midnight feeding. "You need some sleep."

I woke up a few hours later to find Steve making baby faces to the little girl who wouldn't sleep. I nearly wept at the sight of their bonding. "Steve, thank you so much for being such a good dad to her," I said with conviction.

Steve waved away my praise. "She's my girl. What else would I do? Now get out of here before she starts crying for you."

I went back to sleep and didn't wake up until I heard the doorbell ring. It woke the boys, too. Chad, Simon, and I went downstairs to find Deshawn's nose pressed against the glass and Rachael's nose deep in Steve's neck. She, like her dad, was sound asleep.

"Come on in," I whispered to Deshawn. "But we all have

to be really quiet." I pointed to the sleeping couple on the couch. Deshawn giggled.

Dolores stopped by later that day. "The damn landlord just kicked me out," she told me by the door. "Can Deshawn spend the night with you?"

"Of course he can," I answered promptly. "How about you? We've got plenty of room."

"Nah. I'll be alright."

Dolores came by the next day. "I ain't got a place, yet. Can he stay with you awhile longer?"

I told her it was okay, so she walked to the street and reached into the trunk of her friend's Monte Carlo and pulled out a garbage bag.

"Here's his stuff," she said, dropping it heavily on my front step. Her friend honked the horn from behind tinted windows, and Dolores left without talking to her son. I waved good-bye and then approached the bag warily. It smelled like something I took home from a weeklong camping trip.

A few days passed, and no one talked about how long Deshawn would be staying. On the fourth day, while I was transplanting Snow-on-the-Mountain from beside my garage to the front yard under a maple tree, I saw Dolores walking toward the house on the other side of the street. She drew closer but didn't cross over. I stopped what I was doing to greet her, but she only waved and walked on.

Deshawn didn't seem to wonder about his future. He was having a blast with us—going swimming at the Y, visiting the zoo, hanging out at the beach. He slept soundly at night and never asked about his mom, so I didn't worry about him.

A week later, Dolores showed up at our door. "I still don't

have a place, but I'm going to buy him something. Where is he?"

"He's in the backyard. I'll show you."

Dolores and Deshawn walked to a convenience store around the corner. Deshawn came home with a huge smile and a bag of beef jerky. Dolores was gone before I could see her again.

"She makes me so mad," I told Steve after dinner while the kids were out playing. "I don't mind that Deshawn is here, but she should give us an idea of how long he's staying. And she should come visit him more often."

"I have a feeling he'll be staying a long time."

"Yeah, it may take her awhile to find a place. What if she never does?"

"Like I said, he'll be staying here a long time."

I looked at my husband and smiled. I leaned over to kiss him. "You're amazing," I said.

"What?"

"I always complain that you never show your love, but really, you love deeper than most people do. It seems like everyone else's love is based on feelings; yours is based on action."

"Whatever you say," Steve said. A few minutes later he went out to the garage to work on the bookshelf he was building me.

"I was tucking the kids in bed that night when Deshawn dropped the bomb. "I'm going to live in Guatemala."

"Guatemala? Why?"

"My mom has some friends there who will take care of me."

"Well, why go all the way to Guatemala to find someone

234

who will take care of you? You can stay with us."

I saw Deshawn's eyes move slowly up to look into mine. He seemed to be holding his breath. "Forever?" he said quietly.

Only two other promises in my life met the depth of the words I spoke to that young boy: One promise was to God, the other to my husband.

"Deshawn," I said, pulling him close, "if it's what you and your mom want, you may stay with us forever."

Deshawn remained silent for a long moment, his head down. Finally he looked up at me again. "Why can't my mom take care of me?"

I knew so little of Dolores's life. I had no idea how deep her pain was. But at that moment I didn't care. I wanted to shake her. I wanted to scream, "Quit being so selfish! Give up your crack and your boyfriends so that you can be a mother to your child! We all have lousy stuff in our lives. But we deal with it! You don't have the luxury of living in despair, okay? You have a son who needs you!"

But Dolores wasn't around to hear my admonition. She had chosen a different path.

"Listen, babe," I said softly. "Your mom loves you a lot. But she needs to take care of herself before she can take care of you. I promise you that I will pray for her, and I know that God cares deeply about her. As soon as she discovers God's love for her, she will be able to take care of you again, okay?"

"Okay," he said. "I'll pray, too."

A few weeks later, Dolores came to our doorstep again. "I can't come in," she said. "I'm in a rush. I just want to make sure my boy is okay."

"He's doing very well," I told her. "But he misses you."

"I know. But I don't have a place yet."

"He can stay here as long as you like, Dolores. We love having him. But if you think it's going to be much longer, we should probably make this legal. I've been signing his school papers and stuff."

"What do you mean, legal?" she asked defensively.

"I think it would be good if Steve and I could be Deshawn's guardians. As soon as you get settled, guardianship will go back to you. I'm just afraid we're going to get into trouble if I keep signing his stuff."

"Will it cost anything?"

"No," I lied. I knew we would be covering the costs. "All you have to do is sign some papers. I've got them already. Do you have a few minutes to look them over?"

Dolores didn't read the papers, but she signed them.

"Do you have a number I can reach you at so I can tell you the court date?" I asked.

"Court? I ain't going to no court."

"You don't have to if you don't want to. No show means you agree with the proceedings."

Dolores's eyes narrowed. "You better not be screwing me," she said, wagging a finger in my face.

My manners stepped aside so I could lean toward her. "I'm taking care of your son, Dolores," I said softly, threateningly. "If you don't trust me, you shouldn't be leaving him here."

Dolores backed away. "Nah," she said. "I trust you."

I stepped toward her. "What I want more than anything is to see you settled down so that Deshawn can have his mother back."

"I will, I will." She turned to leave. "I'm working on

236

something right now." From the sidewalk she called out a thank-you and then disappeared down the street.

I looked at Deshawn carefully that day when he came home from school. He was energetically telling me about the back flip he did off the teeter-totter and how all the kids wanted him to do it again and how his teacher said he should take gymnastics and not do things like that at school. As I stared into the face of the little person before me, I wondered how his biological parent could not want him desperately.

And I knew Rachael was safe.

MOUNTAIN MOVEMENT

I had been beyond hope before, and that had never stopped God.

*Did you grow up on these streets? Is the steady beat
of rap music your chant of meditation? Are the street
corners your sanctuary? Or is this a place that taught
you despair, a place from which you long to escape?
For me the city was neither home nor prison: It was
a path.*

Would you ever move to Colorado, Steve?" I asked
doubtfully after the dinner dishes had been
cleared away. It was a humid August afternoon,
and the sidewalks seemed to steam under the men and
women who were taking lazy walks, waving to each other
and smelling the food grilling in backyards. We didn't have
air conditioning, so our windows were wide open. I could
hear Rachael's four-year-old laughter drifting over the voices
of her three big brothers as they ran through the sprinkler
in the yard.

"I'd move tomorrow," Steve answered promptly.

"Yeah, right."

"I would," he insisted, glancing up from his book.

"You'd better think carefully about what you're saying. I got a job offer today."

I was working at a large Christian publishing house as an editor of children's books. A former colleague had called me up that day to say that she needed to hire an editor, and she needed to know right away if I would come.

"Are you serious?" Steve asked. "Move to Colorado?"

"Yeah. Colorado Springs. We'd have to go next month."

"Let's get packing."

"Be serious."

"I am. Are you?"

"Well, the job sounds ideal, but it's pretty far away."

"Wow." He got up to get a map. He spread it out on the dining room table. "Colorado Springs! We could take daytrips into the mountains to go skiing. We could go hiking on a mountain trail on a Sunday afternoon. Colorado is gorgeous."

"As long as there would be no humidity." A fan was blowing on us, but my hot skin still felt sticky.

"No humidity. No mosquitoes."

"And no family," I said. "No friends." I dropped into a chair.

"The kids are getting big now," he said. "It's not like they wouldn't know our families. And we'd come back to visit."

"Remember when we were first married how mad I would get when your mom brought us groceries every time she came over? Now I don't know what we'd do without your family."

"She hardly ever does that anymore. We'd be fine without them."

"I'm not talking about the food. I'm talking about them.

242

And we'd be moving farther away from my family, too. What if we got lonely?"

"We'll make friends. You'll probably be having people over every night of the week before we've been there even a month."

"I don't know. I can't imagine finding friends like we have now. Think of them: Maryann and Byron. Tasha. Jon and Barb. Everyone at church. We've been through a lot together. I don't think we'll ever find friendships like that again."

"It doesn't seem likely. But remember when it didn't seem likely we would ever be friends with Jon and Barb again? Or with Tasha? And that all worked out."

I am still in wonder that it all worked out. Our friendship with the Adamses was restored when the four of us were able to see past our own despair enough to care for each other's wounds. For Jon and Barb, this happened when they adopted the sibling group a woman at our church had introduced them to. Jon and Barb found their hearts' desire fulfilled with not just one but with three children they called their own.

My relationship with Tasha didn't heal so quickly. At church we avoided each other—me, because I was afraid of saying anything inappropriate; her, because I already had. When she moved to another city, we lost touch altogether. A few years later, I heard her voice on the other end of the telephone line asking if we could please renew our relationship, and I felt like she had handed me a glass slipper: I was startled and delighted by the gift that fit me so naturally.

"Yes, it all worked out," I answered Steve, "but only

because God orchestrated it—"

"So you don't think God can orchestrate things again?"

"Well …" I didn't have an answer to that.

"Besides, we would still be friends with them."

"Okay. But what about living in the city? Are we supposed to give that up?"

Steve was silent for a moment before he answered. I didn't interrupt his thoughts. "I think it's alright if we leave," he said. "We've fulfilled our purpose here."

I nodded my head. Steve's wisdom had grown over the years so that I now looked to him for spiritual direction. "Okay, maybe God is calling us to something else," I agreed. "But I like it here. Why did he want us here when we didn't like it, and now that we do, we're not called to it anymore?"

"I don't know. I don't think we'll ever really get the method behind God's madness. I just know that we've got a chance to move to the Rockies." He pointed to Colorado Springs on the map and then looked sideways at me. "Pike's Peak is right here, Heather. And the Garden of the Gods. Instead of gushing over fall colors for a few weeks of the year, you'll be looking at a snow-peaked mountain every day."

It did sound like a dream come true. And the job seemed perfectly designed for me. I let go of my fear and jumped wholeheartedly into the adventure.

"Okay," I said, standing up. "Let's do it."

"Seriously?"

"Yes. I'm going to go call right now." I was halfway to the phone.

"Wait. We should think about it some more. What about work for me? I'll have to look for a job," he said.

"You'll find something. Construction is booming there.

244

Or maybe I'll make enough money so you can stay home with the kids."

"That sounds good," he said longingly. "But—"

"Come on, Steve. Let's go for it. Let's step out of all that's familiar to us and see what happens. It'll be fun. It'll be good for us."

"But next month already?" Steve asked apprehensively.

Rachael ran into the house at that moment, dripping water behind her. Her laughter revealed delighted fear; Simon was chasing her with a water gun. She stopped long enough to kiss me and hug Steve, and then she tore out of the house again with Simon right behind her.

"Why wait?" I asked my husband. "Don't you want to see what's going to happen next?"

What happened next was a blur of action. We quit our jobs and started packing. We visited friends and family, crying our good-byes. We sold our house and secured new housing. And then we drove across the country to our new home.

Deshawn came with us. I had contacted his mom to let her know we were moving. "You know I want him back," Dolores told me. "As soon as I get me a place, he's coming back to live with me."

"Okay," I said. I didn't remind her that she had been saying that for three years. "But you're okay with our taking him to Colorado with us?"

"I guess so," she responded.

It wasn't so easy for Deshawn. A darkness of heart seeped into this young child whose outlook on life, as long as I had known him, had been joyful and compassionate. Now, he lashed out in anger at everyone. "I want to go back to Michigan," he spat. "I want to go back to my real mom."

"I think you should tell her that," I told him. I was beyond hoping for reconciliation for them—in the last three years she had rejected him more times than I, let alone he, could bear. But I had been beyond hope before, and that had never stopped God. "Maybe if she knows how much you want her, she'll be motivated to find a place," I offered.

I loved Deshawn as deeply as I loved each of the other kids God had picked out for me—and I didn't want to see him go; but I knew Dolores, even with all her faults, was the one Deshawn was looking to for acceptance.

"She *will* take me back!" Deshawn shouted with accusation in his voice. "You don't think she will, but she will!"

I nodded. "It's important that you try to reunite with your mother. And as much as it hurts me to see you go, I will do what I can to help you." His customary embraces were noticeably absent. "But, Deshawn—" I began. I didn't finish the sentence until he finally looked begrudgingly up at me. "If your mom is not able to take you back, could we please adopt you?"

He walked to the phone without looking at me.

To my surprise, Dolores promised her son the world. "Yes, baby," she gushed. "I've got everything worked out. In two months, at the most, I'll have a place for us. I've already talked to the landlord. And I just started a real good job yesterday. Oh, baby! I can't wait for us to be together again."

We both believed her—he with great joy; I with gladness, fear, and sorrow.

At his request, we returned Deshawn to Michigan right

away so he could get back into the Christian school he had been attending. He stayed with a family from Sherman Street. "Just for a few months," we told them. "He's going back to his mom."

But two months turned to four. Four turned to six. I talked to Dolores more during those months than I had all the years we were neighbors. Coaching her. Cajoling her. Begging her. I wanted Deshawn back with us, but I couldn't bear to see him rejected by his mom again.

I suppose I shouldn't have believed her promises, but I couldn't help it that she failed again.

The school year ended, and Deshawn came home to us. The first thing he said after he welcomed my hug was, "Mom, will you and Dad adopt me now?"

We did, and at that moment, my heart could not contain any more joy.

Every time I look at the mountains, it is a new experience. Whether Pike's Peak is mirroring the sunrise so the entire horizon, east and west, is lit with a multi-colored glow; whether its silhouette is etched for miles onto a darkening sky; whether black thunderclouds are hurling rain onto the Front Range, emphasizing its unchanging strength; whether the brilliant snow is harshly reflecting a late-afternoon winter sun; whether the hills look green and hazy and deceptively gentle—the experience is good.

Mountains reveal vastness, drawing from me an awareness, not of insignificance, but still of smallness. It is the *moods* of the mountains, however, that propel me into reflection— variance displayed on the unmoving; fleetingness passing over the ageless—and I dare to walk forward on unknown

STARTLING BEAUTY

Rape takes too much.

But I, for one,

have gained more than

I have lost.

Rape is ugliness at its basest form. Rape destroys innocence and cultivates bitterness. It steals security and extends fear. It kills hope and fosters shame. Rape leaves no room for beauty.

"My father raped me when I was eighteen," a woman told me in the privacy of her living room. She was the mother of two young children, the wife of a godly man. "I hadn't seen him in ten years, but he came here yesterday and tried to rape me again." Her voice wobbled as she tried to say words that resisted articulation.

My face grew wet as I sat with her in the silence.
"I hate him, Heather," she whispered. "I'll always hate him."
I don't know why I believed him," a twenty-year-old sobbed.
"He broke into my apartment, and I still trusted him."

"What happened?"

"I pushed the dresser up against my bedroom door so he couldn't get in. He stood outside the door for an hour, trying to convince me that he would protect me if I would only open the door. I finally did, and then he raped me."

She curled up on the couch, clutching her knees to her chest.

I put a blanket over her. "He caused your terror and then used it for his advantage," I told her. "It wasn't your fault."

"I'm so scared," she whispered into the air. "If I'm that easy to trick, how can I face life again?"

Who needs men?" quipped a middle-aged woman who had been raped on the first date she attempted after her divorce.

She dropped out of counseling and took up drinking. She left the church and joined a feminist group.

"Not all men are bad," I ventured.

"Ha! You should know better than that!"

"I do know. I know many men who are not like the men who raped us."

"Oh, Heather, don't be so naïve. If they smile now, they'll bite you later."

Rape takes too much.

But I, for one, have gained more than I have lost.

I have been startled by beauty in places it doesn't belong. I see it on a bloodied cross, and bitterness loses its power. I see it on the face of the man who keeps his vows to me, and fear releases its grip. I see it in the graceful dance of a child who was so unwanted, and hope revives its song.

I consider that our present sufferings are not worth comparing with the glory that will be revealed.... I am convinced that neither death nor life, neither angels nor demons, neither the present nor the future, nor any powers, neither height nor depth, nor anything else in all creation, will be able to separate us from the love of God that is in Christ Jesus our Lord.

from Romans 8

YOUR LIFE JOURNEY

STARTLING
BEAUTY

Study Guide
for Personal Reflection
and Group Discussion

Beauty is startling when it appears in the face of stark ugliness. The tiny fingers of a stillborn baby. Trusting relationships in a dangerous neighborhood. A cherished child conceived through rape.

Startling Beauty narrates Heather's journey between despair and hope as she faces pain no one should experience. Relationships are strained and mended; decisions are forced and welcomed; fears are created and calmed; faith is threatened and increased. Heather and her husband, Steve, fall into grace, exchanging their emptiness for God's fullness.

We can't help but marvel at the beauty of this exchange, just as we would ooh and ahh over a beautiful display of fireworks. But the individual bursts of glory don't compare to the beauty of the grand finale, when we see this exchange happening in the lives of God's children.

And God is just waiting to lavish his startling grace on you.

After reading Heather's story and vicariously experiencing the depth of her despair, you may find yourself face to face with your own. Old wounds may be opened, and you don't know where turn. God created a longing within you to step into the restoration he offers through Jesus Christ, but you may not know exactly how to take this step.

Answering the questions provided, privately or with a group, will strengthen you for the journey into restoration. Ask the Holy Spirit to direct you, refer to the Bible passages recommended at the end of the guide, and spend plenty of time in prayer.

It takes incredible courage to pursue healing, but God will not leave you to face this task alone. Romans 5:17 says that "God's abundant provision of grace" restores us. Abundant.

The extent of God's fullness from which he provides for us is limitless.

"And my God will meet all your needs according to his glorious riches in Christ Jesus."
–Philippians 4:19

Chapter One
STATIC IN THE STORM

1. "I've always believed that we each choose our own path, but ... I ... realized for the first time that we don't get to choose the obstacles we face on the journey." Lying on the obstetrician's table, wondering if her baby is still alive, Heather prays, "Oh, God, don't let this be my obstacle. Let me learn about life another way." Do you ever wish you could "trade in" your circumstances? Give an example of how you or someone you know has changed for the better because of a painful life experience.

2. An age-old question that nearly every person confronts in life is this: Why do bad things happen to good people? What experience has forced you to wrestle with this question? How have you resolved it?

3. In this chapter, Heather admits that she often used humor as a "shield," hoping that laughter might keep away the sorrow. What are some other ways people try to protect themselves from the pain of difficult circumstances? Winston Churchill once said, "When you're going through hell, keep

going." When is it beneficial to retreat from pain and when is it beneficial to work through it?

Chapter Two
HEAVY EMPTINESS

1. "Self-pity smothered the joy I longed to have." What motivated Heather to let go of her self-pity? When you indulge in self-pity, what does it take to free you from it?
2. Racism is another issue addressed in this book. For a little while, Heather viewed her inner-city neighborhood romantically, but not for long. She says, "I'm not sure when my attitude changed … maybe I was watching the world instead of heaven." Have you ever known that you were departing from the will of God and suffered the consequences for it? What brought you back?

3. "I didn't enjoy my resentment—I hated it—but I didn't know how to change my heart." If we are unable to change ourselves, how will change occur? What are the advantages and disadvantages of allowing God to change your heart?

Chapter Three
PAINFUL HEALING

1. "Strange. Why have I always thought reconciliation was something sweet and gentle?" What is your definition of reconciliation? Racial issues are not the only arena where

reconciliation needs to take place. Are there relationships in your family or community that need to be restored? How can you move toward reconciliation?

2. As Heather delves deeper into her racist views, she realizes her own part in the problem. She prays, "Something needs to change, God. Is it me? Again?" Sometimes it's hard to admit that we could be a big part of our own problems. What role have you played in your own difficult circumstances?

3. Heather's circumstances did not change, but her attitude did. How did Heather's change of heart affect her and those around her? Why do we hang on to beliefs and behaviors that hurt us, when we know letting go will improve our lives?

Chapter Four
THE PAINTING

1. As Heather describes the terrifying details of the rape, she speaks directly to the man who raped her. Why do you think Heather chose this method of relating her story? What would you like to say to the person who most hurt you?

2. "Perhaps the agony [of the rape] would have been too much for me if I hadn't discovered a Place in myself where the Comforter dwelt.... I entered the Place ... and leaned into Holy arms." What do you think Heather meant by a "Place where the Comforter dwelt"? Have you found that place in your own heart where the Comforter dwells?

3. "'Forgive him, Lord.' The words were not even my own." What was your reaction when you read these words?

4. The title of this chapter is "The Painting." Heather speaks of God's brushstrokes upon the canvas of life. What is taking shape on the canvas of your life?

Chapter Five
VIOLATED AGAIN

1. In the aftermath of the rape, Heather finds herself gripped by fear. Fear is a powerful tormentor. What fears have you overcome, and how?

2. "It was my fault." Even in the midst of her trauma, Heather accused herself of negligence. What did you think when you found out she hadn't locked the door?

3. "What are you folks doing in this neighborhood, anyway?" Do you think Heather and Steve chose poorly by staying in the city? Why or why not?

Chapter Six
ILLUSIONS LOST

1. Heather's strengths, as she lists them, include independence, tenacity, and trust. Was she compromising these strengths by leaning on her husband during this stressful

time? Why is it sometimes hard to accept comfort and strength from others?

2. One of Heather's core beliefs is the sanctity of life. Name some of your core beliefs and explain why they are important to you. Have you ever had a core belief challenged? If so, how did you respond?

3. "Integrity is so much more than claiming noble ethics…. Integrity is living out expressed beliefs. It is making choices that accurately reflect core values." Do you agree with Heather's assessment of integrity? Why or why not?

4. "Etiquette placed me on the bull's-eye of Fear's assault." Why do we allow manners to have so much power over us? How do we balance caring for others with caring for self?

Chapter Seven
KNOWING BETTER

1. "Mark and Lori's love knocked me into grace. I would have fallen sooner had I known how soft the landing would be." Has anyone ever given you the gift of true compassion? How is human compassion a picture of God's grace?

2. As Heather's friends rally around her, she takes comfort in their concern. She gains strength from their prayers. Do you think our prayers for each other really make a difference? Why or why not?

3. The three most influential people in Heather's life all counseled her to take the pill. She did, despite inner misgivings. When making a decision, how much weight do you give to the advice of others?

Chapter Eight
WALKING ON WATER

1. "You just looking for an easy way out of forgiving him," Tasha told Heather. "If it weren't so bad, then you don't need to forgive much. He done you wrong, sister. And you need to forgive the whole awful thing." What are some barriers to forgiveness? Tell about a time in your life when you chose to forgive.

2. "The idea of healing more quickly [by talking about the rape] seemed remote, or perhaps unrealistic." Why do we sometimes resist talking things out when we know we can't heal on our own? On the other hand, sometimes we wallow in our pain, talking rather than actively pursuing healing. How would you advise a hurting person who seems stuck?

3. Heather describes the tangible outpouring of love she received—meals, money, babysitting. How do you help someone when the situation she is facing makes you uncomfortable?

Chapter Nine
DOOR NUMBER FOUR

1. After the rape, Heather realizes that she has lost her "innocent faith"—faith that God would use her to bring healing to the inner city. "It didn't seem so easy anymore," she says. How have you dealt with disillusionment or loss of faith in your own life?

2. Steve suggests that Heather get an abortion, and, in her desperation, she consents to the idea. If she had gone through with it, what problems would have been solved? What problems would have been created?

3. How did God intervene in Heather's life? How has he intervened in yours?

Chapter Ten
COMPROMISE

1. Heather and Steve's pastor, Mark, plays a key role in helping them through the healing process. What qualities in Mark made his counsel trustworthy? How can we cultivate these qualities in ourselves?

2. *Startling Beauty* gives numerous examples of people who have suffered. Describe different responses to pain—whether in this book or in your own experience—and discuss which responses bring the most satisfaction, for the short-term and the long-term.

3. As Heather and Steve work through this situation, they discuss the possibility of adoption. If they had gone through with it, what problems would have been solved? What problems would have been created?

Chapter Eleven
CONNECTION

1. "I ... discovered ... how deep love goes when tragedy binds you together," Heather says. In what way has tragedy connected you to another person, and in what way has it separated you from another person? How has tragedy connected or separated you from God?

2. Heather's two best friends did not always tell her what she wanted to hear, but they usually told her what she needed to hear. When is it worth the risk of alienating others by speaking the truth? How do we earn the right to confront?

3. Heather compares a healthy church to a small town: "There are no secrets." Did you consider Heather's closeness to the Sherman Street community to be an advantage or a disadvantage to her? Would you want to be part of such a community? Why or why not?

Chapter Twelve
DESTINY

1. "God, I'm off death row, but I'm not yet free. Please, please make me better." In the past year, how have you grown spiritually, emotionally, relationally, and intellectually? What things do you still need to change in your life?

2. Steve expresses some honest doubts about God. He says, "It's a joke when people pray for God to intervene.... He just doesn't bother himself with that stuff. God made the world self-sufficient, and then he sat back and let us take care of ourselves." Do you agree with this view? Why or why not?

3. Heather is saddened when Tasha ends their friendship, and she realizes that perhaps she has taken Tasha for granted. What do you think Heather's next step should be? What happens when two people are reunited without experiencing reconciliation?

Chapter Thirteen
BABY

1. "Faith is a journey, but there are definite moments along the way when truth propels a person from one state of being to another. I can name several defining moments in my life." For Heather, one of those moments was when her daughter was born. Can you point to a specific moment when your life was changed by truth?

2. "For some reason, I wasn't surprised at what I found: Steve's wedding ring." Do you think Heather and Steve's marriage improved? If so, how? Have you found that relationships are worth working for?

3. "The next fifteen minutes of my life were filled with laughter and tears as my husband and I watched the miracle playing out before our eyes…. 'A girl!' Steve said through tears." What was the miracle?

Chapter Fourteen
A LITTLE DUTCH GIRL

1. "Don't let your pain be for nothing…. Ask God to bless you in your struggles, to let you grow from them." Can you see that your spiritual or personal growth was affected differently depending on how you responded to painful experiences? Please explain.

2. "Steve, thank you so much for being such a good dad to her," Heather tells her husband. Steve's answer reveals his changed heart: "She's my girl. What else would I do?" Steve moved from wanting to abort the child to embracing her as his own. Have you ever had a radical change of heart despite unchanging circumstances? Talk about it.

3. Heather didn't want everyone to think of her as "that girl who was raped." How can we support others without undermining their dignity?

4. Steve and Heather put their love into action by taking their neighbor boy, Deshawn, into their home. Sometimes God calls us to love one another in ways that are not easy or convenient. Has anyone ever shown selfless love to you? How is your life different because of this person's love?

Chapter Fifteen
MOUNTAIN MOVEMENT

1. Tasha contacted Heather, asking to renew their friendship. Heather says, "I felt like [Tasha] had handed me a glass slipper: I was startled and delighted by the gift that fit me so naturally." Is someone in your life waiting for you to take the first step toward reconciliation? What would it require for you to take that step?

2. Heather chose to tell others about her traumatic experience. Even though there were times she regretted that choice, she healed more quickly because of it. What are some good reasons for sharing our struggles with others? Are there good reasons for choosing not to share our pain with others?

Epilogue
STARTLING BEAUTY

In the epilogue of *Startling Beauty*, we see that God has brought Heather full circle. She is now ministering to others who have been deeply wounded. No matter how you have been wounded, God loves you unconditionally. How would your life change if this love took root in your heart?

The following scripture passages will enhance your study and discussion.

Chapter One: Static in the Storm
1. Gen. 37–45
2. Heb. 12:7–13
3. Phil. 1:6

Chapter Two: Heavy Emptiness
1. John 13:34–35
2. Ps. 119:105–106
3. Ps. 51

Chapter Three: Painful Healing
1. 2 Cor. 5:11–21
2. Matt. 7:1–5
3. Gal. 5:22–26

Chapter Four: The Painting
1. Eph. 4:14–16
2. Jer. 8:18
3. Luke 23:34
4. Phil. 4:4–9

Chapter Five: Violated Again
1. Gen. 4:7
2. Isa. 50:8
3. Gen. 6–8

Chapter Six: Illusions Lost
1. Eph. 5:22–33
2. 1 Peter 3:15–16
3. Titus 2
4. Matt. 10:12–16

Chapter Seven: Knowing Better
1. Rom. 3:21–31
2. Rom. 8:26–27
3. Job

Chapter Eight: Walking on Water
1. Matt. 18:21–35
2. Ps. 109:21–31
3. Jas. 2:14–17

Chapter Nine: Door Number Four
1. Heb. 11
2. Isa. 30:1–5
3. Matt. 10:29–31

Chapter Ten: Compromise
1. 2 Chron. 1:7–17
2. 2 Cor. 4:6–12

Chapter Eleven: Connection
1. Rom. 8:28–39
3. Heb. 10:24–25

Chapter Twelve: Destiny
1. 1 Peter 2:1–3
2. Matt. 21:18–22
3. Matt. 5:23–24

Chapter Thirteen: Baby
1. Isa. 6:1–8
2. Gen. 2:20–25
3. Rom. 8:28

Chapter Fourteen: A Little Dutch Girl
1. Gen. 32:22–32
2. 1 Thess. 5:16–18
3. Heb. 12:1–3

Chapter Fifteen: Mountain Movement
1. Hosea
2. Ps. 78:1–5

Epilogue
Ps. 37

No Greater Love

REAL LIFE STORIES
Two Timeless Books in One

No Greater Love

JOY BATH

WITH SHIRLEY COLLINS

KINGSWAY PUBLICATIONS

EASTBOURNE

First published 1995
This 2-in-1 edition 2008

Unless otherwise indicated, biblical quotations are from the
New International Version, copyright © 1973, 1978, 1984 by the
International Bible Society.
Use is also made of the King James Version
(KJV) crown copyright.

ISBN 978 1 84291 400 7

Cover design: PinnacleCreative.co.uk
Front cover photo C Manamana | Dreamstime.com

Published in the UK by David C. Cook
Kingsway Communications Ltd
26-28 Lottbridge Drove, Eastbourne BN23 6NT, UK
www.kingsway.co.uk

Printed in Great Britain
1   2   3   10   09   08

Foreword

It is never easy to give an answer to the age-old question, 'How does a loving God allow suffering?' It is sometimes even harder to understand why, when someone serves God all their life, suffering follows. *No Greater Love* confesses that it does not try to give slick answers to either of these questions, but it does continually show that despite the hardships and testings of Joy Bath, plus many other characters mentioned in her memoirs, God is always to be trusted. A peace that passes all understanding fills our hearts when we put ourselves into the hands of the Almighty, no matter what happens to us.

Roy Castle
Spring 1994

Introduction

How can one person judge the life of another? It was a privilege to ghost-write this book for Joy. I make no pretence of being the same kind of selfless person she was. She gave her time sacrificially, and I have undoubtedly spent more of my time on earth enjoying myself. We could work together because we were both travelling the same road: we shared the same Christian faith.

In my walk with God I have been impressed by the work of the Reverend Malcolm Herbert. Two decades ago he and I attended the same youth group. Now he is a vicar, currently in Woking. He has spoken these words of wisdom which are relevant to society, and to how it may regard people such as Joy; people the world may consider insignificant: 'We live in a society which majors on success and despises failure. But the world is groaning like a woman in labour. And us with it. We are simultaneously part of the problem and the answer. We are not called to succeed, but to follow Jesus.'

Joy was not a natural writer. Her diaries contained mundane things like, 'Washed my hair. Did the washing up before lights out.' Mixed in with these comments were simple statements such as, 'Helped with a Caesarean section.' She did not boast of her achievements; would not mention how the lives of thousands of patients had been saved through the medical knowledge of herself and her colleagues. To discover the stories behind her daily jottings it was necessary to sit alongside Joy and talk at length. Drawing out the facts from such a retiring and phlegmatic individual was not easy. In the process I discovered a modern-day saint with a terrific sense of humour.

I also spoke to a number of friends, colleagues and members of the Bath family, who provided additional insights into Joy's life. The Bishop of Salisbury told me: 'In the end, when you meet death face to face, there is nothing else in which to put your trust except God.'

Joy Bath trusted God—in life and in death.

Shirley Collins

8

'It won't work! This jack—it doesn't fit our wheels, Joy.'

I watched, helpless, as Debbie Brown, my nursing Sister, tried to lift the pick-up to change a punctured tyre. Too ill to be of much practical help, I felt anxious about our predicament on a dirt road in the middle of nowhere.

The sun rose higher, along with my temperature and Debbie's temper. We were both red in the face when I suggested she ought to stop for a cool drink. In her best Irish brogue she told me to push off—to go and sit under the shade of the nearest bush. I watched my colleague from a distance. Of medium height, slim build and with a fair complexion, we are very much alike: both lacking in muscle power and unsuited to an African heatwave.

It was Sunday 8th March 1992. The weather had been extremely hot almost since the year began, when the rains failed to come. Zimbabwe's worst drought in living memory marked the start of a different kind of aridity in my own life. We were on our way to Harare, setting off early to avoid the intolerable heat of the day. The Elim Mission Hospital truck was due for a service, and I was hoping to find a cure for a prolonged fever, nasty cough, sore throat and various aches and pains which refused to respond to antibiotics. Poorly on and off for about a year, the symptoms had escalated over the previous month until my chest hurt just in breathing.

Debbie persevered for well over an hour. When people get angry, they somehow gain extra strength. In her frustration she found a way to make the jack stay on the wheel. Slowly, inch by inch, one corner of the truck was raised off the ground. The job was three-quarters done when I spotted an approaching bus. It stopped and all the passengers piled out, eager to help.

'You know, I'm actually annoyed those guys arrived after I'd done the hardest part,' Debbie frowned, as the journey recommenced.

'You should demand a discount from the garage. Part of the service has been done already!' Realising the humour of the situation we laughed, relieved to be *en route* once more.

Arriving in Harare around midday, exhausted, grubby and dishevelled, all I could manage was to shower and collapse into bed. Thankfully we were at the home of senior Elim mission workers Peter and Brenda Griffiths; old friends who were not expecting me to provide scintillating conversation over lunch.

Next morning I was well enough to visit the local doctor's surgery for a thorough examination, and go for blood and urine tests. More antibiotics were prescribed—this time for pus on the tonsils. Though I had no idea I could be a risk to anyone, I remember commenting that the young lady who took the blood sample should have been wearing rubber gloves.

Three days passed with Peter and Brenda. The cough and chest pain became much worse so the local doctor advised admission to hospital. An empty bed was found in St Anne's, Harare. While Peter rummaged through Brenda's shelves for a suitable nightdress and dressing gown for me to borrow, I rang my parents in England. About to leave for a holiday in Spain, they sounded really concerned and considered cancelling. Thinking they were overreacting, I persuaded them to go ahead as planned.

Back at the Mission prayers were said for me. Dr Roger Drew, who gave treatment in the early stages, kept in touch with Peter by telephone. Tuberculosis or typhoid might account for my problems. When pneumonia was diagnosed, Roger became alarmed. He needed to visit Harare to buy some electrical equipment so he decided to check on me at the same time.

One morning, as a nurse helped me to bathe, I commented on my sudden weight loss. Two-thirds of the patients I cared for as Matron of the seventy-bed Mission hospital had AIDS. I had begun to look like one of them. The nurse made no reply, but must have said something to the consultant as he came to me requesting an AIDS test.

'It really isn't necessary,' I replied. 'During a visit home in 1990 I had a test, which was negative.'

'You could have become infected since then.'

'We've been careful to wear rubber gloves at work, sterilising them with bleach before re-using. There's been no unprotected exposure.' I thought of my young niece back in England, who organised a glove collection as a safeguard against AIDS infection.

'I'm afraid I must insist you take another test now,' he said firmly.

I had faith in Dr Wiles, and submitted. At least I would be able to prove him wrong.

My rough breathing disturbed some of the other patients. Moved to a side ward, I waited with Roger on Saturday 21st March for the results of the blood test for AIDS. For me there was no stomach sickening anxiety, as I was confident the result would be negative, even though the evidence was ominous. Roger had looked at my latest chest X-ray. It was very abnormal, and an accompanying report raised the possibility of sarcoidosis—a fleshy tumour. But why should someone like me, a non-smoker, develop such a thing?

Whatever the cause, my condition would soon begin to improve, I told myself, and before long I would return to the demanding job I enjoyed so much. It was not to be. I was unaware that Roger already knew the worst. Informed the day before, he had been trying to prepare me to face the truth. Now Consultant Dr Wiles was coming towards us, the gravity of his expression warning that something was wrong. He looked down at the floor for an instant, hesitated, then looked me straight in the eye. 'You've tested HIV-positive.'

'I can't be,' I protested and demanded a retest, adding, 'I don't remember any needle-stick injuries. It must be a mistake.'

'I'm sorry,' he said, leaving me to come to terms with the shock and feelings of disbelief.

Peter Griffiths entered at that moment. It was quite early in the morning, but he had been waiting in the foyer at Roger's request. The three of us sat and wept together for ages. When Dr Wiles returned he said something of great significance, although it gave little comfort at the time.

'For you, Joy, the fact that you are HIV-positive is not a matter for shame, but for pride.'

'Yes,' said Peter. 'You have the virus only because of your calling and dedication to service.'

'You must realise you are seriously ill, and it's best that you return to England as soon as possible,' continued Dr Wiles.

'I'll make the necessary arrangements,' volunteered Roger.

'And I'll go back to Katerere with Roger and tell everyone at the Mission,' said Peter, ever the calm organiser, though he looked shaken.

Roger had a real battle to get me on a plane to Heathrow. Very politely he was told to delay travel until his patient was feeling better. Only when he spoke to the British Airways doctor in London, fully explaining the situation, did things begin to move. In the meantime I really appreciated the visit of a contingent from the Mission around my bedside. Emotions were running riot as we said our goodbyes. No one knew what to say; no words seemed adequate. Pastor Munembe was there, Mai Simango—who had worked closely with me in the Sunday school—all the national nurses, and Debbie.

After the others had gone Debbie stayed behind. Now she was telling me of her long-standing fears that I might have AIDS. Though I knew I would never work in Africa again, the full implications of my physical state had not yet struck home. As far as I was concerned I had contracted the HIV virus and developed pneumonia as a result. The fact that Debbie was talking about AIDS didn't register in my mind. That was one more hurdle yet to be faced.

Three days later, strapped to a stretcher and with an oxygen mask over my face, I made the ambulance ride from St Anne's to Harare Airport. Peter and Debbie were also in attendance, together with Roger, who was travelling with me. It must have looked a fearful scene to other passengers—like something from a television soap—but this was real-life drama. Some doubted I would survive the long journey. They were praying hard that life would still be present by touchdown and beyond, to Southampton General Hospital.

I slept most of the way while Roger watched the in-flight movie, *Terminator 2: Judgement Day*. Charity and mission workers normally take the cheapest seats. Due to my state of health we travelled First Class. Roger joked that he would be returning as baggage. Thanks to his diplomacy, no one on the plane or at Elim Headquarters was aware of the full story of my condition. I wanted my parents to be the next to know, and I wanted to be the person to tell them. When we were able to talk together their reaction was strange, as if my words were fulfilling some kind of prophecy.

'We feel the Lord has prepared us for this. We're not at all surprised,' said Mum. At that moment all I wanted was for them to put their arms around me and hold me tight. I found out later that that was what they wanted too, but at the time it was difficult—I had tubes everywhere, and they didn't want me to break down and cry in case it restricted my breathing even further.

I arrived in England at the time of the Elim Pentecostal Church's annual conference, which was being held at Butlin's, Bognor Regis. Many members were following my career with interest. When those at the conference heard the latest news, which Roger had drafted into an official statement, 4,000 people rose from their seats, joined hands and prayed for me. I believe those prayers had an effect. After responding to treatment for pneumocystis pneumonia (PCP) I was well enough, a few days later, to address the conference via a live telephone link. The nurses were left wondering whether their patient was a new celebrity.

I began to feel more comfortable. Then, about three weeks after the initial diagnosis, the reality of my illness began to sink in. I had attended AIDS courses and nursed AIDS patients for four years. Only now did it dawn on me that PCP plus HIV-positive equals full-blown AIDS; a death sentence. Coming from a pentecostal background I automatically began asking God for healing, and questioned how I could have contracted the disease.

I still have no idea how it happened. There are theories about bleach weakening the protection of surgical gloves, and stories of medics becoming infected through body fluids splashing in the eyes. Or it could have been via my feet—in such sultry weather we were inclined to wear open sandals or flip-flops. There may have been an abrasion or cut on a toe … only God knows. In the end, no matter how much of a turmoil my mind and emotions might be in, I had to learn to leave the incident with the Lord, along with the subject of my healing. Otherwise I could forfeit my inner peace.

With the PCP sufficiently under control I became an outpatient at the end of April, under care of the Royal South Hants Hospital. Arriving home at my parents' house, a celebratory photograph was taken to one side of the car. I had gained some weight, but my appearance was changed. While in Southampton my hair started falling out, sometimes in large handfuls. Consultants advised that the HIV virus can cause this, but it also frequently happens to those who have had a serious illness.

One evening I was trying to wash my hair over the sink, but the hair loss was really bad. Heartbroken, I wondered if I would end up completely bald. My youngest brother Keith heard me crying.

He came into the bathroom and gave me a lovely hug. I realised how fortunate I was to be within a supportive and loving family, when so many AIDS victims are abandoned by relatives and friends.

Roy, my eldest brother, and his wife Jacquie, made an appointment with a wig specialist in Swindon. I could have obtained a wig through the National Health Service, but someone wanted to make a gift, so I bought privately. The hairdresser was patient and professional, and the fitting was confidential, in a cubicle in one corner of the salon. Brushed into a style, the chosen wig looked wonderful. I walked out into the street feeling great, if a little self-conscious.

'Where is it then?' asked Roy, who had been waiting in the car park. 'Did you decide not to buy a wig in the end? Your hair do's very nice.' He was not just being kind, he really hadn't noticed. Several months later my own hair had grown back enough to leave the wig off. It was such a relief to go without it. Though no one ever knew my secret I felt vulnerable, especially when shopping on rainy days in Salisbury market. There was always the fear it might be hijacked by a passing umbrella!

My health continued to improve after being prescribed the drug AZT, though I was kept on the lowest dose to avoid becoming anaemic. A pentamidine nebuliser helped the PCP, providing a fine spray for inhalation. Apart from dry, mottled skin and periods of tiredness, few signs of a fatal virus were apparent.

'Why you, Joy? Your life's been spent serving God and helping others. Why should you suffer in this way?' When they learned I had AIDS, questions like this started coming from many people. I had no pat answers then, or now, but rest in the confidence that God never makes mistakes. He called me and promised to be with me.

2

For as long as I can remember I have wanted to be a nurse. Coupled with this ambition has been a keen desire to travel, inspired by tales of far away lands brought to my parents' home in Wiltshire by visiting missionaries. Pentecostal Christians do not exactly believe in predestination, but a pre-school photograph taken in the 1950s shows a budding medic in best uniform holding my favourite toy Topsy, a black doll.

As I grew up the longing to be a nurse remained, though there was no confidence I would be able to gain the necessary qualifications. The thought of entering my father's business instead, the greengrocery trade, did not seem anywhere near as exciting. On reaching the fourth year at secondary school I sat an English Language RSA examination and, to my astonishment, passed. This encouraged me to stay on a further twelve months. Then came a two-year pre-nursing course at Salisbury Technical College. I managed to get the necessary credentials and began training to be a nurse at Poole General Hospital in 1968.

Three years later, soon after passing finals and qualifying as a State Registered Nurse, I attended an Elim Pentecostal Church conference in Blackpool. Among those speaking at a missions rally were a number of workers from Rhodesia. My memory fails to recall the names and faces of all the speakers, but I remember that a lively young teacher called Mary Fisher was among them. She sang two hymns as solos and had a fine voice and I thought she looked youthful for a missionary—about the same age as I was. I had no idea then that we would one day be together in the same compound, or that she would lose her life in a terrible massacre.

Someone was appealing for doctors to volunteer for service in Katerere, as a married couple who began Elim's work there were reaching retirement age. I thought, 'I could never be a doctor, but maybe they can use a nurse,' and made my way to the front. A number of young people were gathering near the stage to dedicate their various careers to God. When it became obvious that no one was signing up nurses I joined this group, saying a simple prayer.

At the end of the week I went home and began pestering the Almighty about future prospects in a more fervent way. No definite answers seemed to come from above, but Dad offered some divine inspiration: 'It wouldn't do any harm to qualify in midwifery. Surely they'll need those skills in any developing country.' I joined a class in Bristol.

About a year later, when the course had just ended, I received an unexpected visit from the local pastor. A member of the Elim Missionary Council, he had recently returned from a meeting where the Mission hospital in Rhodesia was on the agenda. Matron Joyce Pickering was now the only expatriate there, and desperately overworked. In a letter she had written, 'If you can't find a doctor, please send a nurse with midwifery training.'

When I heard of this plea I had a tremendous feeling of peace. Though only twenty-four and fairly inexperienced, I knew God was leading me out to Rhodesia. The minister went to great lengths to explain all the problems I could encounter. Others tried to discourage me, saying I should wait a few years. In my simple childlike faith I was sure that if this was my calling, God would not let me down.

Once I had said that I was willing to go, everything happened very quickly, with departure fixed for the last week of July 1974. The weekend before there was a farewell service at the Elim church in Salisbury, where it was touching to see nursing friends as well as regular worshippers. As I had been a Sunday school and youth group leader as well as a church member, three official presentations were made. With each came a Scripture reading, prayerfully selected by different people. No one had discussed which verse to choose, but all were the same: 'Have not I commanded thee? Be strong and of a good courage; be not afraid, neither be thou dismayed: for the Lord thy God is with thee whithersoever thou goest' (Joshua 1:9, KJV).

A ripple of amazement went through the congregation. God was making it clear to me, and everyone else, that he was sending me in his strength. It was a wonderful confirmation.

Although it meant travelling on a weekday, the whole family hired a minibus to see me off at Heathrow. Several friends were also there. In those days overseas assignments could last for many years. No one knew for sure when they might see me again. It was a bitter-sweet occasion.

'I still don't understand why you want to spend your life tucked away in some foreign country,' sighed Pearl, my younger sister.

'It's the role I want, just as that is yours,' I said, patting her pregnant tummy. 'I'll want to hear all the news of my new niece or nephew.'

'We're all so proud of you,' cried Mum, hugging my neck one final time.

Less tearful, Dad was concerned for my safety. 'We always thought you'd make a good missionary. Do exactly as you're told by superiors and don't take any risks. There are rumours of discontent and guerrilla warfare.' Behind his words were many shadows. I told him not to worry.

From Salisbury, Wiltshire to Salisbury, Rhodesia. Although the flight lasted sixteen hours, elation kept tiredness at bay. Descending the steps on landing, a surprisingly cold wind blew around my legs. I began looking around for Alan Renshaw, the mission worker who was to meet me. As I pushed my trolley along after passing through customs and immigration, a deep voice called out: 'Miss Joy Bath?'

I turned and saw a tall, thin man with wide shoulders.

'You look just like your photograph,' he grinned. 'We'll have some lunch first, before setting off for Katerere—it's nearly four hours away.'

Alan is a good talker and time went by quickly as we covered the journey of 140 miles, mostly on bumpy gravel roads. I was conscious of passing through acres of quiet, flat land with no one in sight, just tall grasses on either side and mountain peaks in the distance. Now and again there were a few round, brown thatched buildings grouped together.

'They're called *kraals* and are the homes of village people,' explained Alan.

'The large houses in the city looked very grand and European. These are more traditional, what Africa is really all about. But I don't see any animals.'

'Not at this time of day, it's too hot for them. You'd have to come out here at the crack of dawn, or last thing at night. Of course, there are plenty in the game reserves.'

We came upon the Elim Mission in a valley at the foot of a small hill. Around 5.30pm, just before nightfall, I met Joyce Pickering and deposited my luggage at her house, where I would live for the time being. A cheerful but no-nonsense Yorkshire woman, she gave the instant impression of being an extremely capable and practical person; reassuring qualities to find in a matron. Over a grand meal prepared by Alan's wife Anne at their home, in honour of my arrival, the four of us chatted about ourselves and my new surroundings.

'Our complex here is like a little bush town, sprawling over 100 acres,' said Alan. 'Apart from the hospital there's the main church, also serving smaller chapels in the area, and the secondary school, of which Peter Griffiths is the Principal. Most of the teachers are away this weekend at a Scripture Union camp.'

Anne cut in, 'There are limited shopping facilities for basic food and clothing, African style, and you can buy cooking utensils and the like round here. But nothing resembles Marks and Spencer.'

'Joy seems to have brought sufficient suitcases!' laughed Alan.

'Perhaps it's time we unpacked some of the contents,' suggested Joyce.

After helping to clear away the dishes, Joyce and I hurried back to her house to put some of my clothes on hangers. Electricity in the Mission compound came from a generator, which switched off towards the end of the evening. There was about half an hour of power left. As I went to bed that first night in Africa the air was full of unfamiliar noises, including the sound of drum beats in the distance. It was disconcerting to realise I could no longer reach for the light switch.

'What was all that going on in the middle of the night?' I asked Joyce the next morning.

'Nothing to worry about—just a religious sect a way off who hold all-night meetings.'

'It's Sunday tomorrow,' I ventured. 'There's church for us, I expect, with or without the teachers?'

'There certainly is, and you're the special guest! By afternoon the teachers will be back. Today I'll give you a tour of your workplace and show you the house that will be your own after decorating.'

Most of the buildings in the compound were framed at ground level by neat gardens edged with white stones. Exotic fruit trees—lemon, grapefruit, passion, pawpaw and banana— stretched their branches above tin or thatched rooftops. The hospital seemed very different and strange at first. There were far more staff than I had imagined. Trained nurses wore white uniforms and starched caps, while unqualified ones had blue dresses with white collars and cuffs. They all looked clean and smart, and greeted me with a polite, 'Hello, Sister Bath.' I shook that many hands and heard so many names I thought I'd never remember everyone. It was several weeks before I knew each face and name, and could match both together.

The following day, as I walked down to the Mission church, I imagined my parents attending their morning service. I was asked to say a few words and saw before me a sea of black faces, all friendly and smiling. It was enough to dispel any homesickness. I noticed that men and boys sat apart from the women and girls. The right-hand side of the congregation was sparse, as most of the men were away working, only coming home for holidays. The girls had fascinating hairstyles. Many had braids starting at the roots, twisted into different designs with black thread.

Other early impressions still remain with me. Nursing mothers carry their babies with ease on their backs in a special cloth called an *inbereko*. A crying baby receives breast milk immediately, whether Mum is on her own or in company. Families have new babies on average every two years. Older children help in looking after infants, and it is common to see three-year-olds with tiny babies on their backs, jigging them up and down to stop them crying.

That inaugural Sunday afternoon marked the first of many weekly visits for tea with Peter and Brenda Griffiths. They had worked with the founders, Cecil and Mary Brien, so I asked about the early days.

'The story begins in South Wales, in general practice in a small Rhondda Valley town,' started Peter. Knowing this was a long yarn, Brenda reached for the teapot to refill our cups.

'The Briens were considering their future careers, and Cecil drove to Swansea one weekend, to take advice from Rhys Howells, founder of the Bible College of Wales. He was told: "Return home, and do what the senior partner at the practice tells you." Before surgery opened next morning, the boss rebuked

23

him: "This preaching of yours in the streets of the town on your afternoons off is unbecoming to a medical man. You should go to Africa as a missionary." So he did as the doctor ordered!'

'Just like that, eh! But how did the Briens know where to start?'

'They didn't at first. They began by getting some experience at an established mission on the Mvura Dhona range of mountains, overlooking the Zambezi escarpment in the northern border region of Rhodesia. There they both worked as medics, learned the Shona language, and saw many people become Christians. After a time Mary Brien felt God was speaking to her through the Bible. A few verses just seemed to hit her in the eye, as if they were highlighted.' There was a pause as Peter reached for his Bible and thumbed through pages of the Old Testament to read: '"And the Lord spake unto me, saying, Ye have compassed this mountain long enough: turn you northward … unto a land that I will shew thee. … And they departed from the mount of the Lord three days' journey" (Deuteronomy 2:2–3; Genesis 12:1; Numbers 10:33, KJV).

'Cecil and Mary prayed together, asking for God's guidance. They also wrote to a friend back home, the Reverend Leslie Green. He replied almost immediately, saying they must leave their present posts and join forces with an Elim minister and his wife at a church in Umtali. Around then, a white Rhodesian in the congregation there had a strange dream, which he told to that same minister, the Reverend Jesse Williams. It concerned a group of Africans from Chief Katerere's kingdom, carrying empty pots, looking for water.

'The Briens obeyed their message, even though it meant going south rather than north, and on a journey of two days, not three. Travelling in their truck, they slept the first night in Salisbury's Coronation Park, then drove on towards the Mozambique border and Umtali. Jesse Williams told them about the dream, and how it related to a region north of Umtali, in Inyanga North, where no missionaries had ever settled. Cecil and Mary were convinced that this was the place for them. However, they had to wait a while for agreement from the authorities before setting off to work.'

'In August 1951 they eventually journeyed a third day and reached the Gairezi Valley in Katerere, where the road literally ended. Driving between trees and rocks, they came to rest on the banks of the Manjanja River. Now this stretch of water was reputed to be evil, the name meaning "stream of the lion spirit". Pitching their two tents they set up home, later adding a mud hut which became the dining room.

'Immediately they began preaching the gospel to inquisitive tribesmen in the Shona language, referring to Satan as the evil spirit, who took the place of God in people's hearts. "Jesus, his Son, will give you living water," they cried. The message had instant appeal. A young lad, Rhinos Mukwewa, became the first convert in the area. He is now a teacher and a leader in one of the local fellowships.'

'An inspiring story!' I commented. 'But what of their progress in medical terms?'

'It began slowly, as the local people were suspicious of foreigners when it came to healing, preferring traditional methods. The Briens stretched a tarpaulin from the end of their truck over a framework of poles, and started a dispensary. Then there were clinics, where the Bible was opened, the gospel read and patients prayed over before treatment was given. They described to me their first operation, a herniotomy, performed on a table by the light of a hurricane lamp held aloft by an African assistant. Mary, the anaesthetist, put the patient under by dripping ether onto a mask. A valuable microscope was kept steady on top of Mary's ironing board. And things which needed to be cool were placed inside an old safe and submerged in the river until required.'

'The water comes down from the mountains, and the supply has never dried up, even in times of drought,' added Brenda. This was testimony in itself to the fruitfulness of the site. Still, I was thankful that working conditions had improved considerably since then.

'The Mission as it now stands is the result of Cecil and Mary Brien's faith and hard work. Nowadays there could be up to 1,000 people in the compound at times, wouldn't you say?' Peter rounded off the intriguing tale with a look towards his wife, which was also a signal to fetch more tea.

Established almost a quarter of a century before my arrival, the Elim Mission at Katerere had become well-known for miles around as a centre for health and education. In spite of this, I soon realised that the local witch-doctors remained a problem for the hospital. Highly respected members of the community, they had a real hold on people.

It was still common for sick people to go to the traditional healer first. Only if there was no improvement would an approach be made to us, and by that time the patient could be at death's door. Roots and leaves of various plants do have medicinal properties. The problem is that in Africa's long, dry heat these become concentrated, poisoning instead of healing; the equivalent of taking an overdose. We tried explaining this to relatives of patients, but they still had more confidence in their own ways than ours. Many people died as a result, especially children. Their small bodies are more vulnerable to toxins.

There were no strict visiting hours in the hospital. Relatives of patients stayed at the bedside all day, and often slept underneath at night, if home was a long way off. If a person was seriously ill, and there seemed to be no immediate improvement taking place, relatives would assume the worst, asking that the patient be allowed to go home. There they could die in their own surroundings, with traditional rites being performed. We would argue against this—particularly as a longer course of treatment could often save the life—but it was not unusual for patient and family to flee the compound.

In spite of such disappearances, the wards and outpatients' clinic always seemed to be full of people. We dealt with virtually everything from infectious diseases to broken limbs and accident cases. And there was never a shortage of expectant or new mothers with tiny babies requiring attention. Efficient and businesslike, Joyce was panicked by nothing and no one. At work she was firm to the point of appearing stern at times, especially with the staff. In leisure hours she was just the opposite, and full of fun.

It was a relief to discover that all the Elim workers there were ordinary people. In my mind I had the misconception that they might be super-spiritual beings, giants of faith. I came to the conclusion that perhaps the great Christian pioneers—the first disciples, Francis of Assisi, William Tyndale, the Wesley brothers, Billy Graham, and maybe even Cecil and Mary Brien—were somehow different from myself and my new friends. The former were brave innovators; we just carried on with the work.

I was frequently tired, but always happy. With any new job come the staging posts of initial unfamiliarity, the feeling that one cannot absorb any more facts, and the gradual regaining of confidence as tasks are achieved and skills mastered. Through all of these I remained in a positive mood, feeling my role was the realisation of so many hopes and dreams.

The year 1976 saw a number of comings and goings at the Mission, beginning with the arrival of the Evans family in the spring. Philip was a teacher and the new deputy head, and Susanne had secretarial experience, which was needed for Peter's office. With them came their three young children, Timothy, Rachel and Rebecca (although the eldest two were later to be schooled elsewhere). The newcomers arrived twice: the first time they were refused entry on landing, and directed back to England. It seems Phil annoyed the authorities by declaring he would be a conscientious objector in the event of a civil war. Peter Griffiths managed to smooth things over.

Brenda Griffiths was suffering from insomnia. When the school closed for the Easter holidays, Peter decided to combine a check-up at the doctor's in Salisbury with his speaking engagement at a Scripture Union event near Bulawayo. He was confident that Phil could manage things in their absence, but wavered in this opinion after a worrying conversation with a member of the security forces. The latter operated a camp a couple of miles away and it was normal to see army vehicles driving through the compound. This time they stopped, seeking out Peter to bring news that two bands of guerrillas had come over the border from Mozambique. Perhaps he should think again about the trip. There might be trouble brewing.

'Political activists, some said to be Communists and based outside Rhodesia, are stirring the native people up,' Peter told Phil. 'There's been no activity around here so far, but last year the school was visited by two terrorists—in civvies—as part of a general reconnaissance. They were members of the Zimbabwe African National Union.'

'But these boys may be from another faction. Whoever they represent, there's no guarantee they'll pay us a visit. And SU are expecting you—best not disappoint them,' Phil replied. So somewhat reluctantly Peter and Brenda put their things in the car and left.

The Renshaws and others were away on vacation. A single lady, Joan Caudell, was the only other expatriate teacher on site between terms. She was spoken to by a friendly contact in the security forces.

'The Avila Catholic Mission, not far from here, was entered by a group of terrorists,' she said gravely to Phil and Sue, relating the message. 'They were armed, and threatened people.'

'Was anyone hurt?' asked Phil.

'No.'

Peter and Phil had not told all of the remaining Europeans about their misgivings, only Joyce, and Roy Lynn, our caretaker. Now Sue was party to the information, she had disturbing tidings of her own to add.

'I heard some of the African women talking this week. There are freedom fighters in the district. I didn't think anything of the conversation at the time. Could they be a danger to us? I'm scared.'

Oblivious to all this, I was very much enjoying the company of my parents, who turned out to be intrepid travellers. This was their first visit to Africa, and together we climbed the hill behind the Mission for a clear view of the valley. It stretches as far as the eye can see, with the mountains of Mozambique in the distance. While up there we found some primitive bushman paintings, which fascinated my parents. Then Mum's mood changed.

'There's a man behind us,' she whispered as we began our descent. 'I think he's carrying a rifle.'

I turned slightly. 'It looks more like a walking stick. But even if it is a gun, he's probably out hunting.' The man kept his distance and did not bother us, but Mum remained uneasy. When we got back I had a shift to work in the labour ward and forgot the incident.

Meanwhile, Joan had moved in with the Evans family so she would not be alone at night. Ian Smith, the Rhodesian Prime Minister, was giving an important speech on the radio. They listened intently as he declared that the country was in a state of war, a fight for independence. His words added to their fears and all three of them prayed for God's protection before going to bed. The children were already asleep. Not long after the generator went off, the household was roused by a group of men shouting revolutionary slogans.

I was now living in my own place. I had given my parents my bed and was in a small guest room. Exhausted after a long and happy day, I had fallen into a deep sleep. Dogs are a useful addition to any missionary household, and Sandy, my alsatian–labrador cross, was a good security guard, disposer of unwanted reptiles and alarm clock. He could be quite fierce, and his loud barking woke me up.

31

'Who's there?' I shouted through the window. Sometimes the nurses would come and ask me to go to the hospital in the middle of the night. I could see no torchlight, and there was no reply to my call. Disgruntled, I scolded the animal and went back to bed.

Meanwhile, although he had only been in the country for two months, Phil Evans was doing remarkably well in talking his way out of a life-threatening situation. Refusing to open the door, he communicated with the callers by an open window.

'We've had enough of domination by the whites! We are the freedom fighters!' they declared. 'The whites passed laws which don't apply to them, saying we can't have guns, and must carry identity cards. We refuse to have cards, but we will carry guns!' Their weapons were raised in the air.

'This is a Christian Mission and we don't want to get involved in any fighting,' reasoned Phil. Then, in a flash of inspiration, he told them the story of how he was turned back at the airport for being a conscientious objector. This seemed to please the visitors. They calmed down a little, and listened until he had finished speaking. Phil could see white teeth in the darkness outside as they nodded their approval.

One man was not smiling. '"Love your enemies", "turn the other cheek", I know these are the words of Jesus, who also threw people out of a temple—as we will drive out the whites from our country,' he said, with real venom. 'Now, give me your medicines so we can treat our wounded.'

Sue handed over a First Aid box and the guerrillas backed off.

'Be quiet, you noisy dog!' I called to Sandy who was still barking, and I rose from my bed a second time. Hearing voices I went outside, wearing only my night-dress, expecting to see a couple of nurses. From the garden path a group of people were visible, congregating under the large branches of what I called the flamboyant tree. One of the nurses was there, plus an African teacher. The rest were strangers, wearing camouflage battle dress and carrying machine guns.

The nurse was asked to go to Joyce's house, which was close to mine, and bring her out to join us. She arrived breathless, but not from hurrying. It was the only time I ever saw her unnerved. The spokesman of the military group introduced himself as a freedom fighter, before launching into a lengthy speech.

'Eighty years ago the whites came. African warriors fought brave battles, but could not win without guns. We have guns now. We will liberate Zimbabwe!'

'Down with identity cards! Down with Ian Smith!' they shouted in unison. 'Down with ...'

'Yes, we understand,' I butted in impatiently. 'So if you've finished we'll go back to sleep. I've been delivering babies, I'm very tired, I have to be up early tomorrow, and it's cold standing out here.'

'We know you help our people, so you will not be harmed,' replied the spokesman. 'But I have many soldiers—more than these here—and they need medicines and bandages.'

I looked at Joyce. Did he mean the compound was surrounded?

'Can't you bring your wounded down to the hospital?' she suggested.

'No, we must not be seen by the security forces. Come.' He pointed the way with his gun.

'Please let me go indoors to put on a warm coat,' I requested.

'Very well,' he replied. The group waited while I fetched my dressing-gown.

Walking to the hospital, we were told the freedom fighters had already visited Phil and Sue's house.

'What about Roy?' whispered Joyce, but she was overheard. There was a murmur among the troops, then the African teacher spoke. 'They haven't bothered him, because they know he has a gun.'

Roy's house was a little way from the others. He was probably unaware of our predicament.

We gave them everything they asked for, with me all the time grumbling that it was most unethical to supply medicines without seeing the patients. Just before they disappeared into the shadows I was asked if we had a two-way radio.

'No,' I answered truthfully. Neither did we possess a telephone.

'If you tell the security forces about us, we will come back and kill you,' they warned. Then they were gone.

Joyce was shaking like a leaf. I suggested a cup of strong, sweet tea at my house with Mum and Dad. My parents! In the commotion I had forgotten they were there. Hearing the dog bark, they assumed I had been called to attend to a medical emergency. Dad needed rest and was asleep when we arrived back. At the start of their stay he had been disturbed at night when rain leaked through the thatched roof onto his side of the bed. Mum was wide eyed and worrying. A kind of sixth sense mothers seem to have told her something was wrong. As soon as I started relating it all to them, Mum remembered the man on the hill with a gun. Was there any connection? I didn't know.

34

When I was face to face with the freedom fighters I was not afraid at all. In fact I was indignant that they had come at night and woken me up. It wasn't until I started explaining what had happened to Mum and Dad that I began shaking all over. It was as if something clicked within me, and I realised Joyce and I had been in a very dangerous situation. If the terrorists had been drunk, or if they had taken offence at our words, they could have become angry. Who knows what they might have done to us?

I needed to read something from the Bible to calm my nerves and Dad's copy was handy. It was a Gideon publication, so he looked in the front index, where readings are listed for life's situations. Under the heading 'Where to find help when in danger' was Psalm 91. I took the book to read aloud, but became too emotional to continue. Dad carried on at verse 5: "'Thou shalt not be afraid for the terror by night; nor for the arrow that flieth by day.'" The whole psalm was so appropriate. After a time of prayer together we all retired to our beds again. Mum, Dad and Joyce lay awake for the rest of the night. I slept like a log until morning, comforted by those words.

The next day we expatriates left Katerere for Salisbury, in several vehicles and at different times, so as not to arouse suspicions. Roy Lynn returned to keep an eye on things after escorting Joyce to safety. With hindsight I can see that it was unwise of us to up and go, but we were all inexperienced and nervous about the consequences of the nocturnal visit. Had we known our African co-workers better at that time, we would have realised they could be trusted. If we had confided in two leading pastors, Pious Munembe or Ephraim Satuku, they would have led us to make the right decision. The nationals could not understand why the missionaries had left so suddenly. This caused a slight distancing of relationships. I feel we failed them badly.

The guerrillas who had come to the Mission were cornered by the security forces a few days later. A number were killed, and the rest arrested and taken to Salisbury to stand trial. We all met for a conference to decide the future, and voted to return. The single ladies would be allowed to be in their own homes during the daytime, but would stay with the families at night. When Joyce or myself had to be on duty at night, one of the men would accompany us to the hospital and stay there until the work was done. This was tough on them as we could be up for hours, especially if there was a complicated birth happening. Also, the mosquitoes had a good feed as our protectors read by flickering lamplight to keep themselves awake.

The security situation began to deteriorate. Not many days would pass without us hearing of landmine explosions or encounters between terrorists and the authorities. However, all through the war no violence occurred within the Mission compound. It was as if all our prayers for peace in the midst of the hostilities were answered. Perhaps the surrounding circle of freedom fighters had been replaced by invisible angels.

One Sunday I returned from church and was cooking lunch when through the kitchen window I saw army vehicles arrive at the hospital. A civilian lorry had been blown up by a landmine and there were casualties needing immediate attention. The soldiers explained that there were no army medics in the area, so they had come to us for help. Peter took me to the scene with an African nurse. We travelled in convoy in his Peugeot 404. It was all right to be seen sandwiched between their trucks, but to sit with the security forces would lead people to believe we were taking sides.

By a little bridge near Kajozo an ancient five-ton truck was smashed and lying on its side. The driver was breathing his last. Nearby was a young man, moaning loudly. We parked some distance away in case the weight of the vehicles set off more mines, and walked back to the horrific scene. Behind us, the soldiers were watching the bush, guns at the ready, expecting attack at any time.

I ascertained that the man who was moaning had cracked ribs, and moved on. A young mother lay dead on the ground, with her tiny baby still at the breast. It was unhurt, though in need of nourishment. The slogan 'breast is best' is so true in developing countries. Feeding bottles are a death sentence if sterilising fluid cannot be bought, or incorrect proportions of milk and water are mixed. The water must be clean too. I wondered how this little ebony cherub was going to survive without a mother.

Another woman, still alive but unconscious, needed help first. Both legs were broken and bent the wrong way up from the shins, like a rag doll. Ants had already started to burrow into wounds around her heels. Scooping them out, we patched her up as best we could, putting on splints and setting up a drip. A man with a deep leg wound also required a drip. He had lost a great deal of blood. We gave injections of morphine to those who were in pain.

The casualties were taken away by helicopter, which made two trips and could not stay long in the area for fear of attracting the attention of guerrillas. I handed the infant to a rather juvenile co-pilot. He didn't seem to know how to hold a baby, so it was a new experience for both of them. As the chopper took off for the last time the pilot shouted, 'The doctor sends his compliments to the sister for a first-class job!'

The whole thing was a dreadful experience, especially for Peter, who was unused to seeing mangled bodies and had nightmares for months afterwards. We received feedback that everyone except the young man was doing fine. I was wrong about him and he died. He had a ruptured spleen, not cracked ribs. But at the time I examined him, his condition did not seem critical. Generally the person who is able to cry out is usually the least injured.

God works in mysterious ways. It might have been Phil Evans lying there. An hour earlier that Sunday morning he was driving the Mission's two-ton truck along the same road, with a group of churchgoers as passengers. Before reaching the bridge he mysteriously lost control of the wheel and slid off the road. No one was hurt.

On Tuesdays it was my habit to drive to a village called Kambudzi to hold a clinic. When Pastor Munembe told Peter that the place had become unsafe, he came to discuss the matter with me.

'I want you to make the final decision, but I advise you to discontinue working there for the time being,' he frowned. As he stood before me I thought hard.

'Peter, those are poor and deprived people, in desperate need of medicines. I'll carry on running the clinic if you'll come with me.' He agreed, and became quite a useful form-filler in the process, while I carried on with the nursing.

During the first journey we anxiously scanned the road ahead for any signs of landmines, not realising we had already driven over one. We only became aware of it when an army truck behind us exploded. Thankfully the vehicle, unlike ours, was heavily reinforced. The only injury was to a trooper who was blown clear. He had landed on his rear end, damaging his coccyx.

At least one highway, to the district administrative centre at Inyanga, began to look like the lunar surface, with deep holes everywhere. Every so often this fifty-five-mile route was littered with debris, marking the sites where military vehicles had been blown apart. It was time to take certain precautions with our travel. The school lorry carried sand bags on the back and the tyres were filled with water. The Mission truck was fitted with metal plating. For the hospital, a hardy Rhino was purchased; a Land Rover ambulance offering more protection beneath our feet than most standard models. It was open at the top, until a tarpaulin was added, and looked like a white bath tub on wheels, with a red cross painted on each side.

We were instructed only to journey outside the compound by these specially adapted modes of transport, and not to venture out after dark. When going to particularly sensitive areas I had to wear a crash helmet and put cotton wool in my ears. Seat belts had to be worn on every trip. As the war intensified we had to contend with ambushes as well as the possibility of being blown up.

Peter was having a time of prayer and meditation one day when he felt compelled to read the biblical account of Ezra. Part of the story concerns a journey to Jerusalem, past enemy lines. Ezra was too ashamed to ask the king for bodyguards, having previously declared, 'The hand of our God is upon all them for good that seek him' (Ezra 8:22, KJV). So he set off without a military escort, but arrived safely, reporting, 'The hand of our God was upon us, and he delivered us from the hand of the enemy, and of such as lay in wait by the way' (v 31).

Later on, I burst into Peter's office somewhat distraught, with a plea for help. 'I've a patient in labour who may need a Caesarean and can't be treated here. This is her tenth child, and the previous pregnancies have weakened her, so the uterus isn't contracting as it should. It may rupture. With a younger mother I could try fixing up a drip containing a drug to encourage the contractions. But I daren't risk it with this one.'

'Are you saying she has to be taken to Inyanga now?'

'That's right.' I was amazed by Peter's unusually calm manner. Night was falling. He knew the risks.

He said, 'Don't mind me sounding a little righteous, but God gave me prior warning of this. We have his permission to break the curfew.'

We went in the two-ton truck, with the patient and a relative lying down in the back. None of us dared speak for several miles and the silence was eerie. Coming onto the brow of a hill, my heart jumped. Fires were spreading across the valley below.

'It's nothing to worry about,' reassured Peter. 'They're just burning off the stubble in the fields—farmers do it every year about this time.'

Of course! I should have known that, coming from the West Country.

The journey was completed without incident and the woman taken to a government doctor.

Peter was required to report to the police station, saying where we had come from, and giving the name of a hotel where we would spend the rest of the night.

'You were lucky to get through,' remarked the duty officer. The Principal of Elim Secondary School rose to his full, bantam height, determined to give credit where it was due. 'No, the hand of our God was upon us,' smiled Peter rather sanctimoniously.

4

'If any of us are killed in a landmine explosion, will we be classified as martyrs?' The question was hypothetical and said partly in jest, as a group of us met to talk about writing our wills and leaving instructions for funerals in the event of death in service. I felt I would rather be buried in Rhodesia to keep the costs down.

Suddenly, the blades of several helicopters whirred overhead. Choppers were landing in the compound. We rushed out to see what was happening.

'Civilian casualties, in shock, with minor injuries—nine young girls!' shouted a member of the security forces. 'We attacked a rebel camp, not realising they were entertaining their girlfriends.'

Joyce immediately sprang into action. 'Move the male patients into one ward to make room,' she ordered some junior nurses. Then she and I began giving the most badly shocked girls intravenous fluids. But we couldn't find any veins. Having worked in operating theatres in the past, Joyce had seen plenty of varicose vein surgery.

'I need to do something called an intravenous cut-down,' she explained. I marvelled as she made deep incisions around the ankles of two girls, in each case managing to find a vein.

Within a couple of days all the girls were feeling much better. They seemed popular, receiving visits from a number of smartly dressed young men. Later I heard that these were their boyfriends—rebels who had survived the attack. If the security forces had realised what was going on, we would have been in trouble for fraternising with their enemies.

Around this time road travel became so dangerous that Elim turned to the Mission Aviation Fellowship for help. Once a month a government doctor flew out from Umtali to an airstrip near Katerere. Leprosy sufferers received treatment close to the runway, before he made his way to the hospital to see any patients Joyce and I were worried about. Meanwhile the pilot was unoccupied.

On one occasion the doctor examined a physically small girl, who was due to give birth to her first baby. He confirmed our fears that a normal delivery would not be possible, adding, 'Sister Bath, Matron and I can manage without you for a time. Take this patient to Umtali in the plane. You'll be back before I've finished here.'

It was a windy day and the little Cessna was tossed about like a leaf. In addition, the pilot made swerving manoeuvres to avoid being sighted by terrorists. Some of them now possessed ground-to-air and heat-seeking missiles. The expectant mother had never been in a plane before and was terrified. I tried to reassure her, and held her hand most of the way, but was feeling green with travel sickness myself. We deposited her safely at the hospital in Umtali and had an uneventful return trip. To quell my nausea I tried to concentrate on the view, picking out landmarks. The white stones bordering Katerere's brown plots and pathways looked like rows of white teeth around open mouths, beckoning hungrily from below. A dentist's nightmare! Still, it was good to reach *terra firma* again.

The curtailment of journeys by land was unhelpful to Joyce's personal life. She and Roy Lynn were in the early stages of courtship and needed to spend time alone together off site, so they could become better acquainted. Joyce did well to maintain a professional coolness at work, but I detected a warm glow around her whenever the likeable little Irishman was around. Roy was slightly disabled and walked with a limp. By way of compensation he'd been blessed with good looks and the gift of the blarney. Through knowing him Joyce had mellowed, and there was a spin-off into our relationship.

Joyce and I began to pray together regularly for the African nurses. It was her idea. 'Perhaps it will lead them into deeper spiritual matters,' she said hopefully. Although many were Christians they seemed oppressed by the war waging all around us. Some had reverted to carrying pagan charms for good luck. There had even been tentative enquiries about the end of the world coming soon. We decided to invite them to an evening meeting about the power of the Holy Spirit. Attendance was not compulsory, and the staff dining hall provided a non-threatening venue.

Almost everyone not on duty turned up to hear what we had to say. Joyce was about to start speaking when someone appeared in the doorway. There was an emergency in the labour ward.

'I'll go,' I volunteered, rising from my seat. The message of Pentecost would have more clout delivered by the Matron. Joyce opened her mouth to protest, but I was out of the room before she could say anything.

A couple of hours later a transformation greeted my return. Worried expressions had become wide smiles on glowing faces.

Eyes shone and voices were lifted in praise to God. Even the room's atmosphere had changed. Many were sitting in small groups and from their lips came the gentle murmuring of different languages. People were speaking in tongues for the first time!

'The Holy Spirit has come,' sighed one of the ladies contentedly.

'Yes, and I haven't led this kind of meeting before,' beamed Joyce, with tears of happiness in her eyes.

I owned up, 'I'm glad you did, because I wouldn't have known how!'

Peace and joy flowed from that meeting, permeating every corner of the hospital for months to come. Only after Joyce and Roy became engaged, and she left on furlough to prepare for the wedding, did things sour. But the events were unconnected. I thought it was my imagination at first—paranoia brought on by extra responsibilities. Or could it be that some of the nurses were standing around gossiping about my marital status? Perhaps, like me, they were wondering whether a husband was going to appear on the scene. Eventually they came to see me *en masse*.

'We want more money,' said a spokeswoman.

I explained that they were all due for a rise in salary at the end of the following month.

'*I marii*—how much?' she asked. No one was impressed by my reply.

'That is too little,' said a second girl, while another threatened, 'We want more, or we will not stay here.'

'I'm seeing *mufundisi* Griffiths later. I'll mention the matter to him.' Sensing the group was becoming hostile I edged away, while agreeing to take the matter higher.

I was actually going to Peter and Brenda's for supper. When I arrived there they could see I was upset and were very supportive.

'The management committee, which takes advice from Africans, has overall responsibility for salaries. If the staff are not happy they must make a formal complaint,' said Peter.

'I think someone from outside's been causing trouble deliberately,' suggested Brenda. 'You know how Peter McCann is constantly losing things? Well, the other day the boy who works around the house went to fetch firewood, and hasn't been seen since!'

This raised a chuckle. Bearded and bespectacled, Peter McCann looked every inch the absent-minded professor. As a science teacher, he could not be faulted. In everyday living he was a complete scatterbrain, testing the patience of his wife Sandra to the absolute limit.

Brenda went on, 'It would seem the lad's been press-ganged into joining the freedom fighters. There've been a number of similar disappearances.'

'War is always hardest on civilians,' mumbled Peter Griffiths, momentarily becoming eight years old again and reliving German bombing raids on Swansea.

'There are staff problems at the school too,' said Brenda. 'The Renshaws are returning to Britain when their current contract ends. They have a number of family commitments to sort out.'

'But Catherine Picken is coming back here to teach English and sport,' replied Peter, returning to the present. 'She's been away looking after her elderly mother since before you arrived, Joy. And you'll not have to manage senior hospital duties alone for much longer. Wendy White will soon be here.'

After the meal I walked away from their house with mixed thoughts and feelings. The Renshaws were leaving. I would miss their cheery faces and helping hands. I pictured Anne Renshaw fitting Staff Nurse Evelyn's ample curves into a stylish wedding gown. An altered seam here, a pressed hem there, and a lovely head-dress of fabric flowers. The effect was topped off to perfection by a dainty parasol. Anne is like a fairy godmother to African brides. Over the years she has persuaded more than a score of Elim women in Europe to turn out from storage their precious white dresses, lying unused, and donate them to mission stations. Evelyn was marrying Pious Munembe and, as with most converts, wanted a white wedding 'like the English Christian girls'. Her chief bridesmaid looked lovely in a long dress loaned by myself.

That was my first experience of an African wedding and it was a day to remember. After a moving service, the reception was held outside the church. There was much singing and dancing in the hot sunshine. The guests sat at long tables and enjoyed a cooked meal of chicken served in a tasty gravy with the staple grain *sadza*—a versatile maize, on this occasion made into a kind of porridge. I was amazed that there was enough food to go round as it is not customary to send out official invitations for such events; the cooks just have to guess at how many to cater for. Every guest gave a present and the master of ceremonies shouted out what it was. This was followed in each case by applause and cheering, with traditional '*Rrululul!*' shrieking sounds, made by rolling the tongue. The whole process took several hours. Finally a family Bible was presented by Mai Satuku, in a flourish of low bowing movements.

Immediately after her wedding Evelyn became Mai Munembe. *Mai* is a respectful title for older women, who are generally always either married or widowed. The nearest word in English is 'Mrs'. Spinsters like myself, who are old enough to be married but aren't, pose a problem. There is no word in Shona to describe us. By default I have been addressed as *Mai* on many occasions.

I began to think about the new nurse coming out from England, Wendy White. Older than me, she would probably be called *Mai* as well, though she was single. I was looking forward to having an extra member of staff. But Wendy was newly qualified, a university graduate and social worker who had decided to switch careers in mid-life. There would be a lot for her to learn about coping with limited resources and facilities. Would she be capable, and willing, to take orders from me, a younger woman? I dearly hoped so.

A crowd of memories and expectations raced through my mind during the short walk to Phil and Sue's place. I was resident there at nights with Joan Caudell. It was surprising to see Sue outside the house with a bundle of something in her arms. I quickened my pace as it had started to rain. Sue was carrying a load of firewood, and I helped her inside with it. She explained how, like the McCanns', her hired help had also gone missing.

'I do hope those two haven't got themselves into any trouble,' she fretted. I watched as she shook her long brown hair loose from a pony tail. It was quite wet from the rain. Then she busied herself around the kitchen, sorting a pile of Becky's clothes for mending.

'You look really at home here, Sue,' I said, remembering how she had suffered from culture shock after arriving in Katerere.

'Oh, I am. Phil has always fitted in, but it took me a few months to carve out my own little niche. Now we're both sure this is the right place to be. We'll sit tight and ride out the storm, however rough it gets.' She referred simultaneously to the war and the downpour happening outside. The seasonal rains had come.

Three disturbing incidents shook morale at the Mission over the next few weeks. Everyone's faith and staying power were tested. In the south of Rhodesia an armed African in military uniform robbed a Catholic bishop and nun before shooting them dead. A second nun, who was able to hide, escaped detection and gave the authorities a description of the roadside attack and the attacker. In another part of the country a Catholic priest left his house to lead a service, but never arrived at the church. A search revealed no body or clues as to his whereabouts. Then, at a place called Musami, in the direction of Salisbury, seven Catholic mission workers were murdered.

It was with great trepidation that, a few days after this last event, Peter and Brenda Griffiths met Wendy White at Salisbury Airport. They felt duty bound to brief her on the latest developments in the war, giving her the option to back out at the last minute.

'The situation has become much more dangerous,' cautioned Peter. 'For the first time expatriates have been killed. We'll understand if you want to change your mind and return to England.'

The slim, elegant woman listened to what he had to say. Smiling graciously, head tilted to one side, she replied, 'It would take more than that to keep me from the Lord's work.'

Members of the Mission team were not prone to gossiping about one another, but everyone agreed that having Wendy

49

around was like working with royalty. She was an exceptionally devout Christian, while at the same time being a lady from the upper classes: well-bred, well-spoken and schooled in social etiquette (an unusual and rather intimidating combination). She came with excellent references and was a good nurse, but had the annoying habit of always being right.

Shortly after Wendy's arrival I took her off compound to a baby clinic. Heavy rains had reduced the bush roads to rutted tracks of squelching mud, several inches deep. It was hard to drive the Rhino in such conditions. Even on dry roads strength and skill were needed for this vehicle, as the metal reinforcements had raised the height of the steering wheel. One almost had to stand upright to reach it. Consequently, I asked a male handyman—one of Roy Lynn's African assistants—to drive us to Chiwarira that day.

On the way back it began to rain heavily. When we reached a river bed that was normally dry, it had become a mighty rushing torrent. The driver stopped before attempting to go further. Should we wait for the flood to subside, or try to drive through it? Not wanting to be the one to make the decision, I left it to him. 'We'll go on,' he said, biting his bottom lip and looking rather worried.

Halfway through, the engine spluttered and stalled. We were stranded in the middle, and could feel the force of the brown flow buffeting the Rhino. The armour plating was watertight, but we began to move downstream.

'Help us, God!' I cried.

'We should praise the Lord,' declared Wendy.

I thought, *That sounds very good and spiritual, but what can we be happy about at a time like this?*

As if reading my mind, she said, 'Believe he is going to save us, and thank him in advance. Remember, "Faith is the substance of things hoped for, the evidence of things not seen" ' (Hebrews 11:1, KJV).

We praised the Lord in English and in tongues for what seemed like a very long time. Mostly I didn't know what I was saying, but my heart was telling God that I didn't want to die yet. Nor did I appreciate his sense of humour in sticking me in a makeshift boat with Mary Poppins.

The water level appeared to be dropping. Trapped by mud, the Rhino halted. The driver rolled up his trouser legs, climbed out and waded to the bank. He reached it safely and waved to us before running off to fetch help. We were quite close to the Mission, so it wasn't long before he came back in a truck with Roy. They towed us out of the river and home to Katerere. Still the Rhino refused to start. Roy had to strip the engine right down in his workshop, to clear out the debris, before it could be used again. He was not amused.

I regularly wrote letters to my parents containing news of my experiences. They read the dramatic details of this account to my paternal grandparents and the facts were changed down the line. The next thing I heard was, 'Joy was sailing down the river and came face to face with an angry four-legged Rhino!'

In the meantime Peter Griffiths was in hot water with the security forces. Despite the numerous military skirmishes around the Mission, we believed we could continue our work through a policy of neutrality. The previous year we had had no choice but to hand over medicines when the freedom fighters visited. Since then, Peter had been contacted by guerrillas and had not informed the authorities. As a result he was arrested and found himself in court. His defence was as follows:

'News went along the grapevine that we were using vehicles which were reinforced against landmines. One of our ministers received a message, saying some guerrillas wanted to talk with me, and that I should preach at Kambudzi Church the following Sunday and await further instructions there. I was also told to take a collection among the teachers and bring the proceeds with me, to show good faith towards the rebels' cause. I took the service and afterwards shook hands with people at the door, as is our custom. Nothing unusual happened. I was just about to leave when Pious Munembe—the pastor, and headmaster of the local primary school—said there was a teenager waiting for me in the vestry. The young man had a note from "the comrades", telling me that he would guide me to them. When Pious heard this, he offered to go too.'

'The three of us travelled in the cab of my truck for a couple of kilometres, until the lad said it was time to stop. We went on foot into the hills. Arriving at a clearing at the top of a slope we saw two sentries with automatic weapons. Then we came across a platoon of about a dozen armed combatants. I shook hands with them, greeted them in Shona, and went to sit down on the ground. Their leader told me to sit on a blanket, which I saw as an encouraging gesture.

'We were questioned for about an hour, mainly about why we had reinforced our vehicles. They saw this as a sign that we did not trust them to warn us if and when they planted landmines. I said that without a doctor it was sometimes necessary to rush patients off to Inyanga in the middle of the night, when there was no time to wait for warnings. They accepted this explanation.

'I suggested that if we stayed there much longer the security forces might spot my truck at the side of the road, and investigate. The platoon commander asked if I had brought the money from my teachers. I said that if I had asked for money, they would have become upset and might leave the school. Then it would have to close. However, I had brought $100, which came from the school funds. But this left me with a problem. How would I account for the missing money? As a Christian I could not lie, and neither could I enter into my financial statement, "Gift to the comrades."'

'Pious seemed to get a little nervous at this point, exclaiming, "Give them $50!" One of the combatants, who had been sitting on a tripod-mounted machine gun, came to the rescue by saying, "If he can't fiddle the books for $100, he can't do it for $50 either!" The commander seemed to understand, and we were allowed to leave without making a contribution.'

Pious backed up Peter's account, but the prosecution still wanted to know why the meeting had not been reported. Peter admitted he was guilty in this respect, but replied, 'Because I feared retribution on myself, Pious and the teachers. If that happened the school would be finished.' The court was lenient and Peter was freed. This time.

No one wanted to close the school or hospital. Both were providing vital services to the community. Yet we worried about what the authorities would do if the guerrillas made contact again. Then came a devastating blow which caused an urgent reappraisal of our whole position. The five-ton lorry, which was a lifeline for Mission supplies, hit a landmine on the way to Salisbury. Although heavily reinforced it was a complete write-off. The driver injured his back, and the man next to him—who was not wearing a seat

53

belt—plunged through the windscreen and was killed. Another passenger lost a leg. Suddenly the reality of living in a war zone came too close for comfort. The vehicle was needed daily for bringing 1,000 meals to the school. The hospital sometimes used it for transporting large quantities of medicines and equipment. A replacement would be costly, and what if that were blown up too, with further loss of life?

Peter Griffiths was head of the Mission team, but the most senior Elim official in the country was Ronald Chapman, at Umtali. He attended a conference in Katerere with all of us, to discuss the future. Most were totally unprepared for what he had to say.

'Eagle Preparatory School is on the market for rental. It's in an area where there's been virtually no terrorist activity—the Vumba district—only a twenty-minute journey from Umtali. As Field Director for this part of Africa, I propose the secondary school moves there from next term.'

'That's a radical suggestion,' voiced Catherine Picken. 'What about the rest of the pupils?'

'The primary school mainly consists of day children and local teachers. It can remain where it is—there's no sense in uprooting people unnecessarily.'

'Brenda and I have been here about fourteen years, and are soon to go on furlough,' said Peter. 'I think this is the time for Phil to take over as Principal of the secondary school.' Phil looked at once pleased, unworthy and embarrassed. He began fiddling nervously with his spectacles.

'And the hospital?' I shrieked, the high tone of my voice reflecting the anxiety I now felt.

'It can become more of a clinic, run by less experienced nurses who live around Katerere. I understand Evelyn Munembe has sufficient qualifications to take overall responsibility?' Mr Chapman's eyes were staring into mine, demanding an answer. When I didn't give one, he continued, 'It may be the time, and God's will, for expatriates to step back and relinquish some of the work to capable, indigenous leadership. Not only at the hospital, but in the churches too.' He looked around at the collection of glum faces.

I found my voice. 'Yes, Evelyn would be an excellent choice. Wendy and I could …?'

'No definite decisions can be made today. Approval will have to be given by Elim Headquarters at Cheltenham. However, the secondary school will need a nurse cum matron.'

'And a caretaker.' Roy Lynn entered the conversation. 'Joyce and I will be married by then. She could look after any sick pupils.'

Joan Caudell was also going on furlough. For her the choice was simple: she wouldn't be returning in the autumn. It was mooted that Wendy should fill the gap. She seemed very distressed at this idea, saying that while her degree qualified her to teach, God had called her to medical service. 'I'll have to think and pray about all this,' she scowled.

'And what about me?' I asked, almost in tears. Again Mr Chapman looked me full in the face. It felt as if everyone was staring at me, waiting for him to speak.

'You've been here almost exactly three years. Perhaps it's time to look for another position.'

5

Over the following weeks Wendy and I had a lot of heart-searching to do. The unexpected blow we had both received formed a common bond between us. Secretly we prayed that the proposed changes would be blocked by Elim Headquarters, and for a while it seemed as if the favour would be granted. Before his wedding to Joyce in Yorkshire, Roy Lynn represented Katerere Mission at an Elim Council Meeting. The members were unwilling to sanction the splitting off of the school from the hospital. However, it was agreed that their representative, John Smyth, would travel to Rhodesia to assess the situation.

By the time he arrived Wendy had made her peace with God. 'If the decision is made to move to the Vumba, I will take it as the Lord's will for me to go there. After all, I am qualified to teach English and History,' she told me.

'At least you've had some choice as regards your future,' I replied bitterly. Wendy shot me a reproving glance. Still feeling hurt and angry, I could reach no such plateau of acceptance that my first overseas assignment was coming to an end.

When John Smyth saw how things were, he began to realise it was in Elim's best interests for the school to be sited elsewhere. Individually we were all given a chance to say what we felt, before coming together to hear the verdict. The earlier recommendations were confirmed. I had no option but to obey orders and start packing for home. I was heartbroken.

Before the August holidays a second-hand lorry was obtained to ferry load after load of furniture and non-essential goods to Eagle School. On about the sixth trip it hit a landmine. Thankfully, no one was hurt. The engine was destroyed and the cab windows were blown out, but the rest of the vehicle and its contents remained intact. A breakdown truck arrived, complete with military escort, to tow the lorry to Umtali. Unfortunately the driver was none too careful on the dirt roads. Probably driving too quickly in order to get out of the danger zone, he rolled our lorry and did what the landmine had failed to do, completely destroying it and the load.

At the end of term, three buses came to take the boarders to Umtali. From there they would travel back to their homes. About fifty miles down the road the first bus hit a landmine. Two students, Leonard and Daniel, were killed. A third boy, Jotham, lost a leg. Terrified, the remaining youngsters clambered onto the other buses. The second one arrived safely, but the third bus hit another mine and caught fire. Everyone was able to escape through the windows, which had blown out in the explosion. The driver was the only fatality. For the final clearance of essential equipment and personnel the services of a furniture removal firm were hired, protected by a heavy military escort.

A few days later Mary Fisher and I started a memorable holiday in Durban, South Africa. We seldom saw the sea as Rhodesia was land-locked, and we really appreciated a fortnight spent largely on the beach. While we were relaxing in the sun, our peace was shattered by the tragic news of a huge bomb exploding in Woolworths in Salisbury. Eleven people were killed. How long could this carnage go on, we wondered?

Mary was apprehensive and nervous about teaching in the new location. Her large eyes opened even wider in anticipation, as she described the whereabouts of Eagle School.

'It's very close to the Mozambique border. A beautiful setting, high up in the mountains, where the climate is cool and damp—*Vumba* means misty. The tourist guide books liken the area to England's Lake District.'

'Better take your wellies, then,' I advised. Having Mary around was good therapy. Her incessant chatter helped me to come to terms with the fact that I was leaving. And she was such an innocent it was impossible to hate her for having a job I couldn't do for lack of the right qualifications.

To have another string to my bow would prevent me from being in this kind of difficult situation again, I considered. After completing my midwifery course I had toyed with the idea of going to Elim Bible College. Now the opportunity presented itself again. I took this as the way forward and, back at the Mission, enrolled by post for two years of theological study.

Then it was time to say *chisarai zvakanaka*—goodbye—to Rhodesia. I arrived home on 25th August 1977, to be met by a crowd of family and friends. Three years had passed since I'd seen most of them, and everyone was talking at once, trying to tell me something different. A niece had been born to me via Pearl, and here she was, Charlotte, already walking and attempting to join in the conversation. Travelling back to Wiltshire in the church minibus, I did my best to catch the excitement of the moment, but I had a throbbing pain in my head, and ached all over.

Mum had prepared a huge spread for the whole family. I just wanted to have something to quench my thirst, and then go to sleep. The following day I felt worse and had a high temperature. The doctor was called, and he prescribed antibiotics. It was thought I might have flu. Somehow I managed to get to the hairdresser's, and then went on to a big homecoming celebration at church. Attendance was mandatory as the Mayor and Mayoress of Salisbury were guests of honour. Afterwards I collapsed into bed and stayed there. Four days later jaundice started to make itself evident. The doctor came again and hepatitis A was diagnosed. It took a number of weeks to recover, which made me late starting at Elim Bible College.

The two years spent in residence there in rural Surrey were of tremendous benefit in many ways. My relationship with God took on a new dimension. At that time the college was housed in an old mansion at Capel, set within large grounds. There were plenty of places and opportunities for private reading and contemplation. Good thing too, as I had to share a room with three and sometimes four other students.

Settling down to full-time studies was not easy. I found it difficult to concentrate, and the long hours spent poring over books resulted in eye strain. In addition, there were practical jobs for students to do. At first I was on the cleaning rota, which meant one work period before breakfast and a longer session each afternoon, vacuuming long corridors. I hadn't regained my strength from the hepatitis and by the end of each day was completely exhausted. Later I was given lighter duties serving in the dining room, for which I was grateful.

Fellow students didn't quite know how to treat a real live missionary. Some tried to put me on a pedestal, or treat me like a china doll. Determined to show I was normal, I went out of my way to be involved in as many pranks as possible. Water fights and dunking people in baths of cold water soon showed them my true colours.

I was surprised to find little zeal for overseas mission among the theological students. A conversation with one young man left me particularly disturbed. His main objection was that in the middle of the jungle there would be nowhere for him to go for dental treatment if he developed toothache. This seemed a worrying lack of faith and common sense in someone training to be a pastor!

There were a number of foreign students at Elim Bible College then, including a white South African, and black Africans from Kenya and Guinea Bissau. During the holidays it was possible to take one or two to my home. It was fun for them to meet the family and learn Wiltshire English. When winter came they were fascinated by snow—something they had not seen before. One even went outside to roll in it.

As the temperature dropped and strong winds blew around Capel, I reluctantly put away my cotton dresses and brought out thick wollens which hadn't seen the light of day for four years. Still it seemed unbearably cold. Then someone had the bright idea of placing polythene sheets over the windows—a primitive form of double glazing which effectively cut out some of the draughts.

Peter and Brenda Griffiths returned to England shortly after me. It was to be a period of study leave, so that Peter could complete a post-graduate degree. The three of us met at Heathrow to see the Lynns off. Joyce's parents were also at the airport to say farewell. They were concerned for the well-being of their daughter and new son-in-law, even though Eagle School was thought to be in a quiet area, safe from Rhodesia's warring factions. Roy's expertise was badly needed for maintenance work. Joyce would conduct clinics locally when her medical knowledge was not required by staff and pupils.

A selfish little voice inside me was saying that I should be on the plane too. I tried to ignore it. The pair looked so happy and right together. Something Joyce said gave me a hint that she might be pregnant. It was odd that they went through the departure barrier without looking back for a final wave or glance. Peter noticed this too and remarked on it.

I didn't see him or Brenda again until Saturday 24th June 1978. A Midsummer Day etched in my memory for all time. But I was aware that Peter had been sent back to Rhodesia in the spring for a few days, as there were fears of unrest in the Vumba district. On his return, he told me by letter that everyone was happy and wanted to stay at the new site, where they were at least safe from the threat of landmines.

He wrote: 'We came to the firm conclusion that as the school and the young lives in it were important for the future of the country, the work must continue.' Roy—who had experience of living in the strife-torn areas of Northern Ireland—was adamant that 'mission workers just can't keep running away'.

However, the murder of two Salvation Army teachers working in the country, plus a series of anonymous threatening notes sent to our personnel, persuaded Headquarters at Cheltenham to instigate further changes. Elim International Missions Director Leslie Wigglesworth instructed Ronald Chapman to ensure that non-African staff left the school after lessons each day. Accommodation was to be found within the urban safety of Umtali.

The last Saturday in June was Elim Bible College Open Day and Graduation Day for final year students. Peter was to give the address, and planned to speak on the true story of a group of missionaries in Ecuador who were murdered by Auca Indians. Late morning I was busy with last-minute cleaning jobs. A voice came over the tannoy, 'Will Joy Bath please report to the Principal's office.'

I had no idea why I was being summoned, but hurried along there. When I entered, the room seemed full of members of staff and foreign students. The atmosphere was tense and people were looking around nervously. One or two were crying. Wesley Gilpin, the Principal, welcomed me with a nod of his head. Then he began to speak.

'I have to tell you all that a dreadful massacre took place last night in Rhodesia, in a remote region near the Mozambique border. I don't have all the details yet, but it is suspected that the victims were our mission workers.'

My initial reaction was one of peace. It couldn't possibly be my former colleagues, because they had gone to live in Umtali, only commuting to Eagle School during the day. But over the next few hours, as information filtered in from Ronald Chapman and various news networks, it became clear that it was our people. Their belongings had been packed into cases, and the workers were scheduled to move into new homes the following morning. Instead, as dawn broke, their dead bodies were being discovered on a grassy bank near the sports field. The attack was so violent that some were almost unrecognisable.

By the cricket scoreboard lay a mature woman with dishevelled clothing, including a yellow cardigan. In one hand was clutched a matching scarf, which she had intended to put over her greying hair to conceal the fact that she was wearing curlers. A long-handled axe was embedded in the back of her head. Catherine Agnes Picken: an overseas veteran with eighteen years of fine service to her credit. She first worked in the Belgian Congo in the 1950s, but left there because of ethnic troubles.

A young man wearing a trendy purple sweater and trousers was found with his hands tied behind his back. His face had been split open. Philip George Edward Evans: BSc, Phd. Two weeks earlier a premonition had prompted him to send an album of precious family photos to his mother for safekeeping.

The face of another man had been bludgeoned by a piece of wood. But his beard was still visible. Peter McCann: BSc and former student of Elim Bible College.

Spread-eagled on the ground was a woman in a blue top and slippers, her left arm stretched out towards a tiny baby. Eileen Joyce Lynn: SRN, midwife and newly delivered of her own child, Pamela Grace. How often I had watched and learned from our resourceful Matron, a cheeky lock of dark curls poking around the side of her cap as she worked. Her hair was now matted with blood, and beside her the daughter born just three weeks ago had been bayoneted to death.

A few yards away a man in a checked shirt was found, horribly mutilated. Robert (Roy) John Lynn: an Elim Bible College graduate. His eyes had apparently been gouged out, and his body was riddled with knife marks. The man who had refused to run away from trouble had been stabbed in the back at least fifteen times.

Then there was a group of two women and three small children: Susanne Eugena Mary Evans with Rebecca, who was four-and-a-half years of age; and Sandra McCann with her son

Philip, aged five, and daughter Sharon Joy, four years old. All had been beaten about the head viciously. One of the youngsters had the imprint of a boot on her face. The mothers also had bayonet wounds around the neck, and were naked from the waist down.

Under a tree in a nearby copse a young woman in a denim dress, with long dark hair, was huddled in a foetal position. Elisabeth Wendy Hamilton White: SRN, BA, Dip Soc Stud; daughter of a supermarket magnate and granddaughter of the man who pioneered the Mersey Tunnel. Her murder was possibly the most gruesome. She was severely beaten, and bayoneted in the head, neck, chest and groin. That would probably be because she angered her captors by telling them about Jesus. Eloquent Wendy would not have gone down without a verbal fight.

There was one piece of good news. Mary Fisher: triple graduate of Swansea, Brunel and London Bible College, was still alive! A trail of blood led the security forces to a patch of long grass, where she had run to hide. Unconscious and hypothermic, she was rushed to hospital in the capital and placed in intensive care.

Twelve martyrs, and one brave soul fighting for her life. What kind of mindless beings could have sent my guileless friends into eternity so brutally? Whose politics could demand the savage crushing of young skulls, the raping of women and little girls? And why did no one come to their rescue? For some time I was too shocked to cry—my emotions were kept at bay by a questioning mind. I needed to know more.

It transpired that a large group of guerrillas had attacked the school after supper on the Friday night. Some gave the pupils a talking to in the dormitories, while others herded the British teachers out of their houses at gunpoint, to a quiet spot. The noise of the killings, away from the buildings, failed to reach the ears of a South African teacher, Ian McGarrick, who was in his room marking examination papers. It was he who made the grim discovery of the corpses early on that Saturday morning.

By early afternoon my mother arrived at Capel. Though deeply distressed, she kept saying, 'Thank God you weren't there! You're safe!' This finally brought out my grief. The two of us collapsed into a heap and cried for several hours.

The formalities of the day went ahead, but even now I wonder how Peter managed to stand up and speak. The main theme of his talk remained the same: believing in Christ is no insurance policy against death through missionary activities. Only the names of those who died were changed. Instead of mentioning Americans, his words were of our own dear folk.

Many memorial services were held over ensuing weeks. And one verse from the Bible was repeated again and again: 'Except a corn of wheat fall into the ground and die, it abideth alone: but if it die it bringeth forth much fruit' (John 12:24, KJV).

Suddenly, the Elim Pentecostal Movement was at the centre of world events. British and foreign governments, Ian Smith, and leaders of other churches, were all discussing the massacre, adding to the already substantial amount of media coverage. The publicity resulted in many hundreds of volunteers coming forward for overseas service. If interest in missions was lax during my first year at Elim Bible College, the situation was totally reversed after the events of 23rd June 1978.

Tragically, Mary Fisher never regained consciousness and died in hospital. This brought the total number of martyrs to thirteen. People began to remark on how my life had been spared. Was it for some special purpose? I didn't think too much about it then. I never thought my lot would be to go through a different kind of martyrdom. My thoughts and heart were directed towards the families and relatives of those who died. In particular Timothy and Rachel Evans, who woke up one morning at boarding school to find they were orphans. I was only made redundant from my job. They had suffered a much greater loss.

What next? Towards the end of year two at Elim Bible College I was interviewed about my future plans. The Missions Board would not consider a return to Rhodesia. The situation was still dangerous. But there was an opening at a small clinic in India, with scope for gospel ministry. It was mine if I wanted it, but I wasn't sure. My feathers were still ruffled from the pain of being told to leave Katerere. And the loss of my friends weighed heavily on my heart. I thought and prayed about the offer for some weeks, before finally deciding to accept it.

On 11th July 1979 I found myself at Delhi Airport, being met by the small, motherly figure of Olive Jarvis. There were people everywhere, making a lot of noise as they went about their business. I could hardly hear what she was saying for the constant hubbub of excited voices—absolute bedlam. An overnight stop in a hotel provided some peace and quiet. Then it was back into the crowds again and on to the railway station for a 600-mile train journey to the state of Bihar.

Our compartment was full to overflowing, with bodies pressed together on all sides. Some alighted at each stop, but they were replaced by more people getting on the train. It was extremely humid. Such air as there was contained pungent smells. Though I had done my research and knew the population of India totalled over 700 million, the reality of being confronted with a large, jostling portion of humanity was claustrophobic.

It was impossible to avoid making comparisons. Africa is a continent of contrasts—luscious foliage or sun-bleached grasses; modern cities versus wide open spaces. Tribesfolk are distinguished by different physical characteristics and forms of dress. To my untrained eyes everything in India just seemed brown. From the houses to the burnt sienna dust of the roads and railway tracks. The people were mostly the same colour brown and as the majority were poor, so were their once bright clothes: browned with age and accumulated dirt.

Olive watched my reactions with a bemused expression on her face.

'This is the main train route to Calcutta, so it's particularly busy. Bihar is one of the most densely populated places in the world, and one of the poorest areas of India. I've been out here for twenty years and have grown used to the way of life.' There was a pause as the train halted. Vendors with grubby fingers pushed baskets and trays of refreshments through the open windows.

'Be careful what you eat and drink,' she advised. 'You could easily pick up a tummy bug. Even the bottles of water with screw tops probably aren't safe—they tend to fill them in the river.'

I wasn't tempted. Both food and liquid were brown too.

We were based at Dehri on Sone. A tiny, typically Indian town, without street lights or pavements. A high wall surrounded the only church and we went through large iron gates round the side to our single-storey house. It was divided into two: one part belonged to the Indian pastor, the remainder was shared by myself, Olive and a third worker, Sylvia Beardwell.

The house had few amenities. Electricity was fitful and often went off, or was too weak to be of any use. We frequently resorted to candles or paraffin lamps. Running water was only available at certain times of the day, otherwise it meant a trip to a hand pump in the yard. Even when the water came on it was always cold—there was no hot.

We did have a nice walled garden, full of flowers. From it went a raised pathway through paddy fields to the dispensary, our place of work. This was also surrounded by a high wall. The place was primitive. Just one room divided into two was used for consulting and giving out medicines. Opposite was a shelter where women and children waited to be seen.

For cultural reasons it was not possible to see men. And we could only treat minor ailments as there was no doctor or equipment for anything else. Coughs, sores, impetigo, scabies, ringworm, diarrhoea and ear discharges were common. The patients were very poor, in various states of distress and illiterate. We had to find a way of keeping them in line or the last would push to the front and an uproar would result. A system was devised so the first ten who arrived were given blue cards, the next red and so on, to ensure they waited in order.

Usually the clinic was finished by midday. In the afternoons it was necessary to rest, due to the heat. But in the evenings we sometimes went out on visits, or else I would keep busy with language study. What a triumph it was to master the alphabet! Without it I couldn't even board a bus unless I asked someone for its destination—and most people didn't speak English.

The first hymn I learned in Hindi was 'How great thou art'. It was very popular at that time, and sung at most meetings.

Sylvia was younger than Olive, but both ladies were quite a bit older than I was. In Rhodesia the expatriates formed a closely knit community and I enjoyed friendships with a variety of age groups. Here there were just the three of us foreigners, apart from a Scots lady who also resided in the town. Living so closely together, personality clashes and differences of opinion due to the generation gap would erupt now and then. I realised it was important to put things right as early as possible, before they were blown out of all proportion.

Olive was very kind and patient in helping me to adjust to my new environment. Diminutive but businesslike, Sylvia undertook to educate me in cultural matters. I believe this exercised her mind as well as my own.

'The reason we see so many ear patients is close breeding,' she told me one day. 'There is a social structure of castes. The main ones are *Brahmin*—the priests and their families, *Kshatriya*—warriors, and *Vaisya*—merchants. The three are not supposed to mix. Officially, discrimination is banned in this country, but it's part of Hinduism to stay within one's caste, and as most Indians follow that religion, marriages happen within family groups.'

'Aren't some people outside the castes, for example the Christians?'

'Yes. The tribal people tend to be Christian or Muslim. The *Harijan*—the untouchables—are technically the lowest caste, but many have become Buddhists. Sikhs have their own ways and customs, and would like to have their own independent state. They form a very small part of the whole population and are mainly found in the Punjab, to the north west, on the other side of Delhi.'

I found all the Indians intelligent and hard working; even those begging on the streets. But there was a gap in their mentality when it came to crossing social barriers. Not long after that lesson from Sylvia, I saw the dead body of a man lying in the middle of a Dehri on Sone street. It remained there for several days and was decaying by the time a member of the same caste came to take it away.

Some people might liken this situation to the story of the Good Samaritan. It reminded me of one of the opening scenes of a film, *The Magnificent Seven*. An outcast had died, and someone provided a coffin, but the undertaker and his men were too scared to take the body away for burial. They feared they would be shot by racially prejudiced townsfolk. Enter the Christlike hero Chris (played by Yul Brynner) and another brave soul called Vin (Steve McQueen). They drove the hearse, dodging bullets and shooting back at their attackers, until they reached the cemetery gates. A stirring moment in the history of moving pictures.

On another occasion I saw a man severely beaten by way of religious persecution. It stands out in my memory, happening in a land where all beliefs were supposed to be tolerated. However, at Christmas a subtle form of intolerance was shown towards Christians. Buying cards with a nice message was not easy, as most didn't mention the actual festival. Probably the makers were trying to avoid using the Lord's name. 'Season's Greetings' was the norm.

Carol-singing was popular with young church members. A group would set off after dark, cycling around the town and stopping at Christian homes. After singing they would be given food like sweet meats or *samosas*—triangular pastries filled with good things—before moving on. There was much merriment, and the visits went on late into the night. Christmas Day was a public holiday, but as most shopkeepers and market stall holders were Hindus or Muslims, it meant business as usual for them.

The climate was very unkind in Bihar. Summers were too hot and dry; the monsoon season was too hot and wet. With the rain came clouds of mosquitoes. My legs were always covered with bites. Winter was a welcome respite. The only complaint was that it didn't last long enough—only for about four months and then it was back to the burning heat again.

It was a relief to spend our holidays at a hill station. There we had the company of other mission workers, and I spent a few hours each day at a nearby language school. The station was really a spartan cottage, with limited bathing and toilet facilities. We stayed there for about six weeks each summer to avoid the worst of the heat. In the hills the temperature stayed a little cooler, but not much.

To reach the station took a whole day. It involved a train journey, followed by a hair-raising ascent up a zigzag road in a taxi with bald tyres. I closed my eyes so as not to see the sheer drop either side of the steep track. Vehicles could only travel so far, and the last part of the climb had to be made on foot, carrying luggage and all. Once we arrived, it was necessary to fumigate the premises; rats having been the only occupants since our last visit.

Becoming more proficient in Hindi meant I could take on a Sunday school class at Dehri Christian Church. It was fun and when words failed me, actions and visual aids were used to get the message across. Compared to English children they were extremely well behaved.

I also began venturing out to see needy families on my own. A Muslim man was employed to look after the garden and drive our rickshaw—a three-wheeled bicycle with a seat at the back for passengers, and a hood to keep off the sun or rain. Once, on the way to a village, he turned off the main highway onto a side road, pedalling fast.

'Help!' I cried, as I fell out and landed on my head in a ditch. Hearing footsteps, I expected the rickshaw *wallah* to come and pull me out. But he just paced up and down the road until I hauled myself up. It was a long wait, as I suffered slight concussion and felt very dizzy.

'Why didn't you give me a hand?' I demanded angrily.

'It is not the custom for a man to touch a woman,' was the reply. Then he admitted sheepishly, 'But I have done another kind of wrong. I knew there was a problem with one of the wheels before leaving Dehri.'

When we arrived at our destination some villagers kindly made me a cup of tea as I was still giddy. And I was supposed to be ministering to them!

The visit of a delegation from Elim Headquarters caused a lot of excitement. John Smyth and David Butcher flew in from Delhi to a domestic airport. Olive and I went to meet them in a jeep with a hired driver. At some point on the way there the horn failed, so on the way back we stopped at a garage to get it fixed. While no one seemed to check on tyre conditions, it was illegal to drive without a horn. In India you need the horn all the time. We were certainly glad to have it working later on in the journey.

Ambling in the middle of the road was a herd of elephants. Not wild ones, but transport animals for wealthy people.

The passengers were sitting on top. A keen amateur photographer, David Butcher gleefully reached for his camera to catch the unusual sight on film.

'We pose for you,' volunteered the elephant handler in Hindi. He seemed an obliging sort and the passengers were good natured, so John Smyth and I also took some snaps.

'You're very kind. Thank you. Enjoy the rest of the trip,' I said as we prepared to leave. At this, the handler began to get agitated. Arms waving in the air, he ordered the elephants to kneel down, completely blocking the road.

'I don't think they'll move unless you pay him!' laughed Olive.

She was right. We tried blaring the horn for some time. The noise attracted quite a crowd, but the elephants stayed put. We had to give in and pay up before we were allowed through.

The presence of the two visiting pastors meant evangelistic meetings could be held in Dehri on Sone. The Indian minister didn't do much in that line, and as the culture held no great respect for women, Olive, Sylvia and I were restricted in what we were allowed to do.

'We three are absolutely powerless!' moaned Sylvia during a private meeting with John Smyth and David Butcher.

'We're certainly not using the full range of medical and theological training we possess,' I chipped in.

'All we can do is pray,' said Olive.

The pastors agreed and we took time to bring the matter before the Lord in prayer.

Unbeknown to us, God was calling a man from South India— Augustine Jebakumar—to begin a major work in the North. The first we knew of it was when he arrived at Dehri on Sone

74

with a small group of workers, including two young women. They said they were called the Gospel Echoing Missionary Society, GEMS for short, and began working within Dehri Christian Church.

Talented and enthusiastic, they were like a breath of fresh air through the district. Unfortunately, the staid members of Dehri Christian Church felt rather intimidated by their presence. In addition, jealousy developed over funding obtained from overseas for evangelistic campaigns.

God does not only use Christians in the furtherance of his work. A *Brahmin* lady was so impressed by the GEMS that she gave them five acres of land as a gift. It was in a country area, with plenty of room for expansion. The team moved out of town and set up on their own. One of their young women left to be married and I made a real and lasting friendship with the remaining girl, Jeya. We became like sisters. It was great to have someone of my own age to relate to.

After being unwell for some time, Sylvia was sadly diagnosed as having cancer of the bladder. She was flown home to England as treatment in India was difficult to obtain. I was working more and more with the GEMS team and feeling that was where the main thrust of my work should be. It made sense for Olive and me to close the dispensary and join the GEMS at their base. They had started an orphanage, and were about to open a school.

A number of business people had approached the GEMS requesting that a mission school be set up. Standards in government and private schools were poor and it was generally accepted that mission schools provided a high standard of education. Augustine asked if Olive and I would be willing to teach. As nurses we had no experience or qualifications to be school teachers, but no one seemed to mind. I became a teacher of English and Environmental Science, learning how to teach from books. The children were lovely and well disciplined. I felt fulfilled and really enjoyed the experience.

Two pieces of advice I still remember from those days are: real teaching is guidance—helping a pupil to find the answer themselves; and if a lesson hasn't gripped the teacher, it won't interest the child!

Once again, political events had a hand in changing the course of my life. In 1984 India's Prime Minister, Mrs Indira Gandhi, was assassinated by Sikh extremist members of her bodyguard. All foreigners without visas were ordered to leave. That included me. It was a hurried departure, but I believed that obtaining a visa was just a formality.

'I'll soon be back,' I told Jeya confidently.

'I'm not so sure, my friend,' she replied. 'Getting official papers sorted out can be a slow process at the best of times. Now the country is in mourning ...'

Indians can be highly emotional people at times. I decided this was one of those times for Jeya, and chose to ignore her forebodings.

Once home I made an application to the High Commissioner of India in London, requesting a long-term visa. It was refused. I appealed against the decision, backing up my case with letters of recommendation from influential people in India. I never received a reply.

As time went on it became apparent that I was not going to be able to get back. I took a Teaching English as a Foreign Language course in London, and then a short course on tropical diseases in Liverpool. After this, as I'd been out of full-time nursing for ages, I joined a nursing agency in Salisbury, Wiltshire and for a year eased myself back into my favourite profession.

'I don't know where I'm heading, but I don't think I'll ever be returning to Africa,' I told a friend. The reply was, 'It's best to pencil in your plans for the future. Then you can always rub them out if God has other ideas.'

With the spring of 1987 came an unexpected summons to Elim Headquarters at Cheltenham. Brian Edwards had become Director of International Missions and was eager to meet with me. I had assumed he had in mind a general chat about my situation, but it wasn't long before the conversation with this tanned, rather suave man began to centre on Katerere.

'A lot has happened in nine years, Joy. Life in independent Zimbabwe, as the country's now called, is very different.' I nodded in agreement. He went on, 'Under a new government the health service has developed, and that is good. In practice it means more primary healthcare, ante-natal clinics and infant vaccinations. There's also an emphasis on family planning, and attempts are being made to curb the spread of AIDS.'

Leaning forward in an animated manner, he started tapping one end of a ball point pen on the desk. 'Staff at the Elim Hospital are run off their feet serving a population of about 60,000. Apart from the national workers there are currently three Brits there—a doctor and two nurses. A third nursing post has just been made available via the authorities. Can I put your name forward?'

Of course I said, 'Yes!' It was more than I could ever have hoped for.

After all the formalities were completed I flew out to South Africa in July, to be met by Peter and Brenda Griffiths and their two sons. From there we travelled to Zimbabwe, with hardly a silent moment passing between us. I had a lot of catching up to do.

'Salisbury is now Harare, Umtali is Mutare, and Inyanga is Nyanga,' chanted the boys in unison.

'Katerere's stayed the same, in name anyway,' laughed Brenda.

The family had returned to Africa, so that Peter could resume his important work of helping to educate young minds.

'The last time we met was at a youth camp on the Isle of Wight,' I reminded him. 'Not long after the massacre.'

'Yes, let's fill in a few gaps. After coming out here to help prepare for the funerals, I spent some time arranging for the transfer of students to other schools. Although secondary school places were at a premium at the time, people were sympathetic. Places were found for all 300 children, albeit scattered throughout the length and breadth of the land. Splitting them up was providential. Many were able to start Christian groups in schools where none had existed before. But that's not all. Do you know of a lady called Janet Cunningham?'

'Vaguely. Didn't she start an organisation for women?' 'Yes, Homemakers. Well, she invited me to speak at a combined meeting of several groups of Homemakers on the subject of forgiveness. This had become a controversial issue since the media quoted various Christian relatives of our dead colleagues, speaking of forgiveness for those who murdered their sons and daughters. You see at the same time, the average white Rhodesian was crying out for revenge.'

Brenda took up the story. 'Peter was due to fly back to England the day before the meeting. He said he couldn't attend. Then Janet spoke to him again, and the next thing I knew, he'd delayed his departure by two days. She must be a persuasive woman!'

'Ah, but it was the right decision,' emphasised Peter. 'In my talk I pointed out that whatever we think about the idea of forgiveness for murderers, Jesus prayed that those who crucified him would be forgiven. Although we may not be murderers, we are all sinners, and all need the forgiveness of God found only through the cross, when we repent and call out to Jesus to save and forgive us. I made no sort of emotional appeal for people to commit their lives to Christ, but did point out that anyone interested in becoming a Christian could leave their name and address in a book after the meeting.'

'Did anyone?' I asked.

'Yes. Six ladies.'

There was some significance in the number six. Up in the Vumba mountains, God had allowed six grown women to be martyred and find entrance into his heavenly kingdom. Now I was hearing that after the very first external meeting since the massacre where Peter was able to speak of God's offer of forgiveness in Christ, six women had come forward. A shiver went down my spine.

As we came nearer to the Mission memories came flooding back and I went quiet, trying to control my emotions. A few obvious changes had been made, like new houses for staff, but no extra buildings had been added to the hospital. There were still some members of staff I remembered from before and I was amazed how the lilting Shona language all came back. Nurses who didn't know me had quite a surprise when they realised I could understand their conversations.

Dr Adrian Smyly was a primary healthcare specialist. He put a lot of effort into building up the preventive healthcare services to the community. More baby clinics were established and called ZEPIs (Zimbabwe Expanded Programme of Immunisation). They took place in fifteen different locations, including Nyamombe Refugee Camp, a two-hour drive from Katerere. Ante-natal and post-natal care were introduced at the ZEPIs, using the back of a Land Rover ambulance as an examination room.

It was marvellous to see the improvements in healthcare. In the 1970s we had treated sick children every day of the week, but other services were only available once a month. Now parents could bring their children from Monday to Friday for weighing, vaccinations, and treatment if they were sick.

A real bond of friendship and teamwork developed quickly between myself and the other two expatriate nurses Debbie Brown and Bobbie Marcus, the Matron. Evelyn Munembe had given up full-time work in order to have a family, but she was still active in the community whenever possible.

The days were busy and happy, like those during my first term of service before the civil war. If my thoughts strayed too much towards the massacre, there was always some job or other to be done around the hospital to occupy the mind. I wouldn't admit it, but I was putting a lid on deep emotional hurts.

Before returning to Zimbabwe I told a friend who is a journalist, 'God has forgiven the murderers, so I must too. I feel no bitterness towards them.' I meant what I said, but when the words came out in print and I read them, a great gaping sadness welled up inside me. Every now and again, during quiet moments, those words would come back, echoing around my head.

In June 1988 Mary Brien visited the Mission. Her husband had passed away, so she came as far as Nyanga with a nephew, before being collected by Bobbie Marcus and a group of ladies from the church. They travelled in an open pick-up and we heard their approach from some distance—the ladies were singing a song of welcome with great gusto. People came running to the vehicle to greet her.

She was with us for five days, and from the time of her arrival until the time of her departure there was a constant flow of Zimbabweans waiting to see her, singing to her and bringing gifts. On the Sunday morning the church was packed with people wanting to hear her speak. She was an octogenarian, but had plenty of energy to stand and preach the gospel, and she gave an appeal at the end. It was a real thrill—for her and the expatriates—to see so many men respond. Some had made commitments years ago, but had grown indifferent. Others made a stand for Christ for the first time that morning. After the service a party took place outside the church. Representatives of various chapels and groups in the area sang songs and gave their appreciations to her.

I know it is wrong to put people into little boxes, but I marked Mary Brien down as being an old school type; a woman with a strong personality and full of determination. She was staying at Bobbie's house and had problems with the door keys. On finding herself locked in, she was seen climbing through a bedroom window one morning at 6am. Nothing was going to prevent her from joining the nurses for early morning prayers!

Any antagonism I felt towards Mary Brien was undoubtedly due to the fact that she had sussed me out. Somehow, she knew I needed healing from memories surrounding the massacre. We didn't talk much, but she urged me to pray in the manner of her late husband, 'Lord, help us to live in the light of eternity.'

Then it was the tenth anniversary of the massacre. Bobbie and Debbie were suggesting a trip to the Vumba. It was rare for all three of us to have days off together. Oh, how I tried to avoid going, and how glad I was afterwards that I went with them. Sometimes one has to be dragged out of the past in order to face the future.

Each of us had a profoundly moving experience as we stood by the graves of the martyrs. The plots are marked by simple white crosses and surrounded by specially planted jacaranda trees. An eerie stillness pervades the clearing, though it is a beautiful resting place.

Suddenly the silence was broken by the sound of violent sobbing. I realised it was me. At first it was as if someone else was crying and I was an onlooker. I sank to the ground. Cradled in the arms of my friends, there came a point of owning emotions I had suppressed for so long. A part of me had died and was buried with the victims. I needed to grieve.

When I was all cried out, the three of us stood and praised the Lord for bringing us together to work in Zimbabwe. In turn we rededicated ourselves, declaring our commitment to God, whatever it might mean. Then we sang two hymns: 'Here I am wholly available' and, remembering Mary Fisher's voice on flexidisc, 'For me to live is Christ, to die is gain'.

We turned to leave and Debbie remarked, 'They weren't so much heroes as those who simply believed they were called to do a work, and to carry on doing it until told otherwise.'

Bobbie was frowning, 'In my book that's exactly what heroes are.'

The scene from that old Western flashed through my mind's eye once again. 'They were our magnificent thirteen,' I mumbled.

Feeling fresh and clean, I fell silent on the way back to Katerere. I was thinking of some of the great paradoxes of the Christian life. Of Stephen, the first Christian martyr, who, although young, had an amazing ability as an evangelist, only to suffer death by stoning when he was being most effective for God. And James, who, as one of the inner circle of Jesus' disciples, received special revelation and training, only to be killed most brutally by Herod. Even more puzzling was the fact that after Herod arrested Peter, he was rescued by miraculous intervention, only to die for his faith later in Rome. I wondered why his life was spared on the first occasion.

I had been hearing rumours for some time that the man who led the rebel attack on Eagle School was now a Christian. There was formerly no desire within me to investigate the matter further, but the healing experience by the graves had stimulated my curiosity. At a convenient moment when visiting Peter Griffiths at home in Harare, I asked if he knew anything.

'Oh, plenty,' he said, with a mysterious smile on his face. 'I've been waiting for you to say something, but you weren't ready before.'

'Is it true?'

Peter nodded. 'The man, Gary Hove is his name, attended a Bible college here in the city. He wants to be a preacher.'

'You've met him?'

'We've had several chats. I'm sure his conversion was real.'

Peter went on to tell how, one Sunday morning just after Independence, Gary Hove was reading a newspaper in his room at an army camp in Bulawayo. His eye caught sight of an article in bold type, which commenced with the words 'Dear Comrades …' in bold letters. It was actually a paid advertisement inserted by a missionary called Margaret Lloyd, telling of the love of God towards everyone. Then it described the conversion to Christ of a Cuban Marxist called Raphael. At the end was a PO Box number.

'Gary read the piece aloud to some of his buddies. They were all angry that a comrade, albeit a Cuban, should become a Christian. It was decided that Gary should write to Margaret, inviting her to meet all of them so she could answer questions about the Christian faith. This was a ploy on their part to lure her to the camp and kill her. The letter was written, and Gary put it into the thigh pocket of his fatigues.' Peter demonstrated the movement with his own hand.

'Walking to the mail box in the camp, his hand went to his pocket. The letter had disappeared! He couldn't remember exactly what he had said before, but he hurriedly wrote a second letter. By reply, Margaret sent some Christian literature and a Bible. He not only read what she sent him, but also began to visit churches.'

'Hungry for God,' I asserted.

'One night, back at the barracks, Gary and his friends shared a strange religious experience—a vision—in which they all saw a cross. Then Gary alone saw the hand of God coming down, as if in judgement, to smite him. He cried out to God for mercy, and asked to be saved from his sins!'

85

'Incredible!' I exclaimed. This was some story. 'It's just like Saul of Tarsus, who tried fervently to crush the early church, only to find Christ himself, and to become Saint Paul.'

'After the first time I met Gary, I arrived home to find an unexpected visitor—one of my ex-students—Colin Kuhuni.' Peter looked at me as if I should know this name. I didn't, and said as much.

'Colin is a bright young lawyer, trained to sift through evidence and look for facts. He happened to have been a student at the school when our friends were killed. Along with the other pupils, Colin was subjected to a propaganda talk from Gary and his platoon. I told Colin about my meeting with Gary and the story of his conversion. Immediately I had finished, Colin asked, "Tell me what he looks like." This wasn't difficult, as Gary is so tall and angular. When I gave the description Colin said, "He was the man who lectured us on that dreadful night." It seemed that God had brought Colin along that day to confirm I had met with the right man.'

'Phew! Did you question Gary about the massacre?'

'The second time we met. Apparently the whole thing was a revenge attack—there was nothing personal in it. Gary and twenty others carried out the murders in retaliation, after the security forces killed some of his people. I plucked up the courage to enquire how the missionaries reacted when they knew they were going to die, and what they might have said. His reply was that they prayed God would have mercy on their murderers and save them.'

Once again a shiver went down my spine. Almost as an afterthought, Peter said, 'One of the women—it had to be

Wendy—shouted something like, "You can kill our bodies, but not our souls." '

Brenda came in at that point. I had taken up an entire afternoon of Peter's time, when he should have been looking at students' papers. After kissing them both fondly, I started off on the long drive back to the Mission.

The moon was up and full by the time I reached Rainbow Cottage, the little house which had been built for me. It was so called because the decorators had painted each room a different pastel colour, which was extended to the outside window frames. There was time for a toasted cheese sandwich before lights out. I chose to eat it by the blue window, enjoying the moon, and the stars which had come into view beside it. I pictured how those graves in that eerie Vumba clearing would look on a night like this.

"Yes, it would have been Wendy," I said to myself, then went to bed.

Adrian Smyly's term of service came to an end. Everyone was grateful for the improvements he had brought to the Mission hospital's Maternal and Child Health Department. Over a period of eight years the numbers of children treated increased dramatically from 5,000 to over 18,000. In his place came Roger Drew, a young surgeon. He took one look at the operating theatre and declared, 'Some of this equipment is all right. I suppose the rest belonged to Cecil Brien. He probably bought it from Noah!'

The theatre was brought up to scratch, and we were able to do even more for the people of Katerere. Our inaugural major operation was a Caesarean section, performed in the middle of the night. It was the first of many, and we became quite expert. I gave the anaesthetic, Debbie would help with resuscitation of the baby, and a medical student assisted Roger. We had some failures. There are many risks to mother and baby during pregnancy and the birthing process.

One heavily pregnant patient came to the clinic with a vaginal discharge. I gave her something for it, but the infection refused to clear up. It was diagnosed as having been sexually transmitted.

Although she had been delivered of several children already with no complications, this time the poor woman was growing larger every day, with no signs of going into labour. We let her go over ten months, hoping for a normal birth. But the baby grew too big for a vaginal delivery, and a Caesarean section was performed. This was risky because of the infection, but there was no other choice. The baby died, but the mother survived. She was tested and found to be HIV-positive.

We were continually aware in our work of the steady increase of AIDS. In 1990, 132 new patients were HIV tested at our hospital. Fifty-three of these were positive and five died during the year. In 1991, 199 were tested. Eighty were positive and fourteen died. Most of the infections were passed on through heterosexual relationships. Some patients were infants who had contracted the virus from their mothers.

I mentioned earlier that many of the men travelled to large towns and cities in order to find work. They came back for holidays and special occasions. In between times prostitutes satisfied their sexual desires. Many of the women already had AIDS from unprotected sex—often with customers such as truck drivers, who travelled to and from distant parts of Africa. When the men arrived home the virus passed to their wives, and any subsequent offspring. There is a cultural practice in Africa for widows to marry a member of their dead husband's family. As infected women were paired with previously uninfected partners, AIDS gained more victims. In some parts of the continent whole communities have been wiped out.

Eventually every patient at the Mission hospital was treated as potentially HIV-positive, whatever the diagnosis. To protect the staff, rubber gloves were available. We didn't have enough to use new ones with each patient. The gloves were washed, soaked in bleach and dried. Staff were also encouraged to wear rubber gloves when putting up drips and taking blood samples for the laboratory. Nurses were careful to wear heavy duty gloves when handling soiled laundry, and plastic aprons and gloves when changing bed linen.

Faced with the prospect of an early death, some people will try anything in the hope of finding a cure. A married couple from Harare came to Katerere, having heard of a tribesman using herbs on AIDS victims. The husband was very ill and this form of natural medicine made him worse. As a last resort, the wife brought him to us. Bedridden and seriously dehydrated due to continuous diarrhoea, there was little that could be done. The man died. If he had been admitted earlier, oral rehydration might have prolonged his life.

His widow was left with the awful problem of having to transport the corpse back to Harare. Tradition dictated that he must be buried in a family plot. She had no money, so I arranged for the body to be taken to a mortuary at Nyanga. There it could be kept in a refrigerator until she had the funds for the next stage of the journey. I thought that was the end of the distressing story, but after the wife had left with the body—weeping and wailing as is the Shona custom—in walked a daughter. She was unaware of her father's death. When I told her the sorry tale she became hysterical, violent, and had to be restrained.

In some places AIDS patients are treated as outcasts. In Katerere relatives are generally supportive. It is essential that families receive spiritual and medical help when patients leave hospital. An AIDS home visiting team was set up by the Mission hospital to enable the dying to be nursed in their own homes. The team is led by Mr Chitima, a church lay worker, assisted by Mai Sagwidza. She had previous experience in the Mission hospital's Rehabilitation Department. Qualified nurses administer medicines and whatever else is required.

This can involve the washing of open sores with soap and water, or salty water, which acts like a disinfectant; giving fevered patients bed baths of cold water to help cool them; and rubbing aching muscles with soothing coconut oil. Paracetamol is often used as a painkiller. Other remedies utilise resources available locally. For example, the juice of a sliced onion mixed with sugar makes an effective expectorant for a dry cough. Packets of oral rehydration salts are used in the hospital for acute cases of diarrhoea, but for mild cases four teaspoons of sugar and half a teaspoon of salt, added to a litre of boiled water, will do just as well.

Family members learn simple but important skills, like how to turn a weak patient over to avoid bed sores. They can alleviate the discomfort of thrush in the mouth by providing salt water mouthwashes several times a day. The giving of moist meals containing tomato, banana and other kinds of juicy fruits and vegetables, provides vitamins, replaces body fluids, and at the same time helps to soothe sore mouths and throats.

I saw a number of youngsters orphaned through AIDS. The lives of others were touched by the deaths of brothers and sisters, aunts or uncles. One way I could reach out to these children was through Sunday school classes. Mai Simango, a Zimbabwean lady of about fifty years of age, was my partner in this venture. She was a boarding school mistress at Penhalonga, before obtaining a similar post at Elim Secondary School, which had now returned to Katerere.

For their own good, Mai Simango ruled the older children with a rod of iron. But she was very kind and loving to the little ones. They would flock around her buxom figure, seeking a cuddle, like chickens under the wings of a mother hen. When I went to her house to plan lessons we would always end up on our knees. Mai Simango was a woman of great prayer.

On a larger scale AIDS education became part of the general school curriculum. To take effect, the best approach was to give advice at an age before the children became interested in the opposite sex. Older pupils, whose natural passions were already aroused, were less likely to listen to reasoned arguments. Adults, particularly leaders of communities, were targeted through talks and seminars.

For some time Bobbie Marcus' state of health had been a cause for concern. Little had been said in public, though members of Elim churches in Britain and Northern Ireland were aware she had been undergoing tests. She didn't have AIDS. The symptoms related to her mobility and nervous system. Multiple sclerosis was one possible explanation. She was flown home, where more tests revealed a less serious problem. Happily, she fell in love with Pastor David Tinnion and they were married. Bobbie never returned to work in Katerere.

Her departure led to an important event in my life. Saturday 18th February 1989 was highlighted in my diary as a day off. Nothing significant in that. However, the morning was disrupted by a visit from Brian Edwards and Peter Griffiths. The two had arrived at the compound the previous evening and we shared a meal together. It was a pleasant enough occasion, with no sinister overtones. Now they wanted to talk business. Why?

In the kitchen I poured coffee for the three of us, and took it through to the lounge. Brian appeared tense as he took a cup.

'Joy, the hospital needs a new Matron,' he began. 'Evelyn Munembe is back, but with a family of her own to look after, she can't take on a full-time job. Debbie isn't quite ready yet, we feel, to take on overall responsibility. And none of the Zimbabwean nurses has enough qualifications for such a role. But someone else does.' As Brian paused to take a sip of black coffee I caught Peter's eye. He winked at me.

Brian continued, 'We—that's myself, the Missions Board and Peter—would like you to have the post of Sister in Charge here at the Elim Mission Hospital.'

So that was it. An ordinary day had suddenly become rather special. My heart was beating faster as I replied, 'I'd like that very much. I hope I'll be worthy of your trust.'

I shook hands with Brian and received a fatherly hug from Peter. Then it was over to the hospital where Pastor Ephraim Satuku and Roger Drew confirmed the appointment. The rest of the day was spent writing letters home to tell members of my family the good news.

Official announcements were made at the hospital the next day, and prayers were said for me in church. I said my own private 'thank you' to the Lord—the one who put a yearning for nursing and Africa in my heart from childhood. I was on cloud nine and stayed there for several months, until the rains came.

It was mid-November. While driving to Harare one day to collect various supplies, my vision blurred as my head began to swim—with the heat, or so I thought. Concentration was difficult and I had to keep repeating to myself, 'Salaries from the bank, pick up lactogen, enquire about parcels.' A dark cloud followed me back to Katerere, but no rain fell.

A couple of days later I was having supper with Roger and his wife when a dramatic storm came on. We viewed it from the verandah. The lightning was quite beautiful to watch as it forked down the sky. The noise of the rain was almost deafening as it landed on adjoining tin rooftops.

'Good,' I sighed. 'This will clear the air, and hopefully my sickness.'

'I thought you'd been looking a bit pale,' said Roger. 'Is everything all right?'

'It's nothing really. Just a muzzy head and general malaise. Despite taking medication, the symptoms have persisted.'

The change of weather brought no relief. The following day I vomited and immediately felt better. About a month later, while on duty in the operating theatre, I started to feel ill again. If it wasn't the heat this time, perhaps the condition of the woman lying on the table was to blame. Attacked with an axe, she had suffered terrible head wounds. Was I experiencing a surge of emotions in a flashback to the injuries described at the Vumba massacre? No. Hours later, feeling hot and feverish, I popped a thermometer in my mouth to discover my temperature was up. I mentioned the matter to Roger, and was taken aback by his reply.

'You're off on holiday soon. Have a complete and thorough medical, including blood tests.'

'But I'm sure there's …'

'No need to worry? Maybe not. But whatever it is, it won't go away without proper treatment. Look, I don't want to scare you, but with all these AIDS patients coming in—you should have *that* test too.'

94

I was going home for my brother Tim's wedding. Shortly after I sailed through a check-up, and an HIV test showed me to be negative. I heaved a sigh of relief and returned to Zimbabwe. The sickness did not recur. From time to time most members of staff went through a period of anxiety about contracting AIDS. Roger had a particularly nasty scare.

A small boy was admitted, complaining of abdominal pain. A bowel obstruction seemed the obvious cause and Roger began an operation. No bowel contents were found, but the lymph nodes were swollen and bleeding. This could indicate typhoid, tuberculosis, lymphoma—or AIDS. Two nodes were removed for further investigation, and the boy was closed up.

Roger told me, 'The wound was sutured, the dressing neatly in place. I turned my attention to the instrument trolley. All the needles were stuck to an adhesive pad in their container. They had been new, we'd just received them from England. I went to close the lid of the container to make it safe for the nurses who would soon be clearing up. One needle wasn't lying flat on the pad. As the lid came down the sharp end went through my glove and into my thumb. Taking the gloves off, I encouraged the wound to bleed, went quickly to the sink and washed it copiously with water. It looked such a trivial injury, yet I was only too well aware of the potential implications.'

The patient and his family were well-known to us. The father was a part-time shoemaker with a drink problem, two wives and a large number of children. He had tuberculosis, and the others were suffering from malnutrition. All had been tested for AIDS in the past with negative results, with the exception of one of the little girls. This didn't make sense. For a child of this age to be HIV-positive, the source had to be the mother, who had shown up negative. The mother and children were tested again. This time the results were positive. The boy died a few days later.

Now Roger had to be tested. The first blood sample, taken by Debbie, showed he was HIV-negative at the time of the injury. Then it was necessary to wait three months before taking a further test, to see if he had been infected through the needle. In the meantime every sniffle, ache or pain was a source of worry. Thankfully, the second test came back negative too. However, he admitted, 'The sense of relief was not as great as it should be. I'm negative now, but what about the next accident with a needle, or the one after that?'

Roger subsequently went through the dilemma that many other overseas workers have experienced in the face of danger. Fight or flight? He couldn't escape the problem, for all around were AIDS patients.

One morning, walking to the hospital, he saw a group of women sitting on the ground under the shade of a tree. Their tell-tale wailing meant only one thing: someone had died during the night. The notes of a patient were lying on the floor just inside his office door. They had been put there by one of the night nurses. Roger picked them up, sat at the desk and started to read them.

She was only a young woman. Single, but with a child a few months old. She had first come to the hospital complaining of a cough, weight loss and severe diarrhoea. She certainly looked as if she had lost weight, she was so emaciated. An X-ray showed that one side of her chest was full of fluid. Treatment was given, but her condition deteriorated. The previous day Roger had tried draining two litres of fluid off the chest. Obviously it had made no difference. A blood test confirmed she had AIDS. A few days later the child also died.

Another patient, who was pregnant, had such severe vaginal warts, caused through AIDS, that she couldn't deliver normally. She was given a Caesarean section. The baby survived and seemed fine. Though he was feeding, he did not grow at the normal rate, became sickly and ultimately died. Of AIDS.

'At times, I don't feel I can cope with the pressure,' said Roger. 'It must be similar to the predicament you were in during the war. But I think this is worse because this enemy is hidden, and therefore seems more sinister.'

But he did cope, eventually declaring, 'Though I wanted to leave and find a safer occupation, I realised two things: I can't just run away, and no job is without hazards. I could go home and who knows? An accident or unexpected illness could take me. Life is not something we can hold securely in our own hands. What did Jesus say? "For whosoever will save his life shall lose it: but whosoever will lose his life for my sake, the same shall save it" ' (Luke 9:24, KJV).

Meanwhile my own health was fine. However, my temperament was adjusting to some of the non-medical matters a Sister in Charge has to cope with. Like pilfering. Ten litres of diesel oil and two door frames were reported missing from the hospital storeroom. A close check was kept, and smaller items also started to disappear.

On Elim Secondary School's sports day, the people handling the refreshments ran out of sugar. Roger was around, and offered to go and fetch some from a small shop run by Mai Malvira. The sugar was kept in large containers, not pre-packed as in Western supermarkets. After weighing, his purchase was put into a plastic bag. Roger soon realised this was one of our sterilisation bags. Evidence!

Mai Malvira also had a job in the hospital. She was brought into my office for questioning, but denied theft. The explanation was that the bags were being thrown away. I was not satisfied, and suspended her pending further enquiries. The police had to be called in and an officer gave a talk to all the staff. It looked as if Mai Malvira was guilty, but I didn't want her sent to prison. We opted for a disciplinary warning, after which she was reinstated, but she failed to turn up for work. I believe this may have been due to embarrassment. Pastor Satuku mentioned the matter in church, to clear the air, so everyone knew the true story of what had been going on.

A happier occasion was the visit of President Mugabe to the hospital on 24th October 1990. He seemed impressed and stayed for several hours. It was very hot—another of those days when we were eagerly awaiting the rains. Due to the heat and old age, an elderly lady died while he was there. But we managed to steer him away and avoided the distress of letting him see the body being carried out. I believe she died of a heart attack. She only came in with an abscess on her face.

I was ill again in March and April of 1991, with fevers, aches and pains and then a rash—typical of the type common with typhoid fever. Roger started me on the treatment for typhoid and then I was driven in to Harare for further investigations. No conclusive diagnosis was made. If I had been tested for AIDS at that time, I wonder, would the result have been positive?

Next I had a strange rash on my thighs and abdomen in December. The doctor in Harare was most interested, but had no idea what it could be. He prescribed steroids, which seemed to help. As soon as the course was finished the rash came back with a vengeance—just for one day—before completely disappearing. I never had it again.

On 19th February 1992 I was helping in the operating theatre. A man had mangled his hand in a grinding machine and attempts were being made to tidy up his fingers. It was a long and delicate procedure. I started feeling hungry and then dizzy. The room was spinning round. I grabbed at one corner of the operating table in order to stay upright. No one seemed to notice me.

Suddenly, gripped by agonising abdominal pain, I cried out, 'Help! Go and fetch Debbie!' One of the African nurses ran out to fetch her. With my head on the table alongside the patient, I made sure he was kept asleep by shooting anaesthetic into a vein every time he moved. By the time Debbie arrived on the scene I was on the floor. But the patient was still asleep. I was escorted home, took some painkillers, and went to bed. When I woke up I felt fine, as if nothing had happened.

In the days that followed, the problems with my throat and chest developed. The next part of my story you know—the diagnosis of AIDS, my journey back to England and hospitalisation have already been told in Chapter 1. But that is not the end. As a PWA (person with AIDS) I am not just sitting around waiting to die. The following pages show I am living a full life, as actively as possible. And God is leading me into a new understanding of himself and his ways.

9

After living abroad for so many years, I sometimes feel the world has passed me by. Whenever I have spent time at home in the past it has been hard to make many lasting friendships, because I would soon be off to another part of the world. In the same way, I have allowed myself to become distant from my family—to be less involved in their lives than if I had been in England throughout the last twenty years. Some members of the family have been mentioned in previous chapters. Now is the time for you to hear more, as I rediscover them.

My parents Victor and Violet have been happily married for over fifty years. They had six children. Unfortunately the first baby died. Some brothers and sisters are like peas in a pod. The five Baths have varying temperaments and have all done different things.

Roy is the eldest. He used to help in Dad's shop and now works for the Post Office. He lives with his family in Swindon. Jacquie, his wife, is a kind of extra daughter to Mum and Dad, and a sister to me. Originally from Jersey, she was adopted by another branch of the family and is technically my cousin. As a child she was always round at our house, playing with the rest of us. Roy and Jacquie have two grown-up children, Kevin and Mandi.

I came next, born on 17th April 1950. In some churches a child's first communion or confirmation service might be a cause for celebration. The Pentecostal way records when an individual makes their own decision to become a follower of Jesus. I became a Christian at the age of eight, which is quite young, but not that unusual. I received the baptism of the Holy Spirit at the age of sixteen.

Pearl was born after me. She has a husband called Trevor and daughters Charlotte and Geraldine. They all live in Salisbury. When Charlotte realised my second term of service in Zimbabwe was among AIDS patients, she organised a collection service for rubber gloves from local hospitals and clinics. She was just thirteen years of age at the time.

My brother Tim and his wife Yvonne live in Swindon with young Kristian and James. When Tim is not working as a chef, he and Yvonne can often be found in Russia. As part of Messianic Testimony to the Jews they deliver humanitarian aid to needy families in an orphanage, intensive care unit, and the Russian National Centre For Children With AIDS. Their work also involves sharing the gospel with Messianic believers. Russia is currently experiencing a dramatic spiritual awakening, and the Jewish community is no exception to this. Since the collapse of Communism, literally thousands of Jewish people have come to acknowledge Jesus as their Messiah.

Keith, my youngest brother, is married to Debbie. They are about to begin a family of their own. In the meantime he has several hundred four-legged babies to care for. Keith is a shepherd on Salisbury Plain. It's a rugged life, being out in all weathers.

Quite often Keith will come over for lunch. We have so much in common, sometimes our conversation horrifies Mum and Dad, especially if we are all enjoying a meal together. With Keith a shepherd and myself a midwife, the discussion frequently turns to the similarities between the birth of a baby and a lamb. It is natural for us to compare our different experiences, but either Mum or Dad will interject with, 'Please, you two! Not while we are eating.'

On one such occasion Keith was worried about an old ewe, who might have to be put down. She had developed a bad infection. Though Keith would ensure that any treatment was carried out humanely, he was upset at the thought of losing a member of the flock. I am surprised at the compassion and concern Keith shows for the sheep. If one of the lambs is sick or weakly, his wife is given the job of nursing it back to health in their kitchen.

I hate the idea of pain being experienced by any living thing. But for human beings it can come in many forms; physical, mental and emotional; persecution and rejection. It can act as a purifying process. It can be a benefit, remoulding a person and giving new strengths.

A student social worker called Emma has visited me on a regular basis. She is a tremendous girl who, as a sufferer of cerebral palsy, has already overcome many hurdles to reach her current role. I wonder whether she would have been so keen to succeed if she were not fighting a disability.

Some Christians, mostly those who do not understand how AIDS is spread, have made hurtful comments to me. They spit out accusations like, 'You must think we're naïve to say you caught it at work. From an affair, more like.' As a result I have started to feel a closeness to the Virgin Mary. Her pregnancy, while engaged to Joseph, must have prompted winks and nudges from the gossips. If she had told all and sundry that God was the father of her baby, she would either have been locked up for being insane, or stoned to death for blasphemy. Instead she not only bore all the taunts silently and with dignity, but was also able to utter a wonderful hymn of praise, which is nowadays known as the Magnificat. It has become something I recite often in my private times with God:

My soul glorifies the Lord and my spirit rejoices in God my Saviour, for he has been mindful of the humble state of his servant. From now on all generations will call me blessed, for the Mighty One has done great things for me—holy is his name. His mercy extends to those who fear him, from generation to generation. He has performed mighty deeds with his arm; he has scattered those who are proud in their inmost thoughts. He has brought down rulers from their thrones but has lifted up the humble. He has filled the hungry with good things but has sent the rich away empty. He has helped his servant Israel, remembering to be merciful to Abraham and his descendants for ever, even as he said to our fathers (Luke 1:46–55).

To keep things in perspective, I've encountered little negative reaction to my condition. However, I have been guilty of a few wrong attitudes myself towards other people. When visiting Southampton for hospital appointments, I have to report to the Genito-Urinary Clinic. This is more commonly known as the STD (Sexually Transmitted Diseases), VD or Special Clinic. It is embarrassing to sit in the waiting room there, never having had a sexual relationship. And it is not easy to have an unbiased attitude towards other patients. I have tried to reason the matter through, saying to myself that the other people are there because they are sick, and who am I to judge how they became ill?

I had an interesting discussion with Jacquie along these lines, which led to some radical conclusions:

1. I shouldn't ask or even think about how another person contracted AIDS, unless I am prepared to submit myself to their prejudices and suppositions about me.

2. As Jesus was the friend of sinners, he might have shown more sympathy and compassion than I have so far towards other AIDS sufferers. He might have shown more willingness to be identified with them.

3. How can I be more like him? When asked how I came to be infected, perhaps I should just say, 'Through my work in Africa,' and not go into long explanations about being an innocent victim.

I have had five or six boyfriends. The physical side of the relationships has never progressed as far as the sexual act. Even the naughtiest thing I ever did along these lines is really quite innocent. While training to be a nurse in Poole, a mutual attraction developed between myself and a patient. I used to draw the curtains around his bed so we could kiss and cuddle. That was as far as it went. The sheets always stayed between us. It was most unprofessional conduct and I was lucky not to be caught and thrown off the course. Nothing like that ever happened again.

Over the years it has been hard to see those close to me finding partners and getting married, while I am still single. Now I have AIDS there is even less possibility of ever having a family of my own. I often feel I would love to be married; to have someone to care for me and someone to care for. Then I look around and see so many marriages in shambles. Perhaps I am better off as I am.

Reaching out to make new friends at this stage in my life is such an effort. But I know I must do it, and have joined Salisbury AIDS Support Group. I made the first move, contacting the co-ordinator David Penney, and arranging to meet at his office. We chatted at length. He is a very understanding person, concerned for the downtrodden of our society. Among the many posters on the wall of his office, I noticed one which read something like, 'No one ever died of AIDS by caring.' I could accept what the poster was saying, but pointed out that's exactly the way I contracted AIDS. The poster has since been removed.

Occasionally I come across faces from the past. A girl who was one of my Sunday school pupils in the 1970s was recently baptised at Elim Salisbury Church. Although contact had been maintained with people there, she had faltered in her faith since childhood, until she heard me speak at a luncheon. Before being baptised, she walked to the microphone and said, 'Joy's done so much with her life. But over the last twenty years, what have I done with mine? Very little. This moment symbolises a new start for me.' It was touching to think that my testimony could have such an effect on someone else's life.

Since January 1993 I have undertaken a number of speaking engagements at churches and conferences. They have all been valuable in helping people to understand what it is like to have AIDS. I generally feel I should address the problem of why Christians suffer. This is a vast subject, but starting to explore it has helped me, and I trust it has helped others too.

I believe suffering is not a licence for self-pity, but a chance for the sufferer to teach and encourage others. Shakespeare said that all the world is a stage. The audience can see us playing our part well, or badly. If all is well, they receive something positive to take to their hearts and take home. If all they see is hatred and bitterness the message of the scriptwriter is lost; the time spent at the theatre wasted.

There are Christians who believe healing is waiting just around the corner for everyone who is sick. They see the absence of healing as proof of a lack of faith in the promises of God. Their reasoning is based on certain passages of Scripture, for example Matthew 7:7–11 and 21:18–22, which seem to indicate human beings can obtain anything they ask. Then there are the many instances of Jesus healing people miraculously. I do not doubt the abilities of the Almighty, but in becoming a Christian I became a follower of Jesus. He suffered an agonising death, and if that means I have to do the same for some reason, I must say, 'Thy will be done.'

Three passages of Scripture have been particularly helpful to me. Sometimes, as I read these aloud to congregations, I find it hard to control my emotions. The words seem so powerful and simple:

First, 2 Corinthians 1:3–11, especially:

> … the God of all comfort, who comforts us in all our troubles, so that we can comfort those in any trouble with the comfort we ourselves have received from God … Indeed … we felt the sentence of death. But this happened that we might not rely on ourselves but on God, who raises the dead (vv 3b–4, 9).

Second, 2 Corinthians 4, especially:

> We are hard pressed on every side, but not crushed; perplexed, but not in despair; persecuted, but not abandoned; struck down, but not destroyed. We always carry around in our body the death of Jesus, so that the life of Jesus may also be revealed in our body … Though outwardly we are wasting away, yet inwardly we are being renewed day by day. For our

light and momentary troubles are achieving for us an eternal glory that far outweighs them all. So we fix our eyes not on what is seen, but on what is unseen. For what is seen is temporary, but what is unseen is eternal (vv 8–10, 16b–18).

Third, Philippians 1:20–21, especially:

... Christ will be exalted in my body, whether by life or by death (v 20b).

These passages have also helped me to cope with a worsening state of health. Though I am certainly not living every day in the hope that it is my last, I am looking forward to an afterlife I am certain exists.

My parents' house benefits from the famous view of Salisbury Cathedral across green fields. One of my favourite pleasures on a fine day is to walk the rural lanes there, gazing at the water meadows from Britford Bridge. One Saturday I was out walking when I passed a house where a man was working on his car. Parts and tools were all over the pavement and I tripped on them. It wasn't that I was day dreaming. I just could not see them or the ground beneath my feet. For some months I had been experiencing bad headaches and blurred vision around the lower edges of my eyes. Now some of my peripheral sight had gone.

Dr Wilmot in Southampton said a virus named cytomegalo was responsible. If untreated, it could take my sight completely. He arranged for the fitting of a Hickman Line. This is a tube attached to a main vein near my heart, with the outer end about two inches long, sticking through my chest. With a bit of adjustment it remains hidden by my clothing. Five days a week an anti-viral solution called Ganciclovir is slowly injected through the Hickman Line. The process takes about two hours and I can administer the treatment myself. It seems to have helped stem the sight loss, but the headaches are still with me.

Normally supplies of Ganciclovir arrive at home by a special delivery service. But on one occasion a mix-up over the prescription meant I had to collect it from a hospital pharmacy in Southampton. Also waiting for drugs there was an African girl. She looked familiar, but I could not think whether we had met before. Then I remembered a conversation with a nurse which took place before I was allowed home to Salisbury.

'Joy, I don't know whether I should ask you this, but there's an African lady in the next isolation cubicle with the same problem as you, who doesn't know how she's going to cope. Would you have a chat with her?'

'Yes, I will. I'd like to meet someone else with my condition.'

'And you might be able to speak in her mother tongue?'

'Probably not. There are loads of different tribal languages. But I might be able to help in some way.'

I tried to keep my promise, but I was receiving a lot of visitors every day. Each time I was alone, she had someone at her bedside. By the time we were both free she was being discharged and her husband was taking her away. But here she was again, at the pharmacy. I seized the opportunity to introduce myself.

She was feeling much better, and had found a part-time job. We exchanged addresses and in due course she and her husband came to visit me. It was a great encouragement for both of us. And it was comforting for her to chat with another person who had lived in Africa.

I was also put in touch with another PWA, a young man in a more serious condition. I went to see him on several occasions.

He was painfully thin, and had several infections, which eventually killed him.

Since coming back to England I have been able to attend two Elim conferences. At the most recent, intense headaches meant it was only possible to go to a few sessions. One of these was a children's meeting where I gave a talk. Afterwards they prayed for me, particularly a young coloured lad called Gideon. He showed real faith and it made me quite tearful. A younger child had a prophecy from the Lord: 'Jesus wants us to know he loves us all very much. And Joy, he's proud of you.' I was more blessed by the words of these little ones than by the carefully prepared lectures of seasoned preachers.

Work, church services, speaking engagements and conferences. You may be wondering whether I ever relax and have a good time. Members of some religions believe everything on earth has been put here for us to enjoy. To some extent Pentecostals agree with that, but in practice they try to avoid anything which might be termed worldly or extravagant. In doing so we have become separated from some of life's more innocuous pastimes. For most of us, going to church is the highlight of the week. We really enjoy it—possibly because the services are so lively and uplifting. The rest of the time we are too busy adhering to the Protestant work ethic to notice all the good things in the world around us. We have largely forgotten how to have a good time—at least I had until I was forced into early retirement.

Recently I have been on more outings and holidays, have had more fun, than ever before. I treasure memories of walking along a cliff path on Guernsey, followed by delicious crab sandwiches at Vazon beach; joining in a sing-song with others in the crowd during a carnival procession; sunlight sparkling on a calm sea, as I took a ferry to the Isle of Wight; just sitting at home watching the *Last Night of the Proms* on television with a box of chocolates on my knee.

I went to London's Oxford Street and travelled on an open-top bus to see the Christmas lights. What an experience! It was dark and freezing cold, but I was wrapped up warmly. There was a wonderful atmosphere, with the Salvation Army band playing carols and the beauty of the street lights and window displays. The trip was something I had wanted to do for years, but never managed it before. Then there was the joy of having the family together—all twenty-six of us—on Christmas Day.

I have found happiness in all kinds of everyday pursuits. The key is to relax, stop rushing from one task to the next worrying about the future, and enjoy what the present provides. Try it sometime. I only wish I had earlier.

During my enforced stay in England I have had a lot of time to reflect upon my life. I think it was while I was in India that I had a conversation with a fellow missionary about the right time to go home. My condition is fuddling my mind and I am unable to remember who the person was, but their words have remained with me. It was said that a missionary can get to the stage where Asia, Africa or some other continent is so much a part of them they cannot do without it. That's when it is time to return home. I now think that maybe I had reached that stage with Zimbabwe.

10

Fairly recently, while reading part of the Sermon on the Mount (Matthew 6:31–34), I was struck by the words of Jesus, 'Do not worry about your life.' I am sure he did not mean we should not plan and prepare for the future as best we can. He did mean we should not be full of anxiety. He goes on to say, 'Therefore do not worry about tomorrow, for tomorrow will worry about itself. Each day has enough trouble of its own' (v 34).

What really impressed me about this teaching of Jesus was the air of authority with which it was delivered. He was not giving out advice, but commands. And how right he was to place emphasis on this matter. It is pointless to waste our lives sitting around fretting about things which may never happen. On the other hand, if we knew the trials we had to face in life beforehand, we would probably give up on every aspect before reaching adulthood.

Two letters posted from Nyanga just before Christmas 1992 shocked and saddened me. First Roger Drew wrote that Peter Griffiths was seriously ill. Then Peter himself told me that the outlook was bleak. Yet the start of his troubles seemed so small and insignificant.

At the beginning of November Peter was reading aloud, as a prelude to giving one of his regular Tuesday evening Bible studies to a large group of people. He could not pronounce some of the words properly. No one except Brenda seemed to notice, and he put the problem down to being overtired, plus the fact that the passage of Scripture—from Genesis—contained some tricky Hebrew names.

The next day Peter's speech was slurred from time to time. He wrote: 'I rang Debbie Murphree, the GP, and arranged an appointment. Foolishly ignoring her advice to get someone to drive me to her rooms, I drove myself. She found a slight weakness on the left side of the face, which could indicate I had suffered a minor stroke. After the examination she immediately arranged for me to see a consultant, Terry French, the following day.'

A CAT scan arranged through the consultant showed that a part of Peter's brain, about the size of a golf ball, appeared to have died. At least that was the first impression. When he saw the pictures Terry French commented, 'That's a pretty impressive infarct of the brain!'

An infarct is an area of dead tissue caused by interruption to the blood supply. This would probably fit in with the supposition that Peter had survived a stroke.

Peter had wisely asked his son Stephen to take him to this appointment. From Roger Drew's letter came the news, 'Stephen and his wife Anna had been due to fly to Mozambique that day, to begin work with the Leprosy Mission. Thank goodness they were delayed due to a shortage of aviation fuel. Peter had an epileptic fit in the car as they drove away, just outside the grounds of Terry French's office.'

The normally tranquil atmosphere of the consulting rooms was shattered by their return. Stephen, who is a doctor himself, helped to put up a drip and administered diazepam, a sedative, through a vein. An ambulance quickly arrived and Peter was taken to Parirenyatwa, a large hospital in Harare. Stephen was quite distraught by the sight of his stricken father. Of the fit, Peter said, 'Fully conscious throughout, I thought I was dying. I yielded myself to the Lord, thinking he was taking me home to heaven.'

Several more fits happened that day before Peter's condition calmed down. A neurosurgeon, Mr Auchterlonie, said surgical intervention would not be necessary. About a fortnight later, while Peter was still in hospital, he took a sudden turn for the worse, losing strength on his left side. A second CAT scan was done and this time the picture was enhanced by injecting dye. Terry French and Mr Auchterlonie realised that what appeared to be dead tissue was in fact a tumour.

Wrote Peter, 'I was transferred to the Avenues Clinic where Mr Auchterlonie operates from—literally! He did a biopsy of my brain. There was a two-day, agonisingly long wait for the results. They showed the tumour was malignant, and ought to be removed without delay. I signed the consent form for the operation.'

The apparent strokes were caused by the tumour bleeding into itself, swelling rapidly and putting pressure on certain areas of Peter's brain, resulting in paralysis down the left side of the body.

Roger saw him before surgery, and reported, 'Physically, he was worse. The left arm and leg were now also affected. Naturally, Peter was apprehensive about the operation. But he was doing his best to crack jokes—bad ones as usual—and responded well to a comment made by one of the nurses.'

She had come to wish him luck. Peter replied, 'I don't believe in luck. I believe in God. If this is my time to die, I'm ready.'

The operation went well, and the surgeon managed to remove all of the tumour. Peter recalled, 'The following days were just a blur. As a nurse, you'll realise how I must have looked, with tubes going into me and coming out of me in all sorts of places. And I was sedated up to the eyeballs. But in my confusion, God was revealing new depths of his love and graciousness. As I lay in that bed I marvelled at how God loves this world, and me as a part of it, and at how he deals with us in wonderful ways we do not deserve. I reflected with awe on the scene in Gethsemane, when Jesus saw the horror of his approaching death and said, "Father, if you are willing, take this cup from me; yet not my will, but yours be done" (Luke 22:42). Discharged from hospital, I am now at home. Mr Auchterlonie is setting up programmes of radiotherapy and chemotherapy at Parirenyatwa. The battle continues and I ask for your prayers.'

Strength, co-ordination and clear speech were returning to Peter. Progress was slow, but he was hopeful for the future. I was not so sure. It was no surprise when a third letter came through the letterbox a couple of months later, containing bad news. Peter wrote, 'I have been told there is no cure in medical science for my condition. The sort of tumour I had invariably returns. Radiotherapy simply controls the growth rate for a time, and may give me a little longer to live. So, you and I are in the same boat. Tell me how you cope.'

I knew Peter must be pretty low to send out such a plea, so I was on the telephone to him straight away. He didn't seem too bad, but admitted to struggling with despondency on waking each morning, due to thinking about the future.

He said, 'Depression fades somewhat as I become active and involved in the affairs of the day.'

We decided he was suffering from an over-fertile imagination. He was prone to thinking about what would happen if he became disabled to the point of being like a vegetable.

'Thoughts like that are not allowed!' I chided. 'Remember the Briens' prayer?'

'Lord, help us to live in the light of eternity. There are times when I feel I'm beginning to learn to stand where God stands, and to take an overhead view of what's happening in this brief span of time. Then, in my disabled state, I stumble over some object, or falter in a simple everyday task like a clumsy child, and come back down to earth. It's very hard to accept. I've always been such an active person.'

For the next six months Peter and I supported each other with letters and telephone calls. In a way it was comforting to know that such an old and trusted friend was going through the same kinds of thoughts and feelings as myself. At one stage I had half a plan put together to fly over to Zimbabwe and visit Peter, Brenda and others. It was an impossible dream which never materialised. My health would not have stood up to such vigorous travelling.

The tumour began to grow again, and by late summer Peter's condition was deteriorating. Susie Sanguinetti, a friend who worked for the BBC World Service, began typing his letters to me. 'I am now walking around slowly and once more speaking with some slurring of my speech,' I read. The next paragraphs let me know in no uncertain terms that he would not be with us much longer.

I have given the family instructions for my funeral. I want to be buried, rather than stick to the European practice here of cremation. This is because my African friends find cremation a difficult idea. The preacher and leader of the service will be Dr Ken Jenkins, but Pious Munembe and Ephraim Satuku should also speak. They are so close to me and risked their lives for me during the war here.

I want two hymns which have special meaning for me. 'Amazing Grace', because I have become more amazed than ever that God should treat me, and the whole world, with grace we are not worthy to receive. And 'Ungatora Hako Pasi', which Brenda and I had at our wedding. The Shona roughly translates, 'You can take the world and all its joys. We for our part will take Jesus and all he offers. His grace is overwhelming and sufficient for all.'

Now I must go and take an aspirin gargle—a small thing you and I do in common! Your loving and very tired friend and colleague, Peter.

Those were the last words he ever wrote to me and I treasure them, like a person might hold on to an old pair of worn out shoes. Brian Edwards rang me on the morning of Tuesday 10th October to say that Peter had died at 9pm the previous evening. The funeral would be on the following Friday in Mutare, conducted according to Peter's wishes. A memorial service was held in Swansea on 6th November. I was able to attend, with Mum and Dad. A good number came and it was an incredibly moving occasion. Afterwards Peter's mother gave me a long and tearful hug.

We stayed overnight in Wales and travelled back the following day. I drove all the way there and most of the way home. As we left the M4 at Chippenham I moved over to let Dad take the wheel. Exhausted, I was also acutely aware of my failing eyesight. It was getting to the point where it was no longer safe for me to be in control of a car. Just as Peter's treatment had only delayed the growth in his brain, I feared the Ganciclovir was fighting a losing battle within my own body.

Over the next weeks my health began to deteriorate. I carried on with the treatment, but suffered dreadful migraines whenever I was up and about. So I stayed in bed, sleeping for most of the time. When I did manage to stagger about on my feet I experienced weird feelings of weightlessness, as if I were floating above the ground. These symptoms could have been due to stress and grief; reactions to Peter's death. They disappeared when I was presented with a wonderful surprise.

Early one morning the doorbell rang and my parents instructed me to answer it. David Butcher and his wife were on the front step, both grinning from ear to ear.

'We picked up something special for you at Heathrow at the crack of dawn,' he said. 'Come and have a look in our car.'

I was intrigued as they led me through the door and a few paces up the drive. Someone was sitting on the back seat of the car. I couldn't see who until I looked inside.

'Jeya! I never thought it would be you out here.'

'I never thought to leave India—though I did visit Singapore last year—but you, my friend, are worth coming all this way to visit!'

We both wept happy tears and held each other for several minutes. Until David suggested the house would provide a more comfortable place to sit.

Jeya stayed about a week and was a real tonic. We are similar people, in spirit rather than looks, capable of holding deep conversations and discussions. I interviewed her as part of a Sunday service at Salisbury Elim Church and she shamed me by offering this lovely tribute to our friendship: 'God brings many people in our lives to be a blessing for us. God brought Joy into my life to give me joy.'

When it was time for Jeya to leave England I made the journey to Heathrow with her, escorted by Mike and Elisabeth Sherwood. He is an Elim pastor based in Essex, who formerly worked for Brian Edwards in Elim International Missions. Mike's face beamed as Jeya told how the GEMS has grown at an amazing rate in recent years. The work has expanded from Bihar to surrounding states and into the neighbouring country of Nepal.

Our parting was difficult. Jeya is an intuitive girl, and she knew this would be our last contact this side of heaven. It was a lovely day and I was not allowing any thoughts of an untimely death to invade my mind. I just thought this was another of those occasions when her emotional Indian temperament took over. After checking in her luggage, Jeya clung on to me, sobbing. Elisabeth gave her a handkerchief with which to wipe her wet face.

Jeya took a couple of deep breaths and quietened down a little. As we approached the barrier she clasped my hands in her own and said, 'God has told me that he is going to give you a special blessing in glory.'

She meant I would be rewarded in heaven for experiencing a short life. A sense of calm came over the four of us as Jeya walked off to the plane. Mike, Elisabeth and I gave each other a knowing glance. It was a look that said, 'Who knows? Perhaps she's right.'

From then on, my attitude to death changed. I could no longer carry a vague acceptance that for me life would be brief. I knew I would die young. And within me came a firm, almost tangible excitement at the thought of meeting my Lord Jesus face to face.

Hundreds of daffodils line the roads of Salisbury each spring. They were there like a welcoming committee when I came home in 1992 and provided a vibrant sign of hope to me the following year. How uplifting to see their glorious yellow show again as I was taken out for a treat to mark the second anniversary of my return from Africa. The doctors had not expected me to live this long. Now Mum, Dad, Pearl and I were lunching in a restaurant, celebrating the fact that an extra twenty-four months of life had been granted.

Pearl had never been supportive of my desire to work overseas. Nor had she experienced the Christian faith in the same way as other members of the family. When I contracted AIDS she became bitter and resentful. There were arguments and tears. The gap of understanding between my sister and the rest of us widened into a great chasm.

My mother is a level-headed person—an ordinary housewife who is not prone to vivid imaginings. During the meal she announced, 'I had a dream—or rather a vision. It was so real I know it came from God. It means I mustn't worry about what happens to Joy.' Dad and I were told about this earlier in the day. Pearl looked up from her plate astonished, fork poised halfway to her mouth.

Mum's eyes, always big and bright, grew even larger as she described what she had seen. 'I was in the most lovely garden with Joy. There were flowers everywhere. We walked by a great mass of roses. Red, white, yellow, peach, pink—every colour you could think of. Each bloom was perfect. Their combined scent was overpowering. Jesus was there and he came and stood between us. He held one of our hands in each of his own, so we were one either side of him. Then everything went black.'

We all carried on eating for a few moments. Sniffing back a couple of tears, Dad dabbed at the edges of his mouth with a napkin. Mum leaned over to Pearl earnestly. 'I think Joy will be taken before long. But it's all right, because I've been given a glimpse of where she's going.'

'Yes, I believe you have,' replied Pearl thoughtfully. She accepted the statement without question, knowing our mother could never concoct such a story.

After this, Pearl began to visit us more often. She came to stay at the house, to be with me while our parents took a holiday together. We became much closer and even prayed together during that week, which meant a great deal to me.

It was necessary to have someone around, for my eyesight was becoming steadily worse. I first noticed the upper and side vision in the right eye had gone one Sunday morning in church. Pentecostals go in for a lot of hand raising: it is a Jewish custom St Paul helped to perpetuate by saying he wanted 'men everywhere to lift up holy hands in prayer' (1 Timothy 2:8). So we can often be found with our arms held high. On this occasion I realised I could not see my right arm at all.

In addition, breathing difficulties were starting to return; I quickly became breathless when walking. And oral thrush had developed. Time for a visit to the hospital in Southampton. Too weak to walk from one department to another, I was pushed around in a wheelchair. It was humiliating to think how my freedom was slowly being taken away. All the time I was there, my constant prayer was, 'Lord, please preserve the sight in my left eye.'

Bad eyesight or not, I could see that the ward I was in had not been cleaned properly for some time. With the aid of a magnifying glass I wrote out a formal complaint. It took some time. The domestic supervisor and her superior appeared by my bedside.

'Only the bed table is done by the cleaners. The cleaning of the TV table, locker tops and mirror shelf is not our job,' I was told.

'Oh, so who cleans those surfaces then?' I asked.

'The nurses!'

The pair bustled off, giving the impression that a fuss was being made about nothing. However, the next day, when I came back from having an X-ray, my area was spotlessly clean. I have no idea which of the staff was responsible.

The balance between domestic and ward responsibilities is an age-old problem encountered at most hospitals. Unfortunately dust and grime hold germs, and someone has to wipe them away or else patients may be at risk to infections.

There was good news about my eyes. While the doctors admitted there was an advancement of sight loss, they said the virus was now under control. No further deterioration should occur. Apparently the PCP left a weakness in the lungs. An aromatic treatment of menthol and eucalyptus was prescribed for my chest. And I was given something for the thrush before being allowed home.

It wasn't long before the bad headaches returned. This time, though they resembled migraine, they were much worse. The pain extended down the sides of the face to the gums, and was particularly bad around the eyes. With the headaches came nausea, resulting in a loss of appetite. Then the sight in my right eye began to flicker, like a light being switched off and on.

One morning I awoke from sleep with my head on the left, with the good eye closed against the pillow. I could see nothing on the right. I was completely blind on that side. The medics had been mistaken; the virus was not beaten. Terrified at the thought of going absolutely blind, my mind filled up with all kinds of imaginary scenarios. If my parents died, would other members of the family be able to care for me? What if I had an accident, or started a fire while they were at work?

Suddenly, I understood how Peter Griffiths must have felt when his thoughts took off in all directions. Once more I prayed for God to keep my left eye safe and in good working order.

11

Summer clothes were packed away and out came the warm sweaters and trousers. How I hate having to change my wardrobe twice a year. I miss the African sunshine. This time, as I carefully folded up my pretty cotton dresses, I wondered if they would ever be needed again.

Once more I was admitted to hospital in Southampton. The retina of my right eye had become detached, and that was the reason for the blindness. Nothing could be done to restore the lost sight. There was more concern about my breathing difficulties and the fact that I had lost weight. A cough had developed too. I was put in an isolation ward.

As I lay in bed, receiving frequent attention from the nurses, I remembered some of the advice I used to hand out to carers.

'Sit the patient up, raising the head on pillows to assist breathing. People tend to panic when they can't breathe properly, and that makes them even more wheezy. During panic attacks, stay by their side, encouraging them to stay calm and take regular breaths.' Now people were doing the same things for me. I couldn't help but smile.

Far more visitors came than I could cope with. Sometimes I had to ask them to wait outside while I took a nap. Debbie Brown came over on furlough and it was a real tonic to see her. We joked that I was so weak I should be in geriatrics. It was good to learn that since my departure from the Mission hospital at Katerere, new regulations had been made to protect staff against HIV infection.

'Nowadays we go into the operating theatre dressed for a moon walk!' she told me.

'Well, I'm sure it's much safer that way. If only I'd been more careful, perhaps ...' Unexpected feelings of sadness and anger washed over me.

'You mustn't blame yourself.'

'Yes, I must. I was in charge—of myself and the rest of you. This is the price I've had to pay for my negligence.' I started to cry. Tears of bereavement for the loss of my own life.

It was an entirely appropriate moment for a doctor to arrive and tell me I would soon be discharged. Apart from making my last months as comfortable as possible with the help of drugs like morphine, there was little more that could be done to combat the HIV in my body. I was being sent home to die.

My story had previously attracted the attention of the Christian press. On release from hospital, Mum and Dad contacted a secular news agency. Journalists began queuing at the front door; photos appeared in the national press; interviews were given for radio and television. What a way to become famous!

Hundreds of cards, letters and presents arrived from all over the globe. So many, it was not possible to reply to everyone who sent them. From closer to home came a request from the new Bishop of Salisbury, the Right Reverend Dr David Stancliffe.

He wanted to know if I was strong enough to receive him as a visitor. I said 'yes'.

Before he arrived, I indulged in a few musings as to what he might be like. Perhaps he would wear special robes and speak perfect English in a sing-song voice. Would he expect me to call him 'My Lord Bishop' I wondered? All these ideas were quickly dispelled when he arrived in a businesslike suit, with clerical shirt and collar, and announced, 'Hello, I'm David.'

We sat down together. He was easy to talk to, and listened with interest as I told him something of my calling and work in Zimbabwe. He seemed genuinely moved.

'When a bishop is appointed, it is customary for groups of colleagues and parishes to give various items of episcopal insignia as gifts. If it were not so, it would be difficult to make ends meet. Members of the Liturgical Commission—of which I recently became Chairman—said they would like to present me with something.'

He had already been given a fine bishop's ring by the Bishop of Portsmouth, but said he would very much like to have a smaller and more discreet one which could be worn when not on official business.

'A reasonably simple gold band was found, like a man's wedding ring. The hallmark on the inside showed the year I was ordained to the priesthood. It was inscribed in Carolingian script IN TE DOMINE SPERAVI: "In thee, O Lord, have I put my trust." This is a quotation from the last verse of the TE DEUM, which forms part of the Anglican Order for Morning Prayer.' Leaning forward, he took the ring he was talking about from his own hand, to show me the words. I could just about see them with my good eye.

He explained, 'I chose this motto because it is all too easy for bishops as well as other people to start putting their confidence into management exercises, or new schemes, or the institutional church, or whatever, instead of in God.'

I nodded, adding that he could include medicine in that list.

'Joy, there is a sense in which a bishop is married to his diocese, taking on its concerns, its parishes and people. When I was consecrated I received special responsibility for outcasts, the poor and those who cannot help themselves. I have little to share with you, except my care for the poor. You have sacrificed your life for their sake. I want to be identified with that sacrificial quality; that giving of oneself regardless of the cost. So I want to give you this ring. It will be a link between us. Will you accept it?'

I had already been impressed that a Church of England bishop was taking an interest in the trials of a Pentecostal. Now a lump came to my throat as I took the precious possession from him.

'I will be proud to wear it, and encouraged by the message it contains.' He seemed quite humbled. A look of understanding went between us; a bond of acknowledgement had been formed that we were both servants of the same God.

I have worn the ring every day since. It is a little large for my slender fingers. Mum wound some embroidery silk around the inside edge, to ensure it does not slip off.

At the beginning of December each year there is World AIDS Day. In 1994 I used my newsworthy status to obtain more publicity for this event. Some of the stories used the angle that I would be dead by Christmas. Spurred on by the challenge to prove the media wrong, I not only lived through the festive season, but also enjoyed it. I even put on a little weight in the process.

I did miss out on the carol services, though. It is not possible for me to attend church any longer. I am too weak, and can only walk a few steps around the house before becoming tired. Instead, Mum stays home with me on a Sunday and we worship together. Sometimes other members of the family or friends come over and join us. These are times I really enjoy. I still have my voice, and can sing the old hymns and modern choruses as loud as I like.

Early in the New Year someone interviewed me and said the number of AIDS cases worldwide had risen to more than a million. My reply was that it can only get higher. As yet there is no vaccine, no cure. I was also informed that four other nurses have contracted the disease in the same way as myself: victims of their patients.

As Britain moved into a winter of torrential rain, with people being stranded in dreadful floods, one of my worst nightmares came true. The sight in my left eye failed. I am now totally blind. It is so hard to accept. But even this disability has brought unexpected blessings. My hearing is so acute I can hear the smallest sounds. I love to have the bedroom window open and listen to the birdsong. I never really noticed they were there before. It is a mystery to me how such tiny creatures can make such lovely music. I will not be able to see the golden daffodils this year. However, when flowers arrive for me, I can take pleasure in gently running my fingers over the petals. They are so soft and fleshy in a way nothing else is.

The pains in my head and feelings of sickness would be constant and unbearable now if it were not for the morphine intake, which has been increased. It turns me into a giggling girl, but it works. My appetite is extremely poor. I eat less and less. I have become all skin and bone. Every little movement hurts.

Lying still in bed, with nothing else to distract me, I feel God is close all day and night. He is here when the District and Macmillan nurses come to give treatment; when Jacquie relieves Mum or Dad at my bedside; as Roy is heard cutting the back lawn. I pray out loud, 'Lord send someone to make me comfortable.' It feels as if my bones are on the outside of my skin.

Good Friday 1995. The family have church around my bed. It is lovely. I am so full of praise, my arms go up in the air and I shout, 'Hallelujah!' I know I will not live to experience my birthday next week. I do not care. I will be in a better place.

Drifting in and out of consciousness now. Dreams and visions of heaven. Or are they real? I hear Dad say, 'She's going.' Then all my pain disappears as I leave my earthly body behind. My soul is released into the next world. I leave behind me no offspring. This book is my legacy for all those who are children of this age of AIDS.

Note

The risk of HIV infection from social contact or normal day-to-day activity is effectively non-existent. However, health care workers are regularly exposed to risk through accidents with needles, operating instruments or through blood contamination of their own wounds. Despite this, the risk of transfer of HIV from an infected person is still far less than for, say, hepatitis B. For example, an injury from an HIV contaminated needle will result in infection only one time in 200 accidents, compared to 1 in 5 from hepatitis B. Joy may have been accidentally exposed to HIV many times as she worked in an area where the number of carriers is very high. Health care workers can greatly reduce risk of infection by following normal infection control guidelines.

Dr Patrick Dixon MA MBBS
Founder of ACET (Aids Care Education and Training)

Epilogue

Eunice Joy Bath died in the early evening of Easter Saturday, 15th April 1995, two days before her forty-fifth birthday.

On 26th April her funeral service was held in her own beloved Elim Church in Salisbury, attended by almost 300 people: family, church friends, nursing colleagues, school and college associates. Interment followed in Salisbury Cemetery.

Three weeks later a celebration of thanksgiving for Joy's life took place in Salisbury's Playhouse Theatre, attended by over 450 people from all over the British Isles and Africa. Appreciations were given by Mrs P. Rycroft—immediate past Mayor of Salisbury; Doctor R. Drew, Sister D. Brown and the Revd P. Munembe—all from the Elim Mission at Katerere in Zimbabwe; the Revds W. Lewis and B. Edwards—both of Elim Executive Council, and G. Ladlow and M. Hathaway of Salisbury Elim Church.

It was Joy's wish that the inscription on the headstone of her grave should read: 'Greater love has no one than this, that he lay down his life for his friends' (John 15:13).

The Bath family cannot personally reply to all correspondence. Enquiries about Joy, overseas work undertaken by the Elim Pentecostal Church, or questions about the Christian faith, should be directed to:

Elim International Missions
P.O. Box 38
Cheltenham
Gloucestershire
GL50 3HN
England